William B. Sanders

Macromedia®

Flash® MX
Professional 2004

KICK START

SAMS

800 East 96th Street, Indianapolis, Indiana 46240 USA

Macromedia Flash MX Professional 2004 Kick Start

Copyright © 2004 by Sams Publishing

International Standard Book Number: 0-672-32605-1

Library of Congress Catalog Card Number: 2003107886

Printed in the United States of America

First Printing: May 2004

07   06   05   04   4   3   2   1

Trademarks

All terms mentioned in this book that are known to be trademarks or service marks have been appropriately capitalized. Sams Publishing cannot attest to the accuracy of this information. Use of a term in this book should not be regarded as affecting the validity of any trademark or service mark.

Warning and Disclaimer

Every effort has been made to make this book as complete and as accurate as possible, but no warranty or fitness is implied. The information provided is on an "as is" basis. The author and the publisher shall have neither liability nor responsibility to any person or entity with respect to any loss or damages arising from the information contained in this book.

Bulk Sales

Sams Publishing offers excellent discounts on this book when ordered in quantity for bulk purchases or special sales. For more information, please contact

U.S. Corporate and Government Sales
1-800-382-3419
corpsales@pearsontechgroup.com

For sales outside of the U.S., please contact

International Sales
1-317-428-3341
international@pearsontechgroup.com

Acquisitions Editor
Shelley Johnston

Development Editor
Robin Drake

Managing Editor
Charlotte Clapp

Project Editor
Elizabeth Finney

Copy Editor
Bart Reed

Indexer
Julie Bess

Proofreader
Jessica McCarty

Technical Editor
Steve Heckler
Brandon Houston

Publishing Coordinator
Vanessa Evans

Multimedia Developer
Dan Scherf

Designer
Gary Adair

Page Layout
Stacey Richwine-DeRome

Contents at a Glance

Table of Contents

About the Author

Bill Sanders is a professor in the University of Hartford's Interactive Information Technology Program, where his focus is on rich Internet applications and the interaction between Internet creations and people. He has written six other books on Macromedia Flash, including works on Flash ActionScript and Flash Communication Server. He has served as a consultant for several different computer manufacturers and as a developmental consultant for a number of software companies. He has also worked with national and international development and design teams in creating Flash sites.

Dedication

This book is dedicated to the Abrahms Family, whose assistance and generosity to furthering knowledge and understanding serve as a beacon in the night. Marc Abrahms, and his parents John B. Abrahms and Phyllis Blumenthal Abrahms, have my sincere gratitude.

Acknowledgments

In going over all the emails I had collected since Flash MX Professional 2004 saw the light of day, I was dumbfounded by the amount of help I received. Then, after careful examination, I was sure there were others whose help I may have overlooked. So although I have a lot of people to thank, those who were somehow overlooked can include themselves as the recipients of my gratitude.

First of all, Macromedia, the company that makes Flash, provided a truly incredible level of assistance to me. The following folks gave valued assistance when needed, while putting up with a lot of whining and grumbling. They include Alvin Liuson, Barbara Herbert, Brad Becker, Chris Thilgen, Chris Walcott, Colm McKeon, Ed Skwarecki, Edwin Wong, Eliza Laffin, Erica Norton, Eric Thompson, Erik Bianchi, Gary Grossman, Heather Hollaender, Henriette Cohn, Jeanette Stallons, Jethro Villegas, Jobe Makar, Jody Bleyle, Jody Zhang, Jonas Galvez, Karen Cook, Lucian Beebe, Lily Khong, Mark Shepherd, Matt Wobensmith, Michael Morris, Mike Chambers, Mike Tilburg, Nigel Pegg, Nivesh Rajbhandari, Scott Fegette, Sharon Selden, Ted Casey, Tim Slater, Vera Fleischer, Waldo Smeets, and Waleed Anbar.

Second, but equally important, are the fellow Flash developers who have worked with Flash MX Professional 2004. These men and women share their knowledge with unbounded generosity. They include Adam Bell, Allen Ellison, Andreas Heim, Aral Balkan, aYo Binitie, Bill Ristine, Branden Hall, Brian Hogg, Brian Lesser, Burak Kalayci, Chad Corbin, Chafic Kazoun, Colin Moock, Dave Yang, Greg Burch, Derek Franklin, Fernando Flórez, Jen Dehaan, Jonas Galvez, Joey Lott, John Dalziel, Mathieu Anthoine, Melvyn Song Kian Guan, Mike Carlisle, Nik Schramm, Owen van Dijk, Peter Brouwers, Peter Hall, Phillip Kerman, Rafal Niesluchowski, Robert Hoekman, Robert M. Hall, Robert Penner, Robert Reinhardt, Robin Debreuil, Ron Haberle, Saban Uenlue, Samuel Neff, Samuel Wan, Stefan Richter, and Nate Weiss. They are truly an international group showing a worldwide cooperation that contains the seeds of implied world harmony. Although I am most grateful to all these folks, I must add that any shortcomings in this book are due to my own short-comings, and certainly not anything that any of them offered so graciously.

Like most books, this one was a product of a cooperative effort. Under the leadership of Shelley Johnston at Sams Publishing, I worked with a host of talented editors. Robin Drake was a patient development editor, and Elizabeth Finney served as our very capable Project Editor. Steve Heckler and Brandon Houston served as technical editors, two Flash pros themselves, with an eye to all the technical detail. They were a great help. Finally, copy editor Bart Reed did a masterful job of making sure that everything made sense. As always, I am grateful to Margo Maley-Hutchinson at Waterside Productions for bringing author and publisher together.

My wife Delia and dog WillDe are the best companions an author could have, and their support and understanding are always important.

We Want to Hear from You!

As the reader of this book, *you* are our most important critic and commentator. We value your opinion and want to know what we're doing right, what we could do better, what areas you'd like to see us publish in, and any other words of wisdom you're willing to pass our way.

You can email or write me directly to let me know what you did or didn't like about this book—as well as what we can do to make our books stronger.

Please note that I cannot help you with technical problems related to the topic of this book, and that due to the high volume of mail I receive, I might not be able to reply to every message.

When you write, please be sure to include this book's title and author as well as your name and phone or email address. I will carefully review your comments and share them with the author and editors who worked on the book.

Email: webdev@samspublishing.com

Mail: Mark Taber
Associate Publisher
Sams Publishing
800 East 96th Street
Indianapolis, IN 46240 USA

Reader Services

For more information about this book or others from Sams Publishing, visit our Web site at www.samspublishing.com. Type the ISBN (excluding hyphens) or the title of the book in the Search box to find the book you're looking for.

The World of Flash MX Professional 2004

Macromedia Flash MX Professional 2004 (Flash Pro) represents a powerful tool for making professional Web sites. This book views Flash Pro as a rich integration of the traditional Flash tools, which make graphic animation and Web page development both effective and efficient, and the powerful new set of components and ActionScript 2.0, which allow for optimal development and object-oriented programming (OOP). Like any powerful application tool, Flash Pro consists of many elements, and the approach of this book is to explain these elements so that readers can get started relatively quickly creating professional sites for their clients. Some readers will come from a background rich in graphics and design, and others from one strong in development and programming. Still others have skills in both design and development. Because of the different backgrounds of professional creators of Web-based products, this book attempts to meld the different parts of Flash Pro into a single workflow rather than dissecting it into an unnatural dichotomy of "design" and "development." Designers and developers can work as a team to create the best possible Web sites with Flash Pro, each providing their different expertise.

The extent to which designers and developers understand each other's tools and requirements in the context of the overall site will have a strong effect on the resulting Flash Pro application:

- Designers need to know what can be done with ActionScript 2.0, and Flash Pro has some new tools in the Behaviors panel and some components that simplify adding ActionScript 2.0–based functionality. This book shows how to get started easily using ActionScript 2.0 as well as using its most advanced features. The reader can choose the level of scripting most suitable for his or her needs.

- Developers need to understand the important design tools and the roles that those tools play in creating a site using Flash Pro. This doesn't mean that a programmer has to learn to be a designer, but rather he or she needs to be cognizant of the fact that most Flash programming occurs in the context of graphic-based designs. To get the most out of Flash Pro, developers have to work closely with designers and understand something about design needs. Such an understanding won't undermine efficient and effective coding; indeed, some of the code use, such as communicating with a back end and database, may have very little to do with understanding design. However, information put into and retrieved from a database must be entered through an input text field and retrieved through a dynamic text field that a designer has shaped for optimizing the user interface.

Who This Book Is For

This book is intended for designers and developers who want to use Macromedia Flash MX Professional 2004 to create commercial-quality Web pages and sites. As a book in the Sams *Kick Start* series, this text is intended to explain key elements of Flash Pro so that the reader can develop materials at an optimum rate.

The key groups this book addresses are quite varied, but the common thread among them is the focus on creating professional-quality materials using Flash Pro. Because time is money, this book doesn't linger on every nuance of Flash Pro. Rather, each topic is explained and illustrated with examples, graphics, and tutorials, and we move rapidly to the next topic.

The following groups will benefit most from this book:

- **Professional designers and developers who are familiar with previous versions of Flash**—Depending on your area of expertise, you'll find this book covers everything new about Flash Pro. Therefore, by using this book's table of contents and index, you can go directly to those sections you want to learn about. Because this book integrates ActionScript 2.0 into discussions of various Flash Pro functions, you'll see how to integrate document construction with programming.

- **Professional designers new to Flash**—Designers who have created Web sites for clients and want to add Flash to their array of design tools will find many of the design tools, especially the graphic design tools, familiar. If you're a designer, you can use this book to see how to use the design tools to create dynamic Web sites. If you're unfamiliar with programming, the new Behaviors panel in Flash Pro will let you add code without having to learn to program.

- **Professional developers new to Flash**—Those with a programming background in languages such as Java, C++, JavaScript, and even BASIC (including Visual Basic) will find ActionScript 2.0 to be a very interesting and useful language. Because of the wide range of reader backgrounds, I briefly cover some basic concepts, such as object-oriented programming, variables, functions, and other basic terminology. If you're a programmer, feel free to skim those parts that cover familiar ground and spend more time seeing how ActionScript 2.0 is used in the context of creating Flash movies. It is important, though, to look at how Flash Pro deals with graphics and animation as well as with other design issues.

How to Use This Book

Treat this book as a tool, and use it accordingly. You can read it from cover to cover, read it in any order that suits your needs, or just jump in and look up what you need when you need it. You'll probably find it useful to employ some kind of page-tabbing system to mark those sections you need to use most often. (I've devised a color-coded system in which I place a sticky tab in different key pages.) If you're a designer, you shouldn't get bogged down in learning ActionScript 2.0 unless you've purchased this book for that purpose. Instead, you should use other Flash Pro tools to get a job done, including the new Behaviors panel that automatically generates ActionScript programs. Later, when you don't have a job deadline, you can go over the ActionScript sections and learn how to use different code to accomplish new tasks. There's no rush.

Most of the chapters have elements of ActionScript-based and non-ActionScript-based materials. You can go over some, all, or none of the materials in each chapter to find what you need to get a job done. Most chapters contain multiple small projects that employ several of the features discussed in a particular chapter. If you like, you can first code the chapter's sample projects (or download them from www.sandlight.com) and then read the rest of the chapter to see how all the parts come together.

You can quickly find ActionScript 2.0 features, and depending on your background and needs, pick up the new features. It's important to see how the core of Flash works if you're unfamiliar with it so that you can use ActionScript optimally.

The "best" way to use this book depends on how you best learn new material. Because the book is for professional use, it's designed to be sitting next to your computer when you sit down to construct a jaw-dropping creation.

Flash Origins

Flash's initial popularity stemmed from being a very efficient tool for creating low-bandwidth animations for the Web. At the core of Flash is the use of vector graphics and symbols. Vector graphics have less "bulk" because they use vector points and algorithms for drawing lines between the vector points. Such graphics take up less computer memory than bitmapped graphics, which map *all* the bits in a graphic. Figures I.1 and I.2 show how a vector graphic appears on a Flash page and the lack of distortion as the image is magnified.

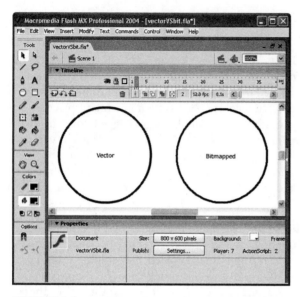

FIGURE 1.1   Vector graphics use less memory than bitmapped graphics.

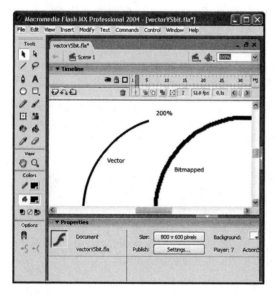

FIGURE 1.2   When bitmapped graphics change in size, they become distorted compared to vector graphics.

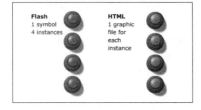

FIGURE I.3 HTML requires the same graphic loaded four times, whereas Flash requires only a single symbol to be loaded.

Flash uses symbols to store information about different shapes that can be used as movie clips, buttons, and graphic images. A symbol represents an object that can be replicated in a Flash movie without you having to send over the Internet the entire graphic that makes up the symbol. Therefore, you can use a single button symbol to create several identical buttons, but because only the button symbol is sent across the Internet, the bandwidth costs are a fraction of what the same number of buttons would be if they were sent as individual graphic objects. Figure I.3 shows a graphic comparison.

Flash also introduced the Timeline, frames, and layers for creating animated movies. The Timeline, with its moving playhead, is a metaphor borrowed from animated films where the cels (the individual movie frames created using drawings on sheets of cellophane) are hand-drawn animations. This greatly simplified the making of computer-based animations for the Web. The automatic in-betweening work (drawings between keyframes) in animation is automatically handled through the "tweening" process in Flash. Therefore, not only is creating animations analogous to the traditional methods favored by animators, but it is far more effective and efficient as well.

As more Web site designers and developers discovered Flash, they adopted it for movie and game animation work and adding flair to their sites. One result was a flood of animated banners and other bouncing and distracting visuals that came to decorate sites and infuriate users. Unfortunately, Flash came to be identified as a narrow animation tool and not a full-site development tool.

With the advent of Flash MX, several user interface (UI) components were added, along with a far more robust version of ActionScript. Designers were able to add these components to their sites easily as well as add their own design colors. Developers could use the new ActionScript to create class-like functions using the `prototype` property. Likewise, a whole new set of ActionScript terms moved the language much closer to the European Computer Manufacturers Association (ECMA) standard, known as ECMAScript. The result was that Flash, while keeping its original core, moved into the realm of a full Web site–creation tool.

We're Not in Kansas Anymore: Approaching Flash Pro

Macromedia Flash MX Professional 2004 represents a quantum leap in the development of Flash. With the basic animation and bandwidth-saving structures still in place, Flash Pro has all the characteristics of a full Web site–development tool. Rather than being just an animation tool, Flash Pro has the capability to replace HTML, XHTML, and JavaScript. Moreover, Flash Pro can accomplish more than the combined traditional tools centered around HTML because Flash contains components, buttons, movie clips, and the capability to work with all the external files that HTML can. This doesn't mean that Flash Pro doesn't use HTML. When Flash movies are published, an HTML file is generated to contain the SWF file. Flash Pro calls for a shift in thinking—that is, you need to think of it as something more than just a tool for making Flash animations. A quick overview of Flash Pro's key features will help.

A Tale of Two Flashes

This is the first time that Flash has been available in two different product packages. In a nutshell, Macromedia Flash MX Professional 2004 differs from the standard version of Macromedia Flash MX 2004 in that Flash Pro contains additional features. If you're considering Flash Pro and using this book to decide whether it's worth the extra cost, this section is for you because it gives you a better idea of what's found in Flash MX Professional 2004 that's not available in Flash MX 2004.

Flash Pro has all the components, classes, and other features that the standard version of Flash has, but it also includes the following new components and classes (I'll discuss some of these shortly):

- Accordion component
- Alert component
- DataBinding package
- DateField component
- DataGrid component
- DataHolder component
- DataSet component
- DateChooser component
- Form class
- Menu component
- RDBMSResolver component
- MediaController component
- MediaDisplay component
- MediaPlayback component

Other features unique to Flash Pro are the Project panel and external data-editing capabilities. What's more, the highly productive Forms and Slide feature is only found in Flash Pro.

The real difference between Flash Pro and the standard version is that Flash Pro is for professional development. The enhancements in Flash Pro cut down on the number of hours required to develop sophisticated documents in Flash, and they more than make up for the cost difference in short order.

Multiple Start Options

When starting Flash Pro, you'll notice a new feature—the graphic list of options (see Figure I.4). Old hands at Flash should familiarize themselves with what's new here. Each of these options is discussed in detail in different chapters in the book, but here a quick overview will show you what's available.

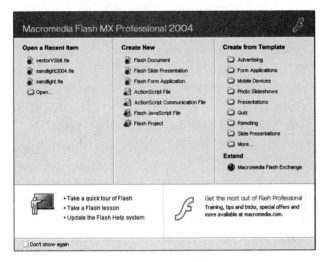

FIGURE I.4   You have a number of different options when starting Flash Pro.

Three columns of choices make the selection options clear. In the first column, the option for opening a recent or other item is now on the Stage instead of only in the File menu. The second column not only provides familiar options from the File menu but also several other previously unavailable options:

- **Flash Document**—Opens a new blank Flash movie.

- **Flash Slide Presentation**—Available only in Flash Pro, this option opens a two-column document ready for using slides (see Chapter 9, "Producing Online Slide Shows").

- **Flash Form Application**—Available only in Flash Pro, this option opens a two-column document set up for inserting forms (see Chapter 9).

- **ActionScript File**—Available only in Flash Pro, this option opens an Integrated Script window for creating Dealing with External Data and Object AS files. It's similar to the Actions panel, but all scripts are saved in external files and not integrated into the FLA source. However, it does support syntax coloring, code hints, and other scripting aids found in the Actions panel (see Chapter 4, "Animations and Interactions).

- **ActionScript Communication File**—Available only in Flash Pro, this option opens an Integrated Script window that is used for creating server-side ActionScript to be saved in ASC files used with Flash Communication Server MX.

- **Flash JavaScript File**—Available only in Flash Pro, this option opens the Flash JavaScript Editor and is used in conjunction with the Flash JavaScript API. You can create JSFL files that can be used with multiple scripts.

- **Flash Project**—Available only in Flash Pro, this option creates a Flash Project file that can be used to coordinate multiple developers/designers and pull together the different files used in a single project (see Chapter 3, "Adding ActionScript to Your Animation").

For those familiar with Flash, these new central options provide far more functionality than what was previously available.

The final column provides a set of templates. These templates are FLA files that you can fill with unique content. For getting a true kick start in using Flash Pro's power, working with templates is a good idea. The following templates are provided:

- **Advertising**—Several different layouts with minimum content are provided as design stages. The layouts represent typical ones you're likely to find in banner ads and other ads embedded in an HTML page or as part of a larger Flash page.

- **Form Applications**—Found in Flash Pro only, these templates help in creating forms quickly (see Chapter 9).

- **Mobile Devices**—These templates help you create Flash movies used in mobile phones and PDAs that can read the new Flash Lite 1.0 player or the older Flash Player 5. Included in the templates are graphic representations of various mobile devices and their display screens to help you plan a movie that can be seen on different devices. Figure I.5 shows the layout for a Nokia phone.

- **Photo Slideshows**—This template allows you to quickly put together a user-controlled or automatically timed slide show.

- **Presentations**—Several layouts provide boilerplates for different style presentations. The materials provide PowerPoint-type presentations using Flash Pro.

- **Quiz, Remoting, Slide Presentations**—Several different layouts with minimum content are provided as design stages.

- **More... (Video)**—The video template uses both media components and forms to show how video can be integrated into different applications.

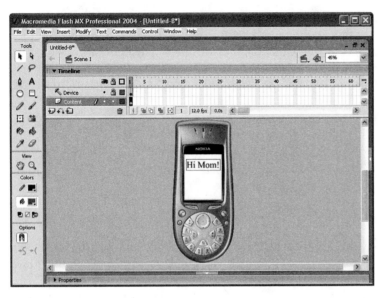

FIGURE 1.5 The work area (or Stage) is made up of the mobile device's viewing area.

Graphic Tools

In developing a site for the Internet, Flash Pro provides graphic tools for creating graphics right on the Stage. The Tools panel has a basic set of tools for creating vector graphics. For those familiar with previous versions of Flash, you'll see that very little has changed in the Tools panel (previously called the Toolbox). The same graphic tools available in Flash MX are still there. The look has changed slightly, but other than the new PolyStar tool, little has changed. Chapter 2, "The Flash Pro Interface," shows you how to use the different tools.

Graphic File Importer

In addition to creating your own graphics in Flash Pro, you can import both bitmapped and vector graphics into Flash. Graphics from programs such as Macromedia FreeHand MX 2004, Macromedia Fireworks MX 2004, Adobe Illustrator, Adobe PhotoShop, Paint, and many other formats can be easily imported and used in Flash Pro movies. New in Macromedia Flash MX Professional 2004 is the ability to import PDF files. Chapters 2 and 3 introduce you to how to work with imported graphic files.

Video Store

As a tool for creating animated movies for the Internet, Flash is unsurpassed. However, it can also import and play digital video files that can be placed into layers where keyframes will be created automatically to accommodate the video. The new version of Flash can also stream external FLV files. Additionally, if AVI or MOV files are imported into Flash Pro, they can be exported as FLV files. Streamed files are important because they're streamed directly from the server; therefore, users don't have to wait while the files are downloaded prior to viewing them. Likewise, because streamed files need not be part of the SWF file, the Flash file will load and play much faster. Chapter 10, "Adding Video and Sound," shows you how to get the most out of video using Flash.

Flash Pro also comes with three new components for placing streaming video into a Flash movie:

- MediaController

- MediaDisplay

- MediaPlayback

Figure I.6 shows a streaming video in the MediaPlayback component. Designers and developers alike can quickly install streaming videos into their Flash productions simply by providing the path to the FLV file entered into the Component Inspector.

You will find support for the following video applications in Flash Pro:

- Avid Xpress/Media Composer
- Anystream Agility

- Apple Final Cut Pro
- After Effects

- Discreet Cleaner

FIGURE I.6 Adding streaming video using the MediaPlayback component.

With this broad range of support plus its own built-in capacity to deal with video, Flash Pro can be an excellent platform for streaming video across the Internet.

Sound Platform

In addition to graphics, both static and animated, Flash Pro handles sound files as well. Sound files, including WAV, AIEE, and MP3 formats, can be imported into Flash. Once in Flash, WAV and AIEE files can be compressed into MP3 format for a smaller-size SWF file to be sent over the Internet.

You can use Flash Pro's sound editor to edit the sound envelope, and using the Property panel, you can synchronize the sound with actions on the Stage. Because the sound is embedded in the SWF file, no separate sound loading is required. Chapter 10 shows how to import sound into Flash and even how to separate the sound from an imported video file.

User Interface

One of the most important features in Flash Pro is the inclusion of user interface (UI) components. The area of computer human interface (CHI) or human computer interface (HCI) is one that cannot be ignored in creating professional sites for clients. Flash MX Professional 2004 includes an expanded set of the UI components originally introduced in Flash MX. Included in the new set are the components detailed in Table I.1.

TABLE I.1

New UI Components in Flash MX Professional 2004

COMPONENT	DESCRIPTION
Accordion	A sequential display component
Alert	An alert window
Button	A graphic push button
CheckBox	A graphic check box
ComboBox	A pop-up menu box
DataGrid	A column-enabled data display component
DateChooser	An onscreen calendar for selecting and displaying a date
DateField	A component that displays a date that can be selected from a pop-up calendar
Label	A text-labeling component
List	A scrollable options box
Loader	A component used to load and display SWF and JPG files
Menu	A drop-down menu with selectable items
MenuBar	A horizontal bar on which you can place Menu components
NumericStepper	A button-operated component that displays numbers the user can increment or decrement by clicking an up/down arrow
ProgressBar	A bar used with preloaders to show loading progress
RadioButton	Used to create a mutually exclusive set of selectable radio buttons
ScrollPane	A window that can contain text and graphics and can be scrolled horizontally and vertically
TextArea (includes a scrollbar)	An expandable area where text can be added, with an auto scrollbar appearing when needed
TextInput	An input text field with depth
Tree	Displays hierarchal nodes of data from an XML file
Window	Displays a movie clip in a window with a title bar and border along with an optional close button

Flash MX Professional 2004 has almost three times the number of UI components Flash MX originally contained. The presence of these components represents Macromedia's commitment to making Flash Pro a truly powerful Web development tool for professional applications beyond animation. By including the expanded number of UI components, Macromedia has shifted the focus toward the professional requirements for an Internet site for business, education, and public service organizations.

Back-End Portal

Flash has longed served as a stable front end for communicating with a back end through a connector. Flash Player 7 contains a security system for external data and files; therefore, Flash can be used as a secure front end. All connections to external data are subject to Flash's sandbox security. This type of security restricts a Flash document from data (including data passed through middleware such as ColdFusion, PHP, or ASP.NET) emanating from a domain other than the originating one. For example, if I use my domain, www.sandlight.com, to store my Flash files, I need to put my database and middleware on www.sandlight.com. The new data components detailed in Table I.2 can be used with different types of data sources.

TABLE I.2

New Data Components in Flash MX Professional 2004

COMPONENT	DESCRIPTION
DataHolder	Serves as a data-holding connector between other components using data binding.
DataSet	Assists in working with data as collection of objects.
RDBMResolver	Used in conjunction with the DataSet component. Assists in reformatting data for appropriate display.
WebServiceConnector	Used to connect to a live Web service such as a stock ticker or the current weather.
XMLConnector	Reads data from an XML file or writes in XML format for POST and GET operations.
XUpdateResolver	This component converts changes made to the data in your application into an appropriate format for updating the external data source in use.

This arrangement improves security. However, if the developer has PHP files communicating with a MySQL database on a Linux server and ASP.NET software communicating with a Microsoft SQL Server database on a Microsoft 2003 server, the sandbox security prevents a single Flash document from accessing both. To resolve this problem, Flash has procedures in place to permit cross-domain access to data. Chapter 11, "Formatting and Calculating," explains how to use sandbox security and how to get around it for cross-domain data access.

Internet Programming Tool

When ActionScript was initially introduced in Flash, it stood as a support system geared primarily toward jumping from one frame to another within a Flash movie. However, as ActionScript developed, making huge leaps in Flash 5 and Flash MX, it took on a life of its own, having much the same functionality as JavaScript plus its original unique Flash functionality. In Flash MX Professional 2004, the change has been so significant that the language has been recast as ActionScript 2.0 (AS2).

ActionScript 2.0 takes its naming convention from JavaScript 2 (that is, being developed to conform to the new ECMA-262 standards for Internet languages). More specifically, ECMAScript Edition 4 (or ECMA-262 Edition 4) is developed to bring true object-oriented programming (OOP) to Flash. For developers used to programming in Java or C++, the new features of ActionScript 2.0 should be very familiar. However, to those who are new to programming or used to the process model dominant in previous versions of ActionScript, ActionScript 2.0 will require some study. Those new to programming will be starting off with a very good and powerful programming model and won't have to transition later on to object-oriented programming.

Also, Flash Pro provides options for nonprogrammers to get started quickly using the new Behaviors panel for automatically generating ActionScript 2.0 code. Although some important changes have been made to ActionScript 2.0, you can still use most of the basic ActionScript 1.0 code and procedures, such as `play()` and `stop()`.

What's New in Flash MX Professional 2004?

This section provides a quick overview of what's new in Flash Pro. Many of these new features have been discussed elsewhere in this introduction:

- Accessibility support is offered in the components and the Flash authoring environment. Keyboard shortcuts allow for non-mouse interfaces. Components allow for improved third-party closed-caption and screen reader programs.

- ActionScript 2.0 is a true object-oriented language in line with ECMA-262 Edition 4.

- The Behaviors panel helps nonprogrammers add ActionScript 2.0 to their documents. Functions include scripts that link to Web sites, control the playback of embedded videos, play movie clips, load sounds and graphics, and trigger data sources. For more information, see "Controlling Instances with Behaviors" in the Using Flash Help.

- Components have been added for data, media, and user interface enhancement.

- Data binding allows you to connect any component to a data source. Data updates and manipulation can be accomplished through ActionScript 2.0 or the components.

- Document tabs make working with multiple documents and documents that use external files much easier.

- File import enhancements allow for importing Adobe PDF and Adobe Illustrator 10 files and preserving vector representations of original source files.

- Find and Replace has been a part of the ActionScript panel in previous versions of Flash, and it is now available for locating and replacing text strings, fonts, colors, symbols, sound files, video files, and imported bitmap files in a document.

- Flash Player detection lets you determine the Player version the user has in his or her system.

- Flash Player performance is enhanced. It now complies with the ECMAScript language specifications. Also, the Player has much improved runtime performance, video scripting, and display rendering.

- Form screens comprise a forms-based visual programming environment for optimizing development.

- The Help system includes a new Help panel with context-sensitive references and ActionScript references, in addition to lessons in using Flash.

- The History panel has been added to the panel set. It tracks user actions for possible conversion to reusable commands.

- Multilanguage authoring using enhanced globalization and Unicode support with any character set assists with international authoring.

- The Project panel allows for team design and development on a single project. File management, version control, and efficient workflow have been added to document development.

- Publish profiles allow the user to save, reuse, and export documents. This new feature aids in cross-document consistency.

- Security is stricter in the Flash Player, including exact domain matching. The Flash Player also distinguishes between HTTPS and HTTP, thus adding further security.

- Screen-based visual development environment, slide screens, and form screens help create slide shows and form-based applications.

- Small font sizes have improved rendering with improved appearance.

- Source code control integration with plug-ins to source control systems such as Microsoft Visual Source Safe help protect source code from decompiling.

- Spell Checker searches your text on the Stage and in movie clips for spelling errors. This is a real lifesaver when you use a lot of text in Flash documents.

- The Start page has been enhanced to display far more options.

- The Strings panel eases the publication of content in multiple languages.

- Templates have been added to Flash for making presentations, e-learning applications, advertisements, mobile device applications, and other templates handy for Flash documents. (The templates are not new, but the content and form are.)

- Timeline effects allow users to apply effects to objects on the Stage. Transitions, fade in and out, spins, and blurs are all made simple using this new feature.

- Video Import makes video encoding easier and offers encoding presets and clip editing.

- Web Services include ready-to-use data connectors for Web services.

PART I

Getting Started in Flash's Work Environment

Getting to Know Flash Pro

Getting the Flavor of Flash

This chapter provides a quick overview of Flash MX Professional 2004. New Flash users should read this chapter in detail to understand the core elements of Flash Pro. Many of the procedures used in this chapter to illustrate the different parts of the Flash environment will be elaborated in subsequent chapters, so treat this chapter as a foundation for what will come. This chapter is for getting the flavor of Flash in context and a kick start in understanding the core Flash environment.

The Stage

The main work area for creating Flash Pro documents is the *Stage*. It represents the visible portion of a Flash movie. Objects can move on and off the Stage, but the viewer sees only what's in the Stage area.

A new feature in Flash MX Professional 2004 is the document tab at the top of the Document window. Each document, including external ActionScript Editor documents, gets a document tab. When you create multiple-document sites or documents that require external files, the tabs make it very easy to switch quickly between the various documents and files. Figure 1.1 shows the Stage and two document tabs (First.fla and Second.fla) at the top of the Document window. In the figure, the mouse pointer is positioned on the First.fla tab.

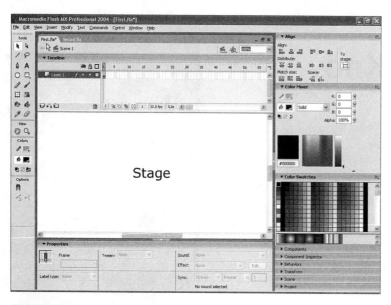

FIGURE 1.1 The Stage is the work area for the selected document.

Multiple Documents for Macintosh Users

Document tabs are not available on the Macintosh version of Flash MX Professional 2004. However, you can have multiple documents open and each has its own window.

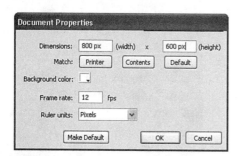

FIGURE 1.2 The Stage size is set in the Document Properties dialog box.

You can adjust the size of the Stage (and thus the size of the Flash window onscreen when the animation is complete) by using the Property Inspector. Click somewhere in the Stage area and then click the Size button. The Document Properties dialog box opens and allows you to enter the width and height of the Stage in inches ("), decimal inches ("), points (pt), centimeters (cm), millimeters (mm), or pixels (px). Figure 1.2 shows the Stage size being set in pixels. Flash provides several units of measure so that designers from other environments can be comfortable with their favorite unit.

The Timeline

The *Timeline* in Flash represents a strip of "film" with frames. To understand how the Timeline works, imagine a film editor with a movable playhead that displays the contents of the current frame on the Stage when the playhead is moved over the frame. Figure 1.3 shows the Timeline. In this example, multiple Timelines (called *layers*) are visible simultaneously. (I'll describe layers shortly.)

FIGURE 1.3   The Timeline, layers, and playhead.

Frames

The frames in the Timeline represent the frames or cels in an animated movie. To understand frames in Flash, it helps to understand the process of traditional animation. Briefly, the traditional manual process of animating requires a master animator and one or more assistants. The master animator draws two different images representing changed characteristics of a scene. The frames in which the master animator draws the images are called *keyframes*. Between the pair of keyframes, the assistant animators (known as *in-betweeners*) draw the frames (or *tweens*) that change the image from one keyframe to the next. This process, called *tweening*, results in a smooth transition between keyframes.

Keyframes in Flash are the frames used to introduce new content in a document. When you move the playhead to a keyframe (or just click the keyframe), the content on the Stage is "entered" into the keyframe. Keyframes are created by clicking a frame and pressing the F6 key or selecting Insert, Timeline, Keyframe from the menu. A blank keyframe is recognizable by a black circle on the frame. If content is placed in the keyframe, the black circle is filled. The initial frame in a layer is *always* a keyframe.

The Flash *playhead* can be dragged to any frame or keyframe. When you select a frame by clicking it, the playhead jumps to that frame. The content on the Stage changes as the playhead is dragged left or right along the Timeline. Content in all layers is displayed as the playhead is moved over the frame containing the content.

You can label keyframes to make your program clearer and easier to debug. To add a label, select the keyframe and enter the label in the Frame window in the Property Inspector, as shown in Figure 1.4.

> ### ActionScript in Keyframes
>
> You can select a keyframe and add ActionScript 2.0 code that will be fired when the playhead moves to the frame. A keyframe with associated ActionScript code has a lowercase letter *a* next to the frame. (ActionScript is discussed in detail in Chapter 3, "Adding ActionScript to Your Animation," and used throughout this book.)

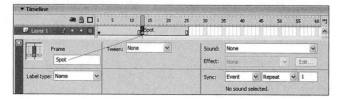

FIGURE 1.4   Property Inspector and labeled keyframe.

A regular frame (just called a *frame*) contains the same content as the keyframe to the left of it. If a frame is part of a tween, it will contain uneditable content generated by Flash's automated tweening process. Tweened frames contain the images equivalent to what the in-betweener artists do in a traditional animation process. However, because the tweened frames contain images with shapes, positions, or some other in-between changes between keyframes, they're "frozen" so that the animation process in the changes cannot be distorted.

Keyframes with no content are blank. If a blank keyframe is inserted in a tween, all tweened frames are destroyed. The best use of blank keyframes is to insert spaces in a layer; in other words, blank keyframes can act as frame "spacers."

Layers

One of the major problems encountered by early animators was the "flatness" of animated movies. To give the movies depth, they placed layers of glass in stacks. Each glass layer would contain a different set of images, depending on the image's depth (position) relative to other images in the movie. Eventually, by placing the drawings on cellophane (called a *cel*), animators were able to move characters in front of or behind one another without having to combine images, and the entire process of creating animated movies was greatly simplified. This technique gave animated movies greater depth and realism.

In Flash, layers work the same way as they do in traditional animation. Each layer can contain different content, depending on that content's position relative to the other images in the movie. When you're animating images in Flash, however, only a single object is tweened in any layer. When objects on the same layer need to be moved independently, you can insert keyframes for each change. However, rather than going though all the work of manually redrawing independently in individual frames, Flash developers and designers typically place all images that need to be changed or moved on separate layers. Although this is not an exact parallel to the traditional layer method on glass panels, it's far more efficient.

Project: Tweening an Animation

The *sine qua non* of Flash is tweening. As noted earlier, tweening is the automated process of filling in the changes between keyframes. The following simple project will help you to see and understand the process. Follow these steps to create a basic shape tween:

1. Open a new Flash document and click Frame 30 to select it.

2. Press the F6 key or choose Insert, Timeline, Keyframe from the menu to insert a frame. Frames are added from Frame 1–29 and a keyframe is inserted in Frame 30.

3. Click Frame 1 and then click the Oval tool in the Tools panel.

4. Draw a circle in the upper-left corner of the Stage, as shown in Figure 1.5.

Oval tool   Oval tool cursor

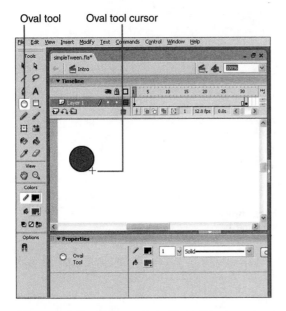

FIGURE 1.5   Circle created with Oval tool.

5. Click Frame 30 and select the Rectangle tool in the Tools panel.

6. Draw a rectangle in the lower-right corner of the Stage, as shown in Figure 1.6.

7. Click Frame 1. In the Property Inspector, select Shape from the Tween drop-down menu, as shown in Figure 1.7. An arrow with a green background appears in the frames shown in Figure 1.8.

Rectangle tool

Rectangle tool drawing cursor

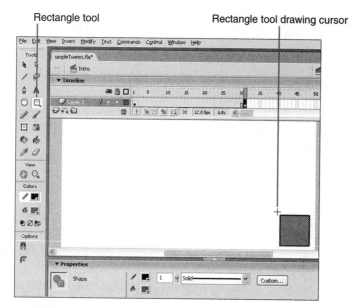

FIGURE 1.6 Rectangle created with Rectangle tool.

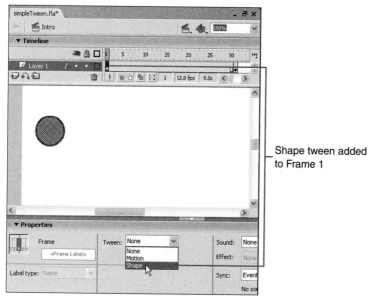

Shape tween added
to Frame 1

FIGURE 1.7 Setting a Shape tween.

Shape tween arrow

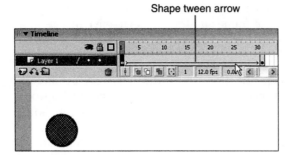

FIGURE 1.8 Shape tween arrow.

8. Select Control, Enable Live Preview. (If Enable Live Preview is already checked, just leave it alone.)

9. Click the first frame and press the Enter key to view the live preview. The circle morphs into a rectangle and moves from the upper-left corner to the lower-right corner.

To understand this process, drag the playhead from left to right to see the different Stages of change that the shape goes through. Each of the frames between the keyframes has a slightly different position and shape. Figure 1.9 shows one of the shapes and positions between the keyframes.

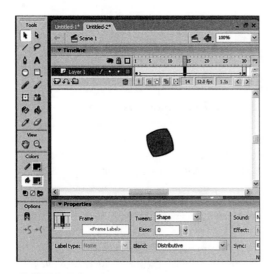

FIGURE 1.9 Shape tween between keyframes.

As noted, if you select any of the frames between the keyframes in the tween, the image cannot be edited. However, if you select a tweened frame and insert a keyframe (F6), the image in the frame can be edited. Chapter 2, "The Flash Pro Interface," provides more details about working with tweening.

Because Flash is set up to have addressable independent objects on the same Timeline and/or different Timelines, understanding levels and Timelines is fundamental to being able to work effectively in Flash. All renderings on the same Timeline change at the rate of that Timeline, whereas objects on different Timelines change at different rates depending on the length of the Timeline and how the objects on that Timeline are set. Figure 1.10 is a rough illustration of how to envision the difference between levels and Timelines in Flash.

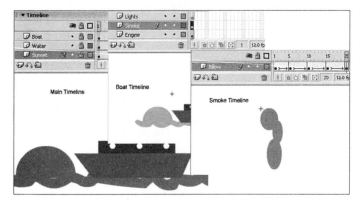

FIGURE 1.10   Levels and Timelines.

Timelines

You can best envision multiple Timelines by thinking of the base movie as a movie clip. Each movie clip has its own Timeline. The main Timeline can be addressed as the root level using the root property. However, because each level has its own root level, the base movie is best addressed as level0. If you load a movie clip into level 25 (_level25), any address to _root will go to the root of level 25. To address the root level of the movie (_level0), from level 25 or any other level, just use _level0 instead of _root.

The Many Roots in Flash

In Flash MX Professional 2004, you can set any movie clip to the root level by using *MovieClip*._lockroot, where *MovieClip* is the instance name of the movie clip. All movie clips loaded into the movie clip with the _lockroot property reference that movie clip using _root. In other words, _lockroot makes that movie clip the base Timeline for all movie clips inside it.

To understand Timeline addressing, imagine an airplane movie clip. The movie clip has the instance name *airplane* sitting on the root level. Inside the airplane movie clip is an *engine* movie clip, and inside the engine movie clip is a *propeller* movie clip. To address the propeller, you could use either of the following paths:

```
_root.airplane.engine.propeller
```

or

```
_level0.airplane.engine.propeller
```

Essentially, when the _levelN property is employed, it's the same as writing "go to the root of this level." This technique is far clearer when you're debugging a script.

Levels

If you have multiple levels in a movie, the root level is whatever the level assigned to the movie clip to be loaded is. So if you load a movie clip on level 12, the root level is assigned the property _level12. Using the airplane movie clip example from the preceding section, you could address the propeller movie clip as either of the following:

```
_root.airplane.engine.propeller
```

or

```
_level12.airplane.engine.propeller
```

As you can see, the reference to _root can be confusing because every level has its own _root property. However, _level12 clearly specifies the main Timeline for that level. The developer specifies the level for the movie clip or loads it into a known level in a given application and thus knows the movie clip's level. New levels are created only when an external movie clip is loaded, an existing movie clip is duplicated, or one is created using the MovieClip class. If a movie clip is loaded to or assigned _level0, the base movie is replaced by the one loaded to _level0. Likewise, if a movie clip is assigned the same level of any other level where a movie clip currently exists, the loaded clip replaces the clip that was assigned the same level. Figure 1.11 shows the basic relationship between a main movie and movie clips loaded at different levels.

▶ For further details on working with movie clips on different Timelines and levels, **see** Chapter 5, "Movie Clip Control."

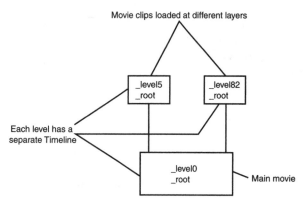

FIGURE 1.11   Levels and Timelines.

Scenes

A *scene* in Flash is a separate area where a new set of materials can be placed. The scene is an organizational tool more than a literal "scene." For example, whenever a background color is changed in one scene, all scenes get the same background color. On the other hand, each new scene has none of the images of a previous scene, and each starts with Frame 1.

Frames in scenes have two different addressing modes: *absolute* and *scene relative*. Because scenes are an extension of a sequence of frames, they can be addressed as the absolute

SHOP TALK

The Titanic Had It Coming

As a professional development and design tool for creating rich Internet applications (known as RIAs), Flash has no peer. Flash was originally designed with the dual goals of enabling the development of animation and doing so at the lowest possible bandwidth costs. Early Flash users, especially hobbyists, made a point of adding animations to every page, to the extent that the blinking, bouncing, and whirling creations were enough to unnerve a tree sloth. Such superfluous moving noise, known unaffectionately as *dancing baloney*, was blamed on Flash and not the near-crazed developers whose boggled minds created these abominations. Critics rightfully pointed out that such animated junk had no place in professional work, intimating that were Flash removed from the hands of developers and designers, the world would be safe for good Web usability.

In addition to creating annoying animations, Flash designers took to creating huge files that lumbered across the Internet at the pace of a hesitant slug. Having learned that vector graphics, especially used in conjunction with symbols, made for smaller files and faster Internet transfer, designers somehow got the idea that an unlimited number of graphics could be animated and quickly displayed on a user's monitor. (For good measure, many of the same designers concluded that if Flash were fast, it would be able to handle bitmapped graphics just as quickly.) When tested on their own computers, the Flash movies appeared lickety-split.

number relative to the number of frames in the entire movie. If you imagine a reel of film filled with several scenes, each frame has a distinct value beginning with 1 and ending with the total number of frames in the reel. Likewise, if you refer to a frame by its position relative to a scene, you can refer to "Scene 5, Frame 7," for example. If each scene has 100 frames, you could refer to the same frame as Frame 507.

Because you address frames only by using ActionScript, such as when you're using the `gotoAndPlay()` and `gotoAndStop()` global Timeline control functions, all references must be through ActionScript. No equivalent setting for Timeline control is possible without using ActionScript. A frame in Scene 5, Frame 7 would be addressed like this:

```
gotoAndPlay("Scene 5",7);
```

If each scene is 100 frames in length, the same position on the Timeline can be addressed as follows:

```
gotoAndPlay(507);
```

Like frames, scenes can have descriptive names that you supply using the Scene panel. For example, the following script illustrates how a scene with a descriptive name and labeled frame provide a clear path:

```
gotoAndPlay("PlanetVenus", "landing");
```

Using descriptive names for both frames and labels helps you keep track of everything in your animation.

Fortunately (or unfortunately), grave developers cautioned designers about bandwidth usage and handed them the infamous preloader. With a preloader, designers could create gargantuan files and, while waiting for these files to load, the users could entertain themselves looking at a preloader animation informing them that their file was loading but not quite ready yet. Unfortunately, neither the developers nor the designers were aware that Attention Deficit Disorder is the norm rather than the exception among Web surfers, and so most of these digital tomes were never viewed by anyone other than the designers themselves. Therefore, as a professional development tool, Flash was suspect.

Since these early days of Flash, both the product and its developers have matured. Good usability was built in with the introduction of UI components, and designers began to realize the importance of using animation judiciously as well as keeping the file size down. Preloaders are likely to be found when loading a portion of a Flash movie, and impatient users only have to suffer a few seconds awaiting the next part of the movie to play. Additionally, many parts of a Flash movie can be loaded progressively so that, after only a moment of buffering, MP3 sound files and FLV movie files begin playing. Rather than being viewed as a tool to create ponderous files on the order of Jabba the Hutt, Flash Pro is much more the orchestra conductor bringing together many different parts to seamlessly inform users and help them get what they want from the World Wide Web.

Flash Files

Before continuing, a word on the different Flash Pro files is in order. As you work with Flash Pro, not only will you generate a number of different file types, you'll also use files that Flash Pro doesn't generate. This section provides an overview of the different files you're likely to work with using Flash Pro.

FLA Files

All editable materials in Flash are saved in FLA files (pronounce it as *F-L-A* or *flaw*). These files contain objects and ActionScript that can be changed by adding, modifying, or deleting materials. After you've saved a document in an FLA file, you can open it again and make any changes you want. In developing a large and complex movie, you might want to consider saving different progressive versions of your movie so that if some portion of a later version doesn't perform correctly, you can open an earlier version where all the parts are correctly working. For instance, you might want to save Mov1.fla, Mov2.fla, and so forth as you develop a movie.

SWF Files

A SWF file (pronounce it *swif*) is a compiled Flash document that can be run directly from a player or on the Web from a browser with a Flash plug-in. A SWF file is created as soon as you have named an FLA file and saved it and then tested the movie. For example, if you save Mov1.fla and then test it, it automatically creates a file named Mov1.swf. When you publish a Flash document, typically you also generate a SWF file. The default publish settings include generating a SWF file.

HTML Files

Another file that may be created when you publish a movie is an HTML file. Like the SWF file, the default publish setting generates an HTML file with the same name as the saved name of the FLA file. So, if you have a document named Mov1.fla, when you publish the movie, it generates a file named Mov1.html. The HTML file contains code to embed the SWF file generated when the HTML file is created. (An HTML file is generated only if a SWF file is selected to be published at the same time.)

AS Files

You can create an AS file directly in Flash Pro by selecting ActionScript File when creating a new document. In previous versions of Flash, to create an AS file you had to either export a script from the Actions panel or create it independent of Flash using a text editor such as Microsoft's Notepad. An AS file is simply an external ActionScript 2.0 file saved in text format. However, with Flash MX Professional 2004, it automatically loads classes. (See Chapter 3 for details.) An AS file can also be loaded using the #include statement in the following format:

```
#include "filename.as"
```

The code loaded performs in the same manner as ActionScript generated in the Actions panel, but instead of being stored in the FLA file, it's in an external text file.

FLV Files

An important file type that can now be generated with Flash MX Professional 2004 is the FLV file. The FLV file is a movie file that can be progressively downloaded, previously accessible only with Flash Communication Server. Now using Flash Pro, these files can be used in lieu of movie files that have to be entirely loaded into a Flash document or played on an external player such as QuickTime or RealPlayer. (See Chapter 10, "Adding Video and Sound," for details on generating FLV files and running them in a Flash document.)

Other Files

Flash Pro generates other types of files and can work with other files as well. You can generate ActionScript Communication (ASC) files in much the same way as AS files, simply by selecting the ActionScript Communication Files option when creating a new file. The ASC files are used to generate server-side communication ActionScript for Flash Communication Server projects. Likewise, you can use the Flash JavaScript File option to create JSFL files. Both ASC and JSDL files are beyond the scope of this book, but you should know that if generating either type of file is important for your work, you can do so from Flash Pro.

In the Publish Settings, you can create the following files in addition to SWF and HTML files:

- GIF
- JPEG
- PNG
- Windows Projector (.exe)
- Macintosh Projector (.hqx)
- QuickTime (.mov)

For static images, the GIF, JPEG, and PNG files provide a way to capture the current image of the movie. Static images only capture the initial position of the movie. The two projector options provide a standalone movie that can be played within a self-contained Flash player and can be useful for movies to be played from CD-ROMs. If you have the updated version of QuickTime, you can generate MOV files that can be played on computers with the QuickTime players.

A final important type of file you can work with in Flash is the MP3 file, a highly compressed audio file. Previous versions of Flash allowed MP3 files to be loaded into a Flash movie, or you could convert other file types to MP3 and play them from within the SWF file as well.

However, even though highly compressed, MP3 files added considerable "weight" (increased file size) to the SWF file. With Flash Pro, you can progressively download MP3 files (much like FLV files) and not have to load them in the Flash file to play them. (See Chapter 10 for details on streaming MP3 files.)

Graphics and Symbols

Graphics used on the Flash Stage can be classified into two main categories: non-symbols and symbols. This section examines each category.

Bitmapped and Vector Graphics

Bitmapped graphics can be imported from sources ranging from digital photos to user-created graphics developed on drawing applications. Bitmapped graphics are weightier than vector graphics in most cases, and Flash has an option for transforming bitmapped graphics into vector graphics (by selecting Modify, Bitmap, Trace Bitmap). Vector graphics are preferred both because of their lighter weight and because of their ability to be changed dynamically without distortion. All graphics created with Flash tools are vector graphics. We'll get into more detail on this topic in later chapters.

Symbols

Symbols are a key element in Flash's ability to send graphics and animations over the Internet using minimal bandwidth. When a drawing is converted into a symbol, only a single symbol is compiled into the SWF files. Multiple instances of a single symbol can be used in a Flash document, but the bandwidth costs associated with the symbol are only "charged" once, no matter how many instances of the symbol are used in the Flash file. Figure 1.12 illustrates the difference between how symbols and drawings add to a SWF's file size.

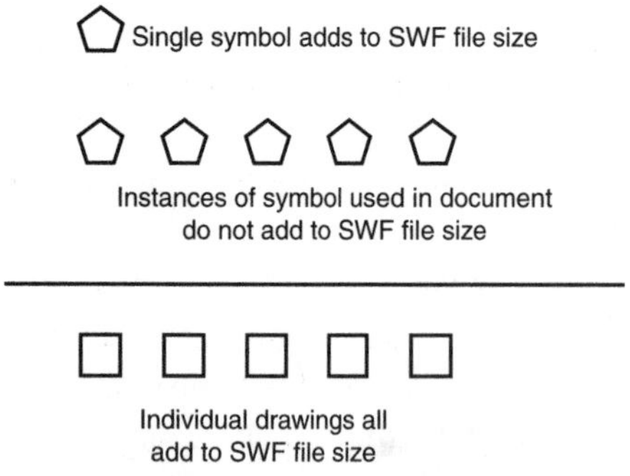

Single symbol adds to SWF file size

Instances of symbol used in document
do not add to SWF file size

Individual drawings all
add to SWF file size

FIGURE 1.12   Multiple instances of a single symbol require less bandwidth.

Movie Clips

Movie clips are movies within a Flash movie. They have their own Timelines and act as independent entities within a Flash movie. They can communicate with other movie clips and with other elements of a Flash movie. In Flash Pro, they're symbols that can be created on the Stage using drawing tools and converted using the Convert to Symbol dialog box, and they're also classes. (Alternatively, you can create them by selecting Insert, New Symbol and choosing Movie Clip. They are placed into the Library panel, where you can drag them to the Stage.) As a class, movie clips can be created dynamically during runtime, and you can link a movie clip on the Stage with a class using the movie clip's Symbol Properties dialog box. For example, Figure 1.13 shows two movie clips on the Stage of a main movie.

Movie clips   Movie clips in library

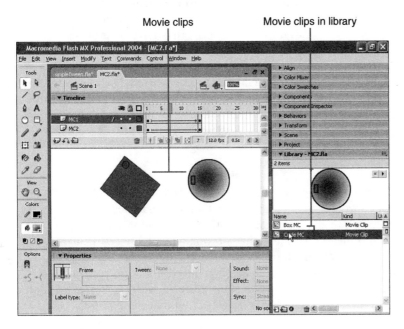

FIGURE 1.13 Movie clips have their own Timelines.

On the main Timeline, the two movie clips are rotated (rectangle) or moved up and down (circle). Within the rectangle movie clip, on the movie clip's Timeline, a ball moves from corner to corner. The circle movie clip has a rectangle that moves from side to side. Chapter 5 provides more details about this important Flash feature.

Buttons
Button symbols are the original user interface (UI) elements in Flash. In addition to the button symbol, Flash Pro also has a Button component, which has different characteristics than a button symbol. In the Actions toolbox in the Actions panel are two sets of terms. The traditional button symbols related to ActionScript are found in the Actions toolbox (Built-in Classes, Movie, Button). Button components are found in Components, Button.

A button symbol has a unique Timeline that's divided into four frames—Up, Over, Down, and Hit—and each state can have a different image in the button or associated actions. Figure 1.14 shows a button in the edit mode with two layers and keyframes placed in each frame of both layers.

The Hit frame is invisible when on the Stage, but it determines the amount of area around the button that constitutes a "hit" or an extended or reduced portion of the button that reacts to mouse movement and clicks. Chapter 7, "Tools for Use with Text and Text Components," examines uses of the button symbol in navigation.

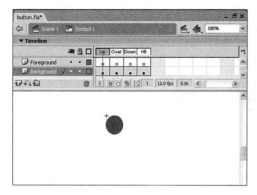

FIGURE 1.14   Button Timeline.

Graphic Symbols

Graphic symbols are for multiple static images or for animations used repeatedly on the main Timeline. They are the least dynamic of the symbols. Ironically, they have their own Timelines in the symbol editor, but unless enough frames exist on the main Timeline, a movie clip, or the movie itself, any animation in the symbol will not operate. That's because this type of symbol is tied to the main Timeline. Figure 1.15 shows three instances of a graphic symbol on the Stage.

Font Symbol

The only symbol not found as a selection in the Convert to Symbol dialog box is the font symbol. A font symbol is created when you have a font you want to export *and* use in different Flash documents. This is not quite the same as the information about a font that's installed in a SWF file that carries the font information with it so that a computer without a particular font in its system can display the font. Rather, the font information in a font symbol is placed into a library that can be copied into another FLA. For example, if you have a font on your desktop system but not on your laptop system, you can place a copy of the file with the font symbol on the laptop and then import it into the FLA files being developed on the laptop.

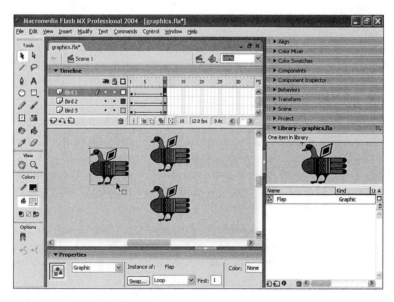

FIGURE 1.15   Graphic symbols.

Text

Text in Flash MX Professional 2004 provides added support for small font sizes. Essentially this means that you can view clearly small fonts in the 8-point range. It also supports a subset of CSS, enabling the designer to include CSS style definitions. The rest of dealing with text is very much like Flash MX. The Properties Inspector is where all the text sizing, font selection, style definition, and other Flash text formatting takes place.

In addition to the standard text fields, this latest version of Flash has a TextField component as well as some other components that deal with different types of text. However, Flash still has three main types of text fields: static, dynamic, and input.

New to Flash is the ability to include graphics in text fields. This new feature, discussed in Chapter 6, "Viewing and Entering Information with Text Fields," allows designers and developers to integrate graphics with a story in text. Chapter 6 also shows how text fields are used with the TextField and TextFormat classes.

Static Text Fields

Static text fields are used primarily as text labels in the main Timeline or in movie clips. This type of text can be animated and changed dynamically, but only along certain dimensions. For example, a static text block can be motion tweened from one side of the Stage to the other, rotating as it goes. However, the static text block cannot have tweened colors.

Text blocks can be made into hot spots and linked to URLs. Static blocks of text can also be broken apart into graphics and reconstituted as virtually any kind of symbol and used exactly as a given symbol could be used in any style.

To see a simple example of how you might use a static text field, this next project adds to the earlier project in the chapter where a ball was tweened into a square. Open the FLA with the shape tween and use the following steps to add text:

1. Add a layer by clicking the Insert layer icon. Name the layer **Text**.

2. Click the Text layer and select the Text tool.

3. Click the Stage to the right of the circle and in the Properties Inspector set the type to 24-point Arial (or Helvetica on a Mac). Then click the Align Center icon near the right side of the Properties Inspector. Type in the message **Amazing Magic Circle Transformed to Square**, as shown in Figure 1.16.

FIGURE 1.16   Adding text to the Stage.

Dynamic Text Fields

Dynamic text fields are the "data output" fields of Flash. Everything from database data to simple calculation output can be placed in dynamic text fields. Used with Flash Communication Server, for example, dynamic text fields can display chat room outputs.

See Chapter 6 for detailed information on using dynamic text fields. Especially important is the section on using CSS in text fields.

Input Text Fields

User-entered text is placed into input text fields. As part of rich Internet applications, the input text field is the most interactive element in Flash because it allows the developer and designer to create environments that change with the needs of the users who visit the site. Everything from usernames and passwords to large descriptive blocks of text can be entered here. Again, see Chapter 6 for detailed information on using input text fields.

Video

One of the key new features in Flash MX Professional 2004 is the enhanced use of video. Including video in a Flash movie is nothing new, but the ability to progressively download video from an FLV file is very new. Until now, short of using Flash Communication Server, the ability to display a video required the entire video to be included in the Flash movie. Not only does this take a huge amount of memory, but loading the SWF file tries users' patience.

Flash Pro not only provides the ability for progressive downloads but also provides three different components that help designers and developers to easily include videos from FLV files. Likewise, new Flash classes such as `NetConnection` and `NetStream` give flexibility to development using an FLV-based video component.

See Chapter 10 for detailed information on loading FLV files into Flash.

What's Next?

This chapter has put a lot of information into a very small space. For professionals new to Flash, it has provided an overview of the different parts of Flash Pro. At the same time, it was a quick review of features for Flash veterans, with an eye to what's new in Flash MX Professional 2004. The next chapter provides a quick overview of the workflow in Flash.

In Brief

- Flash development primarily occurs on a "Stage" and in a code-writing panel.
- Flash is modeled on a film analogy that includes a Timeline, frames, scenes, layers, a playhead, and a process called *tweening*.
- Symbols allow Flash to use a single drawing in multiple instances but add only the size of the single drawing to the overall file size.
- Movie clips are movies that can be added to a main movie for multiple animation.
- Text fields in Flash allow dynamic, static, and input text in a Flash document.

The Flash Pro Interface

This chapter reviews the menus, tools, and panels used in the basic Flash interface. Experienced Flash users need not spend much time on this chapter except for reviewing the new features in Flash Pro. Many of the new features are minor or consist of new arrangements of old features.

Selected examples show how one or more of the processes are used. However, the examples are short and focus on new features.

Menus

As with most program updates, a new version of Flash means changes to a familiar menu structure. You'll encounter the new options as you go along, but I'll briefly summarize the main menu structure for readers who are new to Flash and those who might like a quick review.

File

The File menu contains options for creating, loading, importing, saving, and generally dealing with files of all sorts. With this menu, you can import MP3 files, compile and publish Flash files, and more.

Edit

The Edit menu contains a fairly standard set of editing commands found in most applications, such as Undo, Cut, Copy, and Paste. However, the menu also contains certain editing options unique to Flash, such as Cut and Copy Frames in the Timeline submenu.

The most important new options in this menu are the Find options, including Find and Replace and Find Next. These options are for large text fields and help you locate terms within the fields. (Spell-checking options are often in the Edit menu in other programs; in Flash MX 2004, they're in the Text menu.)

The Undo and Redo options are now context sensitive. If you're working with the Oval tool, for example, Undo/Redo will only affect the oval being drawn. By the same token, if you're working with the Text tool, changes would only be to the text field under construction.

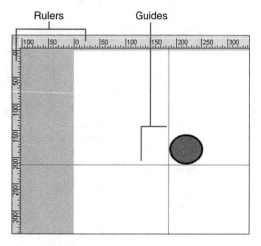

FIGURE 2.1 Creating the guides by dragging from the rulers.

View

The View menu displays different parts of the document. Many of the view features are related to understanding other aspects of using Flash. For example, the Guides submenu requires that the Rulers option be selected. Then the Guides can be dragged from the top and side of the Stage where the rulers can be seen. Figure 2.1 shows the guides and rulers on the Stage.

Some View menu options don't require other operations. For example, selecting the Show Grid option results in the grid appearing on the Stage. The rulers are not required and no dragging is needed. Overall, though, other than the reorganization of the options, the menu is the same as in the previous version of Flash.

Commands

Commands is a new Flash menu. You can use it in conjunction with the new History panel to generate commands made up of several steps taken to create some portion of a Flash document. Because this menu is new, its use needs to be illustrated with an example.

Imagine a series of Flash pages requiring 30 frames and three layers you have to complete. Instead of going through the process of adding the 30 frames and three layers for each new page, you can use a single command to do the same thing. Use the following steps:

1. Open a new page.

2. Select Window, Other Panels, History from the menu bar.

3. Add a total of 30 frames by pressing the F5 key 29 times.

4. Add a total of three layers by clicking the Insert Layer button twice.

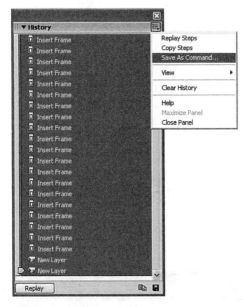

FIGURE 2.2 Creating a command.

5. Select all the steps in the History panel by dragging over all of them.

6. Click the pop-up menu in the History panel and select Save As Command, as shown in Figure 2.2.

7. Type **SetUp303** in the Command Name text box in the Save As Command dialog box.

That's all there is to it. When you open the Commands menu, at the bottom of the menu right below Run Command, you will see SetUp303. When you click the command, it automatically inserts 29 frames and adds 2 new layers. Therefore, if you click the command with a new document, you will have 3 layers and 30 frames. If you click the command a second time, you will have an *additional* 29 frames and 2 more layers, for a total of 59 frames and 5 layers.

> ### Not Always the Easiest Route
>
> Adding frames by repeatedly adding single frames is far less efficient than selecting a frame in the Timeline (for example, Frame 30) and pressing the F5 key once. However, the History panel cannot determine a frame number, so the desired number of added frames or keyframes must be done one at a time. You'll find other limitations in working with commands; however, by using single steps you can usually create the commands you want.

Control

The Control menu contains several options that control moves in and around the movie. You can also select most of these options by using keyboard shortcuts. For example, pressing Enter for a Live Preview test is far more efficient than going to the menu every time this control is required. Likewise, pressing the period key (.) or the comma key (,) to move forward or backward through the Timeline is a quick shortcut. Most of the other options on the Control menu are selected and left alone, such as Enable Live Preview.

The only new option in this menu is Test Project. A Project file is one that contains more than a single file. In the current version of Flash MX Professional 2004, the key use of the Project panel is keeping files together. As such, the Project option is very handy for keeping files with accompanying class.as files organized. To test a project, simply open the Project panel, select the project name you want to test, and select Control, Text Project.

Window

The Window menu can be seen as a long-term storage menu for panels. Most developers and designers create a panel set they use by placing the panels they typically work with in the panel docks or on the Stage and then selecting Save Panel Layout from the Window menu. Once a panel set has been saved, it's typically opened when Flash is launched; if not, a favored panel set is chosen. During typical projects, the Window menu is seldom used if the user has planned a good panel arrangement for his or her project—making the Window menu a "set and forget" menu.

Most of the new features of the Window menu are in its organization, and its new options are simply new panels, such as Project, Screens, Component Inspector, and Web Services. The Common Library submenu no longer contains a Sounds library, but it does contain a Classes library.

SHOP TALK

Old Habits Die Hard

Not long ago I was watching a relatively new Flash user fly through a project using a number of shortcuts I'd never seriously considered using. For example, I'm a frequent user of the F keys for shortcuts. (What would I do without the F8 shortcut to open the Symbol Conversion dialog box?) Also, although I use more generic shortcuts, such as the standard cut-and-paste keyboard shortcuts (Ctrl+C and Ctrl+V on my PC; Cmd+C and Cmd+V on the Mac), I rarely use the single letters available for acquiring tools from the Tools panel. Likewise, until recently, I hardly ever used context menus, and now it's my preferred way of doing several tasks.

In part, my habits were formed because I use both a Windows PC and a Mac. The one-button mice on Macs require a Control-click (*not* a Command-click) to do what a right-click does on a Windows PC. So rather than having to worry about using one method or another, I settled for not using the context menus at all. (I don't claim that this was a brilliant decision. It's just what I did.) However, a couple years ago I bought a Wacom tablet for a wireless mouse and drawing stylus and hooked it up to my Mac. The Wacom mouse for the Mac has two buttons, so I started using the right-click option on both platforms. The one-button optical mouse shipped with every Mac is probably the most beautiful mouse ever devised, but I'll never use it because I'm hooked on my two-button Mac Wacom mouse. (Let's face it, when it comes to getting a project done, a pretty mouse may not be the most important consideration.)

Don't get me wrong. If you like your one-button mouse and use Control-click with the speed of a gazelle or avoid context menus all together, that's your prerogative. Besides, an option is

Help

The Help menu is much expanded and very complete in most cases. A significant and easily overlooked new option is Transfer Your Software License. Macromedia allows users to install Flash Pro on two computers. If one of the computers on which the software is installed is being replaced by a new one, the user can remove Flash from the old computer, transfer the software license, and then install the software on the new computer.

The Reference button on the Actions panel links to the Help panel. If you select a term and click the Reference button, the Help window appears, with the selected term in the window. I've found that it's easiest to use the Help panel by keeping it out of a dock and calling it up using the F1 key or clicking the Reference button.

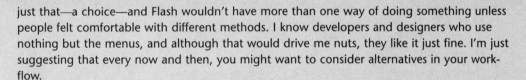

just that—a choice—and Flash wouldn't have more than one way of doing something unless people felt comfortable with different methods. I know developers and designers who use nothing but the menus, and although that would drive me nuts, they like it just fine. I'm just suggesting that every now and then, you might want to consider alternatives in your work-flow.

An overlooked submenu can be found at Edit, Keyboard Shortcuts. This opens the Keyboard Shortcut window. Not only can you find all the different shortcuts in one place—such as the period (.) key, which moves the playhead one frame forward, and the comma (,) key, which moves it one frame back—but you get a mind-boggling set of options. For example, if you're accustomed to using Photoshop, you can select the Photoshop keyboard shortcuts. Likewise, you can select shortcuts for previous versions of Flash, back to Flash 4, and other applications you may feel more comfortable using.

But there's more. Some designers and developers I know have their own personalized set of shortcuts. You may have noticed when you open the File menu there's a new option for Save and Compact, but there's no keyboard shortcut. Using the Keyboard Shortcuts window, you can add your own shortcuts or change existing ones. Any unused key combinations can be added as a substitute for a menu option. You don't have to make any changes, but you should know that you can. If you're tired of "menu diving" for an oft-used command, just go in and add a shortcut for it. (By the way, the keyboard shortcut for inserting a keyframe is F6, and it's Shift+F6 to delete one. F7 inserts a blank keyframe, and Shift+F7 deletes a blank keyframe. For some reason these shortcuts are not listed in the menus.)

Tools Panel

The Tools panel is the main source of instruments for creating and changing drawings on the Stage. Experienced users will find almost no differences between the current Tools panel and former ones, with a single exception: The Tools panel now contains a dual selection in the Rectangle tool. Figure 2.3 shows the new PolyStar tool being put to work creating the star in Chile's national flag.

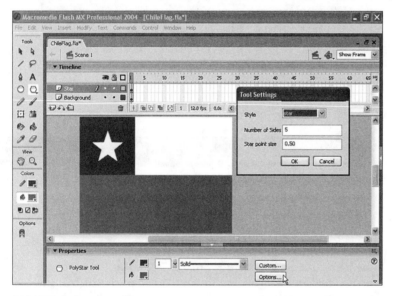

FIGURE 2.3   The PolyStar tool can be used for everything from making stars on flags to creating a pentagon.

Here are the steps to creating that nifty flag:

1. Open a new Flash document and add a layer so that you now have two layers.

2. In the bottom layer, use the Rectangle tool to draw a 200×200 blue rectangle in the upper-left corner of the Stage. Then draw a 400×200 red rectangle in the bottom half of the Stage. Lock the Stage.

3. Select the PolyStar tool from the Tools panel. In the Property panel, click the Options button, and in the Tools Settings dialog box, select Star from the Style pop-up menu. Then, type **5** for the number of points and **.5** for the star point size.

4. Click the top layer. In the middle of the blue square, draw a white star that's about 100×100. When you're finished, your drawing should look like what's shown in Figure 2.3.

The new PolyStar tool has options to set the style as a star or polygon, the number of sides, and the star point size. Although the tool itself seems like very little as far as creating shapes on the Stage, its options make it a very flexible and valuable addition to the Tools panel.

Figure 2.4 shows the Tools panel with all its tools. Each of the tools is labeled, along with any applicable letter shortcut. The Arrow tool has been renamed Selection tool, but experienced Flash users will find little difference otherwise from previous versions.

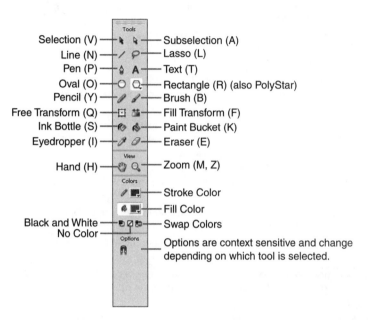

FIGURE 2.4   You can select tools by clicking or using single-letter shortcuts.

Although this book is not designed to go into drawing lessons using Flash tools, Table 2.1 describes each tool's use briefly, along with the options that appear in the Options section of the Tools panel when a tool is selected.

TABLE 2.1

Flash Tools

TOOL	DESCRIPTION
Selection	Used for selecting objects on the Stage in unlocked layers. By selectively locking and unlocking layers, you can easily select objects on lower layers. The tool cannot select objects on layers with the visibility off, even if the layer is unlocked. Clicking a keyframe selects all objects in unlocked layers in the keyframe. Options include Snap to Objects and the straighten and smoothing tools.
Subselection	Used for revealing anchor points on any drawing. You can use the tool for adjusting curves by dragging anchor points. It contains no options.
Line	Used for drawing lines in straight segments. Property Inspector options include color selection, stroke size, line type, and custom styles. It also contains the Snap to Objects option.
Lasso	Used for selecting irregular shapes. Magic Wand, Magic Wand Properties, and Polygon Mode are available options.
Pen (Bezier Pen)	Used to draw Bezier curves. Property Inspector options include stroke and fill colors, line size, and styles.

TABLE 2.1

Continued

Text	All text properties are in the Property Inspector. Includes all font styling and formatting as well as the three key types of text: static, dynamic, and input. (See Chapter 5, "Movie Clip Control," for details on using text fields.)
Oval	Used for drawing ovals and circles (holding down the Shift key forces a circle). Property Inspector options include stroke and fill color selection, stroke size, line type, and custom styles. Also includes the Snap to Objects option.
Rectangle/PolyStar	Used for drawing rectangles, polygons, and stars (holding down the Shift key forces a square). Property Inspector options include stroke and fill color selection, stroke size, line type, and custom styles. It also contains the Snap to Objects option.
Pencil	A freeform drawing tool that uses the stroke color. The Property Inspector contains options for line size and style. Also contains Straighten, Smooth, and Ink options.
Brush	A freeform drawing tool that uses the fill color. The Property Inspector contains fill color selection and smoothing values. The Tools panel options include Paint Normal, Paint Fills, Paint Behind, Paint Selection, and Paint Inside. Brush shape and size menus are also options.
Free Transform	This tool is used to change shapes, move center points, and skew images. Options include Snap to Objects, Rotate and Skew, Scale, Distort, and Envelope.
Fill Transform	This tool is used with linear and radial fills to change the light focus, fill center, and relative position.
Ink Bottle	This tool colors the stroke in drawings. Besides changing an object's color, the Ink Bottle tool can change its stroke size and shape as well. It contains no options.
Paint Bucket	Used to change the fill color of drawings. Options include Don't Close Gaps, Close Small Gaps, Close Medium Gaps, and Close Large Gaps. Another option is the Lock Fill Modifier, which causes gradient fill to appear to cover several drawings.
Eyedropper	The Eyedropper tool is like a magic color changer. When it's dragged over a color, the color in the color box changes to the color the Eyedropper touches. It contains no options.
Eraser	Used to remove drawings using several context options. Erase types include Erase Normal, Erase Fills, Erase Lines, Erase Selected Fills, and Erase Inside. The Faucet option automatically erases fills and lines. Also, several sizes and shapes are available as options.
Hand	Placing this tool on Stage and dragging moves the viewing position. It contains no options.
Zoom	You use the magnifying glass icon to zoom in by clicking and zoom out by Alt-clicking (or Option-clicking on Macintosh). It offers the Enlarge and Reduce options.
Stroke and Fill Colors	Stroke colors are the colors of lines, and the fill colors are the colors within the lines. If a drawing has its lines deleted or is created with the Brush tool, the drawing may have no stroke color at all. When you're using the Oval, PolyStar, or Rectangle tool, a stroke line is automatically included along with a fill color, unless one or the other is turned off. (A rectangle in the color swatches pop-up box with a red diagonal line indicates that the stroke or fill is turned off.) No options are available.
Black and White	Used to change the stroke color to black and the fill color to white with a single click. No options are available.
No Color	Indicates that the selected stroke or fill has no color. No options are available.
Swap Colors	Used to reverse the stroke and fill colors. No options are available.

Panels and Toolbars

Flash users need to be able to work comfortably with an array of panels and toolbars, which I describe in this section. Later chapters cover the use of these features in detail as they're employed to create objects.

Toolbars

Depending on the project, Flash Pro's three toolbars will be more or less useful. Your individual working style will dictate how and if any of the three are to be used. About the only drawback of any of the toolbars is screen clutter.

Main Toolbar

The Main toolbar is not particularly "main," per se, but it does have handy icons for opening new or existing documents and for saving documents. Likewise, often-used tasks such as freely transforming and aligning objects on the Stage are included. Figure 2.5 shows the items on the Main toolbar.

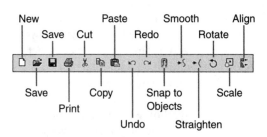

FIGURE 2.5   The Main toolbar.

FIGURE 2.6
The Controller toolbar is used like VCR playback.

FIGURE 2.7   The Edit toolbar.

Controller Toolbar

The Controller toolbar is a VCR-like set of controls for playing, fast forwarding, stopping, and rewinding a test file. Figure 2.6 shows the Controller toolbar.

Edit Bar

The Edit bar shows the scene currently selected and provides a drop-down menu for selecting scenes. It also contains a pop-up menu for selecting the zoom size of the Stage and objects on the Stage. Although not much appears to be on this toolbar, as shown in Figure 2.7, it's one of the handier tools, especially when the document contains more than one scene.

General Panels

The first set of panels in the Windows menu is either used with virtually all documents, such as the Property Inspector and Library panels, or used with tasks that require specialized panels, such as the Projects and Screens panels.

FIGURE 2.8 The Project panel displays all files associated with a project so that all the files can be seen and accessed easily.

Project Panel

The Project panel is exclusive to Flash MX Professional 2004. When it's used with projects that have more than a single file, the Project panel is very handy for organizing all the parts. Eventually, this panel may be developed into a base for collaborative development, but with this release, its most important function is to simplify working with different files in a single project. Figure 2.8 shows a simple project made up of two files. When you double-click any of the files shown in the Project panel, that file is loaded into Flash.

Property Inspector

The most-used of all the panels is the Property Inspector. It needs to be placed where you can get to it easily, such as docked at the bottom of the screen beneath the Stage. This context-sensitive panel changes depending on what object on the Stage is selected. Figure 2.9 shows the Property Inspector when a movie clip symbol has been selected. The *most* crucial aspect of the Property Inspector is the instance, name window where instance names are placed. Instance names are important because all movie clip and button instances created on the Stage are addressed by their instance names in ActionScript. When a symbol is created, the name used is for the symbol. However, every instance of that symbol, whether a button or movie clip, must have a unique instance name. Otherwise, it's impossible to specify which instance a script references.

FIGURE 2.9 The Property Inspector is context sensitive. The display varies depending on what's currently selected.

Screens Panel

The Screens panel is unique to Flash MX Professional 2004. It only appears when either a Flash slide presentation or Flash form application is in the document window. Rather than appearing in the dock, the panel appears on the left side of the document and can be toggled on or off in the Window menu but cannot be dragged anywhere on the screen like other panels. Figure 2.10 shows a typical Screens panel displayed in a Flash slide presentation before content has been added.

See Chapter 9, "Producing Online Slide Shows," for more details on creating slide shows.

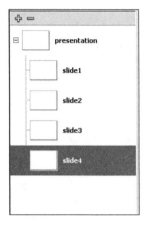

FIGURE 2.10 Screens panels are blank when they're first added to the screen set.

FIGURE 2.11 The Timeline is characterized by frame markers and a playhead marker indicating the current frame.

Timeline

The Timeline is largely unchanged from previous versions of Flash. It contains the frames, keyframes, playhead, layers, and other motion picture–like editing features. Although the Timeline can be dragged to anywhere on the screen, typically, it's in the dock above the Stage. Figure 2.11 shows a typical Timeline with labeled keyframes and a tween.

Library Panel

The Library panel is virtually identical to the Flash MX Library panel, except that it now automatically loads into the dock on the right side of the document. The library holds all the objects in the movie, from which instances can be dragged to the Stage. Besides standard objects such as movie clips, buttons, and graphics, the library also stores font and embedded video objects. The pop-up menu on the Library panel is important not to overlook; from this menu, you acquire embedded video and other objects, as shown in Figure 2.12. When you drag a component to the Stage, all the different parts that make up the component are placed in a folder in the Library panel.

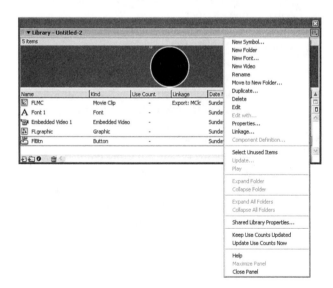

FIGURE 2.12 The Library panel contains symbols, components, graphics, sounds, videos, and embedded videos.

FIGURE 2.13   The Align panel shows a number of icons symbolizing different types of alignment options of Stage elements to one another or to the Stage itself.

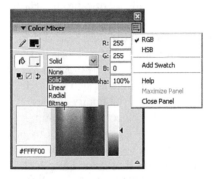

FIGURE 2.14   The Color Mixer panel provides several ways to mix colors.

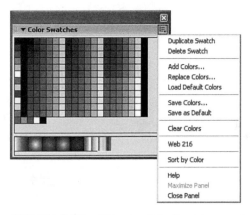

FIGURE 2.15   Using the Color Swatches panel, you can define your own color palette.

Design Panels

The design panels are a reorganization of panels from Flash MX. All the design panels are used in creating and arranging objects on the Stage.

Align Panel

This panel is essential for organizing objects on the Stage. Each of the icons on the panel align, resize, or distribute objects relative to others selected or to the Stage. Both drawings and symbol instances can be aligned, but all layers to be aligned need to be visible and unlocked. Figure 2.13 shows the panel, unchanged from Flash MX.

Color Mixer Panel

With no significant changes from previous versions of Flash, the Color Mixer panel provides different ways to create colors and gradients. The color mixing can be done using either decimal or hexadecimal with either RGB (Red, Green, Blue) or HSB (Hue, Saturation, Brightness). You can set the opaque level by changing the Alpha value. Once a color is mixed, you can add it to the Swatch panel by selecting Add Swatch from the pop-up menu. Figure 2.14 shows the panel with both its menus open.

Color Swatches Panel

Also unchanged from previous versions of Flash is the Color Swatches panel. Its most important use is to set a color palette to use with a document or projects. Once you have created a palette by adding swatches using the Color Mixer, you can save the palette by selecting the Save option from the pop-up menu. When the same color palette is to be used with another document, it can be loaded from this panel. Figure 2.15 shows the panel with a color palette along the bottom of the solid swatches. Note also that different kinds of gradients can be selected from the Color Swatches panel.

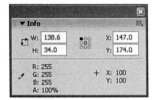

FIGURE 2.16 The Info panel provides dimension and positioning information for both the object and mouse, but also provides color information for whatever the mouse is positioned over.

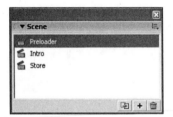

FIGURE 2.17 The Scene panel makes adding and arranging scenes easy.

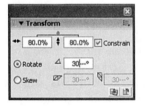

FIGURE 2.18 The Transform panel makes it simple to make precise changes to an object's size, rotation, and skew.

Info Panel

Much of the functionality of the Info panel has been usurped by the Property Inspector. However, it still remains an important panel for quickly and dynamically getting information about objects on the Stage. Unchanged from previous versions of Flash, the panel displays color (RGB and Alpha) and _x and _y values as the mouse is moved across the Stage. By changing the center point from the upper-left corner to the center of the object, designers can gather information about placement parameters. Figure 2.16 shows a typical Info panel with its values.

Scene Panel

Although the Scene panel is fairly simple, it's essential when you're working with documents with multiple scenes. Using the Scene panel, you can easily rearrange, add, delete, and rename scenes. Figure 2.17 shows a typical set of scenes in the Scene panel.

Transform Panel

When you want to change the size, angle, or skew of an object on the Stage, and you want a precise value, use the Transform panel instead of the Free Transform tool. For example, rather than attempting to drag an object to a 90-degree rotation with the Free Transform tool, you can simply select the object and type **90** in the degree window with the Transform panel. Figure 2.18 shows an object that has been reduced to 80% of its original size with the constrain box selected so that the change is proportional. Also, it shows the object has been rotated 30 degrees.

Development Panels

The panels associated with developmental tasks such as writing ActionScript 2.0 are organized into the Development Panels submenu in the Window menu. Two new panels, the Component Inspector and Web Services panel, are included in the folder.

Actions Panel

Significant changes have been made in the Actions panel. First, rather than including Normal and Expert modes, the Actions panel now has a single mode. (The Normal mode has largely been replaced by the Behaviors panel described in the next section.)

The left side of the Actions panel includes the Actions toolbox and new Script Navigator. ActionScript 2.0 is written in the right pane of the panel. Scripts are typed in the right pane with optional line numbers included. You can also add script by double-clicking the terms in the Actions toolbox or clicking the Add (+) icon above the script-typing area. In longer scripts, you can use the Script Navigator to jump to different parts of a script. Although scripting individual buttons and movie clips outside of a frame script is discouraged as a practice, if scripts are written in such a manner, you can easily switch to different scripts by using the Script Navigator. Figure 2.19 shows a script referencing a user class. (Chapter 3, "Adding ActionScript to Your Animation," contains more detail on using ActionScript 2.0 and the Actions panel.)

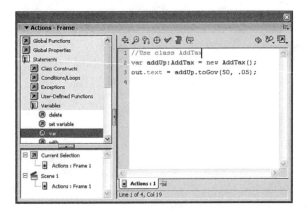

FIGURE 2.19   The Actions panel is used for adding ActionScript to a movie.

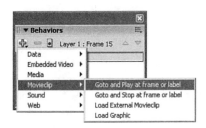

FIGURE 2.20   The Behaviors panel contains built-in code blocks for accomplishing a number of different tasks.

Behaviors Panel

The Behaviors panel replaces the Normal mode of the Actions panel. If you're just learning ActionScript or prefer to focus on design, you'll find the Behaviors panel to be quite helpful. Basically, the panel is used to automatically create blocks of code that can be used for different tasks. Chapter 3 describes the use of this panel in detail. Figure 2.20 shows a typical set of selections in using the Behaviors panel.

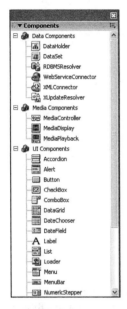

FIGURE 2.21 The Components panel in Flash MX Professional 2004 contains Data, Media, and UI components.

FIGURE 2.22 The Component Inspector changes context depending on which component is being used.

Components Panel

Components are packages or prebuilt objects with high and dynamic functionality. They greatly simplify and increase productivity of rich Internet applications. Flash MX Professional 2004 has a large set of components both in comparison to Flash MX and to Flash MX 2004. In addition to UI components, Flash Pro has Data and Media components. The parameters for components are set in both the Property Inspector and Components Inspector. The various components are discussed in subsequent chapters where their use is most relevant. Figure 2.21 shows the Components panel in Flash Pro.

Component Inspector

The Component Inspector is a new panel in Flash MX 2004. It's used to set parameters, bindings, and schemas for different components. Like the Property Inspector, the Component Inspector is context sensitive and changes depending on what component has been selected. Figure 2.22 shows the Component Inspector with the MediaPlayback component selected on the Stage. The Component Inspector is discussed with the use of various components throughout the book.

Debugger Panel

The Debugger panel is used in conjunction with the Control, Debug Movie selection. Depending on the nature of the script in the Actions panel, the levels used and the objects in the document, the Debugger panel displays different information.

To use the Debugger panel, write a script in the Actions panel. Then, rather than selecting Control, Test Movie, select Control, Debug Movie from the menu bar. Figure 2.23 shows typical results you can expect to see in the Debugger panel.

Output Panel

The Output panel has two distinct and different functions, but it generally serves as a debugging tool. All trace statements as well as all programming errors send results to the Output panel. Figure 2.24 shows a typical scripting error—attempting to place a script for a button instance in a frame script.

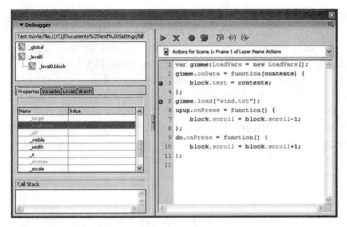

FIGURE 2.23   The Debugger panel assists in locating and repairing bugs in a script or movie.

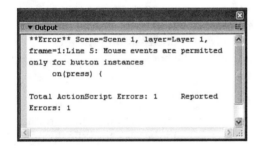

FIGURE 2.24   The Output panel showing a scripting error.

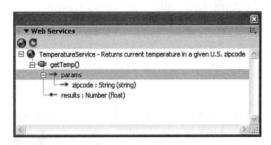

FIGURE 2.25   The Web Services panel is used in conjunction with the WebServiceConnector component.

Web Services Panel

The final panel in the Development panels grouping is the new Web Services panel. By adding a Web service address to the Web Services panel, you can set up connections to a Web service. Figure 2.25 shows a typical Web service connection displayed in the Web Services panel.

See Chapter 12, "Dealing with External Data and Objects," for more information about using Web services with the WebServiceConnector component.

Other Panels

The other panels make up a residual category of Flash MX 2004 panels. The following is a brief overview of each one:

- **Accessibility**—This panel is used to select which accessibility feature you want turned on.

- **History**—This is a new panel used to record each action taken on the Stage. It's used with the Behaviors panel. (See Chapter 3 for details on how this panel is used with the Behaviors panel.)

- **Movie Explorer**—The Movie Explorer panel is similar to the script navigator, but it resides as an independent panel and provides more information about a document. It can be used to locate different links and levels and is especially useful in a complex document.

- **Strings**—This is a new panel used in authoring multilanguage text. This addition is especially important for projects to be used in the international market.

- **Common Libraries**—Buttons, Classes, and Learning Interactions make up the three common libraries. The Sounds library has been removed, but the Classes library has been added in Flash MX Professional 2004. The classes include `DataBindingClasses`, `UtilsClasses`, and `WebServiceClasses`.

Saving and Publishing Flash Movies

Saving an FLA file (source code) is unchanged from previous versions of Flash (File, Save), but in projects where user classes are developed, both an FLA and AS file need to be saved in the same folder. All movie testing (Control, Test Movie) generates a compiled SWF file. Selecting File, Publish generates both SWF and HTML files in the default Publish Settings.

The publishing options have increased. Naturally, with Flash Player 7 available, one more player can be selected; however, you'll also find Flash Lite 1.0 as a player option. Flash Lite 1.0 is for playing on mobile devices such as PDAs and mobile phones.

Another new publishing option can be found in the Flash tab of the Publish Setting dialog box. First, you can select between ActionScript 1.0 and ActionScript 2.0. If you have several old UI components from Flash MX, you'll want to select both ActionScript 1.0 and Flash Player 6. In addition, if you have placed your class AS files in a separate folder, you can select the Settings button and provide a classpath URL.

What's Next?

The workflow in Flash Pro is very similar to previous versions of Flash, but Flash Pro can easily incorporate far more robust projects than in earlier versions. This chapter has briefly covered the menus, panels, inspectors, and other tools and elements of the Flash interface used to create documents. New Flash users as well as experienced Flash users encountering new elements, such as the Project panel, the MediaPlayback component, and other new Flash Pro features, will find more details on using these tools in subsequent chapters.

In Brief

- Flash provides a wide range of options within the menu structure for creating Flash documents.

- Flash tools can be used both to create original drawings and to transform imported drawings using vector graphics.

- The context-sensitive Property and Component Inspectors provide multiple functions without cluttering the work area.

- Multiple toolbars and panels let you arrange your workspace to best match your project needs.

- Several functions found in menus can be acquired through the use of keyboard short-cuts.

Adding ActionScript to Your Animation

The Role of ActionScript 2.0 in Flash Pro Development

In this seventh incarnation of Flash, ActionScript has taken on a new version name for the first time. Flash MX Professional 2004 introduces ActionScript 2.0, heralding a line of demarcation between all previous versions of ActionScript, now called ActionScript 1.0, and the new version using the ECMAScript Edition 4 standards. By following the European Computer Manufacturers Association (ECMA) standards, ActionScript 2.0 is consistent not only with other Internet languages that meet the standards, such as JavaScript 2.0, but with the wider world of object-oriented programming languages such as Java and C++.

ActionScript 2.0 is an integral part of creating a wide range of documents in Flash Pro. Rich Internet applications rely on ActionScript 2.0 because it can be used to call up external files, control objects on and off the Stage, and create interactivity in Flash movies. However, ActionScript 2.0 is only one of many tools that make up Flash. Therefore, although the documents you create with Flash will typically contain ActionScript 2.0, they are also made up of different objects created with the array of other tools found in Flash Pro.

> **New in ActionScript 2.0: The Behaviors Panel**
>
> Readers who are not programmers and have no aspirations along those lines should take heart. Flash Pro provides a new panel, the Behaviors panel, that automatically generates simple but effective code for you. Using the Behaviors panel is covered in this chapter. However, the other examples of ActionScript 2.0 throughout the rest of the book employ the more standard Actions panel.

In subsequent chapters, you'll use ActionScript 2.0 to create different parts of a Flash document that are needed for various tasks. The uses of ActionScript 2.0 are centered around typical parts that one would incorporate into a professional Web site using Flash Pro as the primary development tool. Therefore, when describing how to create effective I/O structures in Chapter 6, "Viewing and Entering Information with Text Fields," for example, I'll explain how to use different types of text fields, the TextField component, and ActionScript 2.0 for dynamically using the `TextField` and `TextFormat` classes along with the information entered into a text field. This integrated approach requires that you see ActionScript as just another tool—and not the only tool—for making a Flash document.

Object-Oriented and Procedural Programming

Those who know OOP already or who really don't want to be heavily involved in programming can skip this section. This section is important for readers who are new to object-oriented programming (OOP) and who want to optimize their scripts using ActionScript 2.0. To optimally work with ActionScript 2.0 and OOP, I recommend reading a book on OOP to fully understand the object-oriented approach to programming. An especially valuable book that deals with Flash MX 2004 and OOP is Jeff Tapper's *Object-Oriented Programming with ActionScript 2.0* (New Riders, 2004, ISBN 0735713804).

To begin understanding OOP, you need to know a little about what the OOP approach replaces. Originally, programming took a *procedural* approach. The procedural approach executes a series of procedures sequentially. Chances are that if you've programmed extensively in ActionScript 1.0, many of your programs are procedural. For simple programming, the procedural approach works fine. However, as programmers began encountering larger programming tasks, they found that large projects involving multiple programmers were problematic, and they needed a new approach. ActionScript 1.0 had some relatively simple OOP structures, and many ActionScript programmers took full advantage of those structures. So for some, OOP in ActionScript 2.0 certainly is not a brand-new topic.

Real-World Modeling

Rather than dealing with procedures that could be accessed from anywhere in a program, OOP developed the idea that programming should better reflect the real world in the problem-solving work accomplished by the program elements. To reflect real-world models,

OOP took the *object* as its central concept. Objects in the real world have *characteristics* and *behaviors*—nouns and verbs, as it were. For instance, you may know a person who has brown eyes and brown hair, is 6 feet tall, and likes to jog and eat Mexican food.

These are some of the characteristics of the person:

- Brown eyes
- Brown hair
- Six feet tall

These are some of the behaviors of the person:

- Jogging
- Eating Mexican food

Obviously, people have more characteristics and behaviors than those listed, but most of the objects you deal with in Flash are made up of just a few characteristics and behaviors.

In the parlance of OOP, an object's characteristics are called *properties* and its behaviors are called *methods*. One way to think of properties is that they are something like a variable that can have different values. If one of the characteristics (properties) of an object is "hair color," you can have red, blonde, black, brown, or even blue, just as a variable called hairColor can have different hues. The methods of an object are something like functions in a program. They call for some kind of behavior. Imagine an object in a Flash movie that simulates jogging by rapidly increasing the pace of movements of the arm and leg parts. The object might include both walk and jog methods, and when the jog method is called, the object moves faster than if the walk method is called.

Classes and Objects

In ActionScript 2.0, you create a class typically saved in an AS file, and you use instances of that class in your scripts written in the Actions panel. Think of a class as a mold, and when you need to use the class, the mold pops out an object (an instance) with all the characteristics of the mold. So, if you have a "person" mold (class) with brunette hair who jogs, to bring that person to life, you create a new instance of the jogging brunette. The mold (class) itself simply describes what the objects it creates can do. The objects themselves are the instances created in the Actions panel. Depending on whether you're a purist, you can accept different definitions of classes and objects. The most common, and probably most useful, conception of classes and objects is one that treats an object as an *instance* of a class. A purist definition follows the reasoning that a class is an object from which other objects can be created, and although that conception is perfectly correct, treating objects as instances of a class helps differentiate between the creating term (class) and the term in use (object) in a program.

Project: Creating a Class in ActionScript 2.0

For those familiar with OOP from ActionScript 1.0, where prototype classes were created, you will find creating classes in ActionScript 2.0 both different and in most respects easier. You can still create a class using the prototype function, but otherwise all user classes are created in an external AS file. Likewise, extensions of built-in files are created in the same external kind of file. Only a single class or extension of a class can be created in a single file. However, a document can have as many files containing classes as you need in a program. The name of the AS file must be saved as the name of the class. The names of classes, as well as the AS files containing their definitions, begin with a capital letter. For example, if you define a class as Car, the name of the AS file would be Car.as so that it can be compiled correctly.

Creating a Class in an AS file

Use the Script window to write your class AS files. Open a new Script window by selecting File, New from the menu and then selecting ActionScript File from the General tab. You can write AS files in virtually any pure text editor, such as Microsoft Notepad, but the Script window provides both code hints and script formatting that make scripting much easier.

To help you understand how a class works in Flash MX Professional 2004, a simple example is in order. In this example, the class has a single property (a string for the name of a color) and a single method (a statement that outputs the values of the property). Follow these steps:

1. Using the new Flash MX Professional 2004 Script window, save the following script with the name ColorShow.as:

```
class ColorShow {
//Property
 var colorName:String;
 function ColorShow(someColor:String) {
 this.colorName = someColor;
 }
 //Method
 function outNow():String {
 return colorName;
 }
}
```

When you use a class in a program, you need to place the AS file with the class definition in the same folder as the FLA file. The class is compiled into the SWF file when published; therefore, the SWF file need not be in the same folder as the AS file.

Creating a Path to a Class File

If you have programs with several classes, you may find it more convenient to place all the classes in a subfolder. For longer-range planning, you may decide to place all your classes in a folder separate from all your Flash projects so that they can be used by any single project. Part of OOP includes reusability, and the ability to access classes anywhere on the developer's hard drive is a good feature where reusable code is concerned. To create a path to your class file, use the following steps:

1. Create a class file and save it to your hard drive.

2. Create your FLA file, save it, and then select File, Publish Settings from the menu bar.

3. In the Publish Settings dialog box, select the Flash tab.

4. Select ActionScript 2.0 in the ActionScript Version pop-up menu.

5. Click the Settings button next to the ActionScript version to open the ActionScript Settings window. Click the plus (+) button beneath Classpath in the ActionScript Settings window.

6. In the live text box beneath the plus (+) button, type the path to your class AS file. For example, if you're placing all your classes in a subfolder within the folder (named `classes`) containing your FLA file, type in **classes/** for the class path. Figure 3.1 shows what you get.

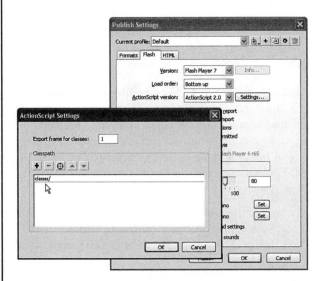

FIGURE 3.1 You can create any path to your AS files that you want.

2. Now that the class is written and you've decided on the default path, you can create a Flash document that uses the class. The following script, written in the Actions panel, creates an instance of the class named showOff:

```
var showOff:ColorShow = new ColorShow("Green");
display_txt.text = showOff.outNow();
```

Because this script creates an instance of the class, showOff is the object (instance) in the object-oriented program. Moreover, using similar short scripts that use the class, you can re-create other objects to display any value you want.

3. On the Stage, place a dynamic text field and give it the instance name display_txt. Now, whatever color name (or any other string for that matter) that you place in the ColorShow() argument appears in the output window.

Using this simple example, we can now look at the key features of OOP. Three key concepts make up the foundation of OOP:

- Encapsulation

- Inheritance

- Polymorphism

Each will be described briefly, but you are encouraged to look at a more detailed work on OOP to fully understand their use and value.

Encapsulation

In some office construction, rooms are added as modules. A big crane lifts a prebuilt room and sets it in place with the other rooms. This module is a self-contained entity, even though it's part of a larger structure. You can think of encapsulation in OOP as a self-contained module. It contains the data (properties) and functions (methods) to get something done, just as the different rooms in a module-built building have self-contained capsules used for different purposes. As such, classes in OOP are independent, but they can interact with other instances of the same and different classes in a program.

In our example, the *property* colorName is a string that is determined by the value placed in the class argument (someColor). To be fully encapsulated, the instance cannot be exposed, so a *method*, outNow, is included to provide the value of the property. With both the property and method, the class is fully encapsulated.

Inheritance

Dog breeders work to make sure their pups inherit the best traits of a given breed. Some breeds are bred to protect their owners' family and property, whereas others are bred to get along with people. A breeder may want to improve the temperament of his dogs, and so he might breed more dogs who include a good temperament even though some other trait, such as size, may not be optimum. Whatever the breeder does shows up in the way the litter looks and acts. The pups inherit the characteristics of their parents.

Inheritance in OOP works the same way. A class can inherit the characteristics of a class from which it sprang. A "parent" class is called a *superclass*, whereas the "children" of an existing class are called a *subclass*. The subclass inherits all its superclass's characteristics, plus it can have unique characteristics of its own.

In Flash Pro, several classes are built in, and you can use a built-in class or a user class to create a subclass. For example, suppose you want a method in the Array class that will return the top element but not remove it from the array, like the pop method does. Also, you want to know when the array is empty, so you want a method that tells you that as well. Using inheritance and the extends statement, all of this is possible (see Listing 3.1). First, create an AS file with the class definition as an extension of the Array class. You want to return the top element in the array; because array element references begin with 0, you want to find the length of the array and subtract 1 to get the top element. Next, all you need is a method that returns a Boolean true if the array is empty.

LISTING 3.1   Adding New Features to an Existing Class (Stack.as)

```
//Stack class
dynamic class Stack extends Array {
 var Stack:Array = new Array();
 function top() {
 return this[this.length-1];
 }
 function isEmpty():Boolean {
 return this.length == 0;
 }
}
```

To test this script, you need to see whether the new method top() will indeed return the top element in the array without removing it. First, invoke the top() method and then check the length of the array. If the length of the array is the original size, everything is working. Next, after using the pop() method three times to empty the array, use the isEmpty() method. The script in Listing 3.2 requires a multiline dynamic text field with the instance name zoo_txt on the Stage.

LISTING 3.2   Using the New and Inherited Features of an Extended Class (StackTop.FLA)

```
var popMe:Stack = new Stack();
popMe.push("Lions", "Tigers", "Elephants");
zoo_txt.text = popMe.top()+newline;
zoo_txt.text += "Length:" + popMe.length + newline;
zoo_txt.text += popMe.pop()+newline;
zoo_txt.text += popMe.pop()+newline;
zoo_txt.text += popMe.pop()+newline;
zoo_txt.text += "Empty:" + popMe.isEmpty();
```

When you test the new class, Stack, you will find that you can now successfully use all the inherited characteristics of the Array class plus the new methods you added to the subclass, Stack.

Polymorphism

The third element of the OOP foundation is polymorphism. At its simplest, *polymorphism* simply means taking on several forms. In programming, polymorphism refers to using the same method or operation to do different things. One context generates one action, and another context generates another. For example, anyone who has used the add operator (+) in a program is aware that in one context the operator adds two values, and in another context it concatenates strings. The following shows a simple example of polymorphism with the add operator:

```
29 + 31 = 60
"29" + "31" = 2931
```

As the context changes, so does the meaning and use of the add operator, but the operator looks exactly the same no matter what it's doing.

Perhaps the most appropriate way to think about polymorphism is in terms of parent classes (superclasses) and child classes (subclasses). Suppose you create a parent class called MotorVehicle. The MotorVehicle class contains an internal combustion engine method for locomotion, called useEngine(). If you create three different subclasses using the MotorVehicle interface—Airplane, Automobile, and JetSki—all must include the useEngine() method, but each provides the useEngine() differently. If all the subclasses adhere to a common MotorVehicle interface, they all have a useEngine() method. Therefore, the lines

```
JetSki.useEngine();
Airplane.useEngine();
Automobile.useEngine();
```

result in different actions appropriate to each subclass, even though the term used, useEngine(), is identical.

Polymorphism is a far more robust and complex concept than what has been presented here, and you'll find more than a single type of polymorphism (such as coercion, overloading, parametric, and inclusion). To learn more about OOP in general and polymorphism specifically, take a look at a good book on object-oriented programming. In *this* book, when polymorphism is employed in a script, its use will be noted. (Virtually all uses of classes employ encapsulation, and inheritance can be easily spotted by the use of the extends term; therefore, the use of encapsulation and inheritance need not be noted.)

Using the Behaviors Panel

Some Flash developers and designers don't give a hoot about OOP and only use ActionScript 2.0 for relatively minor chores. If you're among that number, you'll find the Behaviors panel in Flash to be just the tool you've been waiting for. It provides built-in code for non-programmers so that all you need to do to get the code you want is to select the task you want accomplished, and the Behaviors panel will whip up the code you need in no time at all.

Project: Loading External JPEG Files into a Movie Clip with the Behaviors Panel

The code from the Behaviors panel can be placed in buttons, movie clips, or frames. Depending on what you've selected when you begin using the Behaviors panel, you will see different selections. To get started, the following steps show you how to create a document that will load external JPEG files into a movie clip. Before you get started, though, create three JPEG files with the names ad1.jpg, ad2.jpg, and ad3.jpg. (In the example, old-time advertisements are used; hence, the name "ad#.jpg" is used.) Here are the steps to follow:

1. Open a new document and create three layers, naming them, from top to bottom, Buttons, MovieClip, and Background.

2. Add the desired background in the Background layer. In the MovieClip layer, use the rectangle tool to create a 50×50 square. Select the square, press F8, and change it into a movie clip symbol. Select the movie clip on the Stage; in the Instance Name box in the Property Inspector, type the name **jpgLoader_mc**.

3. Select the Buttons layer and create a button by drawing a circle, pressing F8, and selecting Button in the Symbols dialog box.

4. Open the Behaviors panel, select the button on the Stage, and click the add (+) button. When you click the add button, you'll open the Behaviors menu. Select the Movieclip menu and then the Load Graphic option in the submenu, as shown in Figure 3.2.

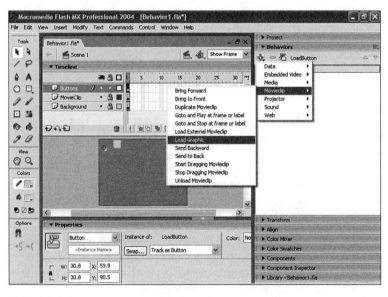

FIGURE 3.2 Selections available from the Behaviors panel's Movieclip submenu when a button is selected.

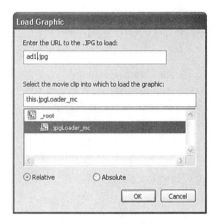

FIGURE 3.3   The Load Graphic dialog box.

5. When you select the Load Graphic option, the Load Graphic dialog box opens. In the first text box, type the name of the first JPEG file you want to load (**ad1.jpg**, in this example). Then select the jpgLoader_mc icon and make sure that the Relative radio button is selected. Figure 3.3 shows what this dialog box should look like when correctly filled out.

6. Select the button and open the Actions panel by pressing the F9 key. Notice that a script has been written for you. Figure 3.4 shows what it should look like.

7. Add two more buttons and repeat steps 4 and 5 so that the remaining two JPEG files can be loaded. Label the buttons appropriately. Figure 3.5 shows what your completed movie will look like when you run it and click one of the three buttons.

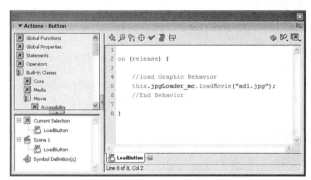

FIGURE 3.4   The Actions panel with code written by the Behaviors panel.

FIGURE 3.5   A different JPEG file loads into the movie clip as each button is clicked.

Project: Loading an MP3 with the Behaviors Panel

The scripts created by the Behaviors panel that go into frames are a different set of selections, and a more limited set as well. However, that doesn't mean you won't be given some terrific code.

The Behaviors panel has fewer selections for scripts associated with frames because both buttons and movie clips have far more events associated with them. For example, a button recognizes events such as being pressed and released, mouse rollovers and drag-overs, and whether the event is on or off the button. A frame essentially has the event of something entering the frame. Nevertheless, some great scripts can be generated automatically for frames. This next example is quite simple, involving a single frame and script. Before starting this example, get a musical MP3 file and name it `class1.MP3`. Place the MP3 file in the same folder where you'll be saving your FLA file. Here are the steps to follow:

1. Open a new Flash document and click the first frame.

2. Click the add (+) button on the Behaviors panel and select Sound, Load Streaming MP3 file. In the resulting dialog box, type the name of the MP3 file and a reference name (with no spaces). Figure 3.6 shows what the dialog box should look like prior to you clicking the OK button.

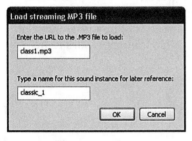

That's it. You're done. The MP3 file has now been imported into your movie, which you can check by looking in the library and the Sound menu. That is important because your movie will load considerably faster, and the sound will be "streamed" (actually a progressive download) into your movie as the user starts playing it.

FIGURE 3.6 The Load Streaming MP3 File dialog box.

To set up the streaming MP3 file, the Behaviors panel generated the code shown in Listing 3.3.

LISTING 3.3 MP3 Streaming Code Generated by the Behaviors Panel.

```
//Load Streaming mp3 behavior
if (_global.Behaviors == null) {
    _global.Behaviors = {};
}
if (_global.Behaviors.Sound == null) {
    _global.Behaviors.Sound = {};
}
if (typeof this.createEmptyMovieClip == 'undefined') {
    this._parent.createEmptyMovieClip('BS_classic_1',
    ➥new Date().getTime()-(Math.floor((new Date().getTime())/10000)*10000));
    _global.Behaviors.Sound.classic_1 = new Sound(this._parent.BS_classic_1);
} else {
    this.createEmptyMovieClip('_classic_1_',
    ➥new Date().getTime()-(Math.floor((new Date().getTime())/10000)*10000));
    _global.Behaviors.Sound.classic_1 = new Sound(this.BS_classic_1);
}
_global.Behaviors.Sound.classic_1.loadSound("class1.mp3", true);
```

You need not know what the code means, nor do you have to learn how to code. All you need to do is to select the correct options in the Behaviors panel, and you'll accomplish the necessary tasks. (Your clients don't need to know you can't code!)

Using the Actions Panel

The Actions panel along with the Script window are at the heart of the scripting you'll be doing. All external coding is done in the Script windows, and the internal code preserved in FLA files is created in the Actions panel. Because the Actions panel in Flash Pro has changed slightly since the last version and some readers are new to its use, the following quick overview serves as both a review and a brief introduction to the Actions panel.

To familiarize you with using the Actions panel, this next little project is handy if you're trying to figure out what 25 degrees Celsius is in Fahrenheit degrees. It uses two text fields and a couple buttons, but otherwise it's all coded. Don't worry about understanding the conversion algorithms. Also, this project doesn't employ any classes; it's just a little warm-up exercise. Figure 3.7 gives you an idea of how the developmental environment looks to help you position the different parts.

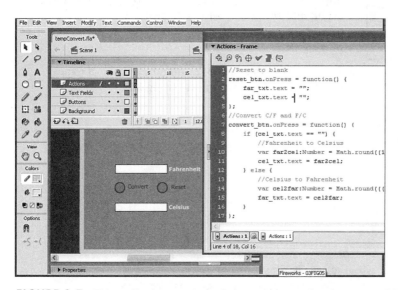

FIGURE 3.7 This application uses ActionScript to convert values between Celsius and Fahrenheit.

Use the following steps to re-create the application:

1. Open a new Flash document and create four layers. From top to bottom, name them Actions, Text Fields, Buttons, and Background.

2. Use the color code #6A0012 for the background color. Select the Background layer and draw a rectangle with a 10-point stroke with the dimensions W=385, H=280. Use #F0DD38 for the stroke color and #D68614 for the fill color. Center the rectangle horizontally and vertically on the Stage. Lock the Background layer.

3. Select the Text Fields layer. Using the Text tool, add two input text fields, positioning one above the other. Select the top field. In the Property Inspector, type the instance name **far_txt** and then do the same for the bottom text field, using the instance name **cel_txt**. If it's not selected, click the Show Border Around Text button in the Property Inspector. Lock the layer.

4. Select the Buttons layer and draw a circle with a 22.2 diameter using a 2-point stroke. The stroke color is #6A0012 and the fill color is #838F8E. Select the drawing and press the F8 key to open the Convert to Symbol dialog box. Choose Button for the Type setting and name it what you like. Open the Library panel (Ctrl+L/Cmd+L) and drag a second instance of the button to the Stage. Place both buttons between the two input text fields. (Refer to Figure 3.7 for a guide.) Provide the instance name convert_btn for the button on the left and reset_btn for the button on the right. Lock the layer.

5. Unlock the Background layer and add labels using the Text tool and static text, as shown in Figure 3.7. Lock the layer.

6. Click the first frame of the Actions layer and add the following script:

```
//Reset to blank
reset_btn.onPress = function() {
    far_txt.text = "";
    cel_txt.text = "";
};
//Convert C/F and F/C
convert_btn.onPress = function() {
    if (cel_txt.text == "") {
        //Fahrenheit to Celsius
        var far2cel:Number = Math.round((100/(212-32)*(Number(far_txt.text)-32)))
        ➥*100/100;
        cel_txt.text = far2cel;
    } else {
        //Celsius to Fahrenheit
        var cel2far:Number = Math.round((((212-32)/100*Number(cel_txt.text)+32)
        ➥*100)/100);
        far_txt.text = cel2far;
    }
};
```

To test the movie, enter a number in either input text field and click the Convert button. The application converts the value to the opposite temperature unit of measure. Before each conversion, click the Reset button.

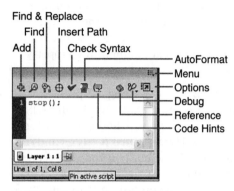

Find & Replace
Find   Insert Path
Add   Check Syntax
                              AutoFormat
                              Menu
                              Options
1 stop();   Debug
                              Reference
                              Code Hints

Layer 1 : 1
Line 1 of 1, Col 8
Pin active script

FIGURE 3.8   The Actions panel's buttons.

Writing Code

Open the Actions panel by pressing F9. The panel has three parts: On the left are the Actions toolbox, where the code can be found, and the Script navigator, which shows icons of different actions and objects in your document. The right side of the panel contains the Script pane, where you write your code.

Above the Script pane are several different buttons to aid you in writing code (see Figure 3.8).

Table 3.1 briefly describes what each of these buttons do along with comments as to their relative usefulness based on the author's experience, but feel free to use them in any way you want.

TABLE 3.1

Code Aid Buttons

BUTTON	DESCRIPTION
Add Item	I rarely use this button. When you click it, a series of menus and submenus let you fish for the code you want. Using this button may aid some, but it's really a residue of early versions of Flash ActionScript, and more of a hindrance than help. If you want to automatically add code, you will find it far easier to use the Actions toolbox and double-click the term you want to use.
Find	Use this button in longer scripts when you want to find a term. Just click the button and type the term you're trying to find.
Find & Replace	This button works like a find-and-replace operation in a word processor. Type the word to find and the replacement word. The only limitation of this button is that you can't select a portion of the script (as you can in a word processor) and just find and replace terms in a limited section of a script. So remember, when you use the Find & Replace button, everything in the script will be changed. (Keep the Ctrl+Z [Undo] shortcut handy when using this option.)
Insert Path	This is another one of those buttons left over from earlier versions of Flash that may have limited utility. Where you have lots of addressable objects on the Stage and want to find the path to an object, this can come in handy. With the new Script Navigator, though, this button has less use than before.
Check Syntax	Before you test your movie, give this button a click. If it finds errors, it will show the nature of the errors in the Output window. Don't rely too heavily on the Check Syntax button, though, because your code can have correct syntax and still not work the way you want.
Auto Format	This is one of my most-used buttons. It cleans up your code so that it's easier to read. If you have an error in your code, this button won't format it for you, so you then must click the Check Syntax button. Usually I find it easier to click this button first rather than the Check Syntax button because if there are no errors, you'll have your code nicely formatted.
Show Code Hint	Even though this button might be thought of as a beginner's button, I use it all the time. With strong typing in variables in Flash Pro, this button becomes indispensable. For example, if you type **var myHotVar:**, a list of data types appears. Although user-defined types won't appear, you'll find that getting used to strong data typing, along with the rest of ActionScript 2.0, is greatly aided by the code hints.

TABLE 3.1

Continued

BUTTON	DESCRIPTION
Reference	If you select a term in the script and click the Reference button, the Help panel appears with information about the selected item. This is extremely handy, especially when you're getting to know the new code used for the ActionScript 2.0 components.
Debug Options	The main debug option you'll probably use is setting breakpoints. A *breakpoint* allows you to stop a SWF in the middle of being played where the breakpoint has been placed. You can also remove a breakpoint using this same button. (Generally, I find it easier to just click the line number where I want a breakpoint, and one is inserted.)
View Options	This button opens a menu to select set-and-forget options. Included are View Esc Shortcut Keys, View Line Numbers, and Word Wrap. All these options are helpful, and line numbers are essential when you begin writing longer code. I use Word Wrap, but it can be toggled off if you have an especially long line of code that's better viewed using the horizontal scrollbar at the bottom of the Script pane.
Pin Script	When you have several objects on the Stage and you keep forgetting their instance names and have to click them to recall their names in the Property Inspector, you'll love this feature. When you "pin" a script, it stays put while you click different objects and layers. With multiple scripts, it's possible to use multiple pins. Pin Script is a toggle button, so you can just click the pin icon to turn it on or off.

The pop-up menu in the upper-right corner of the Actions panel contains duplicates of the Actions buttons and preferences found elsewhere in Flash. However, it has a number of handy options you can use even if many are redundant (see Figure 3.9).

FIGURE 3.9   The Actions panel's pop-up menu provides a wide number of options you will find valuable.

Variables

> **Case-Sensitive Code**
>
> An important new feature in ActionScript 2.0 not found in ActionScript 1.0 is case-sensitive code. Writing code in ActionScript 1.0 meant that variable names only had to be spelled the same to be considered the same instance of the variable. Hence, `myVariable`, `MyVariable`, and `myvariable` are treated as equivalents in ActionScript 1.0, but in ActionScript 2.0 they're considered to be different variables. When writing code, be sure to observe case sensitivity.

Like all computer languages, ActionScript 2.0 variables are data containers. However, unlike ActionScript 1.0, the data that a variable can contain in ActionScript 2.0 must conform to a type. For example, if a variable is declared as a String type of data, when you place a Number type in the variable, the number will be treated as a string. In ActionScript 1.0, a variable changes depending on its contents. Most other OOP languages, such as Java and C++, have a similar form of data typing, called *strict* or *strong* data typing. To declare a variable, you include the type of variable using this format:

```
var variableName:DataType = value;
```

For example,

```
var moneyIn:Number = 123456
```

declares the variable named `moneyIn` as a Number and assigns it the value `123456`. If you later decided to assign a String to the `moneyIn` variable, you'll get a Type Mismatch error. Try the following script to see what happens:

```
var moneyIn:Number = 123456;
moneyIn="Dough";
trace(moneyIn);
```

The Output window signals a Type Mismatch error. However, you can assign hexadecimal values to a Number type variable. The following script works without an error because the hexadecimal value is automatically translated into a decimal value:

```
var moneyIn:Number = 123456;
moneyIn=0xFFFF;
trace(moneyIn);
//Output = 65535
```

Code Hints to the Rescue

You should write your scripts with Code Hints enabled in the Actions panel and Script window. This way, when you declare your variables, as soon as you type the colon at the end of *var variableName:*, a list of all the data types appears. While you're getting used to the different data types available, you'll find this pop-up menu invaluable.

Data Types

The most general data type categories include the following:

- Primitive
- MovieClip
- Object

The MovieClip data type is the only one that refers to a graphic element you create on the Stage. It can be a little confusing because movie clips are objects, and you can declare a movie clip object to be either an Object or MovieClip type of data. Object data types can either be built in or user created (custom). A detailed categorization of data types is shown in Table 3.2.

TABLE 3.2
Data Types and Assigned Values

DATA TYPE	DESCRIPTION
String	Refers to sequence of characters enclosed by quotation marks. For example, `var someName:String = "\"Delia\""` returns `"Delia"`.
Number	Double-precision floating-point value. Responds to math operators.
Boolean	Includes values of `true` and `false` or 1 and 0.
Object	A collection of properties that have variable-like values. You can arrange objects inside one another (nesting) and access them through the path using dot (.) operators (for example, `ObjectInstance.prop1.prop2.prop3`). All methods in the Object data type are available to object instances.
Null	This data type has a single value, `null`, which is the same as no value.
MovieClip	This data type refers to movie clip symbols in a Flash document. All properties, methods, and other controls are available to instances of the MovieClip data type.
Undefined	When an existing variable has no value, it's treated as undefined, which is the single value of this data type.

When you type a data type, the pop-up menu shows far more data types, including all the built-in objects and components.

You can add all custom classes as data types. For example, suppose you have a class named `Clients`. This is a custom class that won't show up in the pop-up menu when you're declaring a variable. For example, the following script is perfectly acceptable:

```
var FarShores: Clients = new Clients();
```

Therefore, keep in mind that although the pop-up menu is important for getting to know the built-in data types, all custom classes can be used as data types.

Converting Data Types

Sometimes you will want to convert a variable from one data type to another. One of the more common situations where such a conversion would be desirable occurs when using input text fields. All data entered into a text field is automatically typed as strings. When using text fields for entering numeric characters requiring math operations, you need to

SHOP TALK

To OOP or Not to OOP

To OOP, or not to OOP: That is the question:
Whether 'tis nobler in the compiler to
Grind the code with objects, properties, and methods,
Or to sling a sea of procedures,
And by so doing end the script?

With apologies to Shakespeare, therein lies the nub and rub of whether to use OOP. Computer engineers may see the question as moot because the benefits of OOP are so many and (to them) so obvious. As noted at the beginning of this chapter, OOP indeed has much to offer, and as an approach to big projects with multiple programmers, OOP has become a virtual necessity.

However, is OOP really necessary for little programs that are often associated with modules used for Flash pages for the Web? After all, if a few lines of code will solve the problem and get the job done, why take the long way around, creating a class in an AS file and then writing code in the Actions panel that uses the code that could have been created as procedures in the first place? The truth of the matter is that a few procedures often do the job just fine, and you can rest assured that the OOP police won't be at your doorstep if you knock out a simple application without even thinking about OOP. In the real world of business development where a client needs a module immediately and doesn't know OOP from elephants, no one's going to know whether your code is OOP compliant or not. (Well, maybe some OOP Nazi whose idea of a good time is to decompile code to check for good OOP practices; however, those guys usually can't get out of the asylum long enough to be a real problem.)

Such exigencies aside, where using procedural programming to meet a deadline is more than a convenience, developing good OOP practices has other consequences than being politically make data type conversions prior to the math operations. The following code shows an example of making such a conversion:

```
btn.onPress = function() {
    var productCost:Number = Number(product_txt.text);
    output.text = productCost += (productCost*.05);
};
```

Likewise, sometimes you need a double conversion. The following script begins with text to be converted to a number to be converted to a string for hexadecimal output:

```
btn.onPress = function() {
    var conHex:Number = Number(product_txt.text);
    output.text = String(conHex.toString(16));
    };
```

correct. Using OOP makes me stop and organize my work. Put otherwise, it forces me to plan. Procedural programming practices allow the coder to muddle through with a lick and a promise, and usually something workable comes out the other end. As projects grow in size and complexity, especially if site maintenance requiring regular updates and changes is built in to a contract, the fly-by-the-seat-of-your-pants methods begin to take their toll. Without foresight and planning, every little change could require major program rewriting. So rather than spending a little time at the onset of a project planning, the developer finds himself tacking together an increasingly onerous site.

A friend of mine who is a self-taught programmer latched onto OOP and modular programming on his own. He explained that it just didn't make any sense to spend a lot of time working out code only to have to redo the same or similar code for every client. So, he began making classes from his procedural code. He took what worked well, and then taking the core algorithms from the code, he reworked it in OOP format. He planned way ahead. Instead of waiting for a client to give him specs for a new project, he culled the needs of his former clients and created classes and modules that dealt with typical site requirements. He was able to meet his clients' requirements much quicker but also with better-quality code. Because most of the modules and classes for typical needs were already built, he could spend his time meeting unique client needs.

My advice is to get used to OOP at your own pace. Because OOP is as much an attitude as a set of procedures, start with the simpler aspects of OOP. Instead of wringing your hands about whether you really understand polymorphism, just take little steps. A very first step is to stop and think about a project as being made up of different objects with certain characteristics and behaviors. Next, rather than beginning a project in the Actions panel or even the Script editor, begin with pencil and paper. Sketch out client requirements and think about the objects you'll need in your program. As you take these steps, you'll ease into OOP and write far better programs.

You can use any of the conversion functions in Table 3.3 to convert data types.

TABLE 3.3

Conversion Functions

FUNCTION	DESCRIPTION
`Number()`	Converts data into real numbers. This function is especially useful in converting numbers from input text fields into real numbers.
`Array()`	Converts contents into array elements; for example, `Array("nuts","bolts", 21);`.
`Boolean()`	Converts to `true/false` but also 1/0; for example, `Boolean("apples"=="oranges");`.
`Object()`	Converts numbers, strings, and Booleans to objects; for example, `Object("A String");`.
`String()`	Converts numbers, Booleans, and strings to text (for example, a Boolean becomes the string `true` or `false`). An object is returned as a string representation of the object. Movie clips are returned as paths using slash syntax (not available in ActionScript 2.0). Also, as illustrated earlier, you may need to make more than a single conversion, even in a relatively simple operation.

Operators

ActionScript 2.0 works with a rich set of operators for generating a wide set of actions. The Flash MX Professional 2004 operators are organized into six subfolders with two general operators outside of all but the Operators folder.

For those unfamiliar with ActionScript 2.0 and operators, the following examples are included to provide a guide in the use of operators from different categories.

General

The two general operators are used in several different situations. The following script shows uses for both:

```
var Price:Number = 123;
var Discount:Number = 25;
//Double quotes
var Buck:String = "$";
//Parentheses
var total:Number = (Price-Discount)+(Price-Discount)*.06;
var formatIt:String = Buck+total;
output.text = formatIt;
//Displays $103.88
```

You'll also find parentheses in conditional statements, but their use still serves to group a number of statements. The single quote (') acts the same as a double quote in designating a string.

Arithmetic Operators

This set of operators is fairly straightforward. The only unusual operator is the addition sign (+) because it is used both for concatenation of strings and adding numeric values, as mentioned earlier. For arithmetic operations, the data type must be Number or some other data type that has real values. (The string "2" cannot be divided, for example, whereas the number 2 can.) The following example shows a typical application of these operators:

```
var total:Number = (7 *5) + 55 - (7/2);
```

The modulo (%) operator can be especially useful for formatting dollars and cents. It divides the left operand by a specified modulo value and returns the remainder. The following example shows how a number can be reformatted using the modulo operator:

```
var totalPurchase:Number = 432.5456;
var dollars:Number = Math.floor(totalPurchase);
//Use modulo
var cents:Number = Math.round(totalPurchase*100)%100;
var zero:Boolean = cents<10;
if (zero) {
    var cents:String = "0"+String(cents);
}
output.text = "$"+dollars+"."+cents;
```

Assignment

Assignment operators have two forms. Typically, the single equal sign (=) serves to assign values to variables. This is a single assignment operator. Compound assignment operators assign the value of the left operand with the results of the operation between the left and right operands. For example, the following shows adding tax to a product using a compound operator:

```
var tax:Number = .06;
var price:Number = 6.70;
//Compound assignment
price += tax;
output.text = "$"+price;
```

The add and assign (+=) compound operator adds the value of the price and tax variables using the compound operator shortcut rather than the following:

```
price = (price + tax);
```

Compound operators can be seen as ways to complete two operations with a single operator.

Bitwise Operators

To understand using bitwise operators, you need to take a look at a good book on binary math.

Some quick practical applications can be seen in shifting bits left and right by a given value. For example, a shift to the left by 1 (<<=1) doubles a number, whereas a shift to the right by 1 (>>=1) rounds the value by terminating all fractions. The following example illustrates this process:

```
var first1:Number=18.64;
var left1:Number= (first1 <<=1)
var right1:Number=(first1 >>=1)
//Output value 18
output.text=right1;
//Output value 36
output2.text=left1;
```

Some programmers make good use of bitwise operators, but most programmers and programs don't require any bitwise operators. However, if you need them, they're available.

Comparison Operators

Comparison operators are typically employed in conditional statements and Boolean variables. The test for equality (==) is often confused with the assignment (=) operator, so you need to pay attention when using one or the other. For example, the following script compares the contents of two variables:

```
var Num:Number = 7;
var Str:String = "7";
if (Num == Str) {
    trace("same");
} else {
    trace("diff");
}
```

Although the string "7" and the number 7 are different, the test for equality (==) finds them to be the same; however, if you use the test for strict equality (===), they're found to be different. Strict equality tests for both value and data type, whereas the equality operator only tests for value. All the operators defined as "strict" test for both data type and data contents.

Logical Operators

Not counting the bitwise operators, ActionScript 2.0 has only three logical operators. They return a Boolean value. Like comparison operators, these operators are typically found in conditional statements. The following example uses all three operators:

```
var cats:String = "Meow";
var dogs:String = "Bark";
var fido:String = "My Doggy";
var bowser:Boolean = (cats == dogs);
```

```
if (!bowser && cats == "Meow" || dogs == "Meow") {
 trace("It's true!");
}
```

The logical NOT operator (!) along with both the logical AND (&&) and logical OR operators deal with Boolean logic.

Miscellaneous Operators

Three types of operators are stored in the Miscellaneous Operators folder. First are the increment (++) and decrement (--) operators. These operators serve to add 1 to or subtract 1 from variables. This example adds 1 to the value of x each time it passes through the loop:

```
for (var x=1; x<12; x++) {
trace(x);
}
```

Second, this folder contains a ternary operator (?:). This unusual operator acts like a shortcut for a conditional statement with an else statement. For example, the third line of the script

```
var income:Number = 5000;
var bills:Number = 4300;
var funds = (income>bills) ? trace("Ok") : trace("Yikes!");
```

does the same thing as the following script:

```
if (income > bills) {
    trace("Ok")
    }else{
    trace("Yikes!")
}
```

The third type of operator in the Miscellaneous folder deals with comparative instances of data and classes. The typeof operator returns the data type of a variable. However, the instanceof operator generates a Boolean result relative to the object being queried. For example, the following script returns true because whatsNew is an instance of the String class:

```
whatsNew= new String("Day") instanceof String;
trace(whatsNew)
```

The instance name, whatsNew, contains a Boolean value and *not* the string "Day". That's because the operator instanceof directs the outcome and not the instantiation of the String object.

Finally, the void operator serves to create an undefined variable from a defined one. For example, the following script creates a string variable, called idNow, and then declares a second variable, cancelId, using the void operator with the first variable:

```
var idNow:String="Cimbel";
trace(idNow)
var cancelId=void(idNow);
trace(cancelId);
```

When using the void operator, don't use the Void data type. The void operator and Void data type are different ActionScript 2.0 terms. For example, the following line generates an error:

```
var cancelId:Void=void(idNow);
```

The Void data type is used with the :(type) operator in developing classes.

Built-in Classes and Objects

In the first part of this chapter in the discussion of OOP, one conception of classes and objects posits that objects are instances of classes. For the sake of both clarity and consistency, all references to classes are either built-in classes, such as those listed in the Built-in Classes folder in the Actions toolbox in the left side of the Actions panel, or custom classes. Objects are simply instances of either the built-in or custom classes.

This section reviews the concepts of built-in classes in ActionScript 2.0 and their constituents. As noted in the OOP discussion, an object, and hence a class, is made up of properties and methods. However, some built-in classes also include constants, events, listeners, and even other objects. To demonstrate each of these class elements, samples from several different built-in classes in the following subsections examine the meaning and use to the parts used with the classes.

Properties

Most, but not all, built-in classes have properties. Some classes, such as Boolean and Date, only have methods and a constructor but no properties. More typically, though, you'll find classes associated with a few or several properties. For instance, the String class has only one property, length, whereas the Button class contains 23 properties.

You use a property with an object by referencing the object's instance name and assigning different values to the property. This is pretty much like assigning values to variables. For example, the following script uses properties from the TextField class in an object with the instance name output_txt:

```
output_txt.text = "Text here";
output_txt.textColor = 0x00ff00;
output_txt.backgroundColor = 0xffff00;
output_txt._x = 250;
output_txt.borderColor = 0x0000aa;
```

Figure 3.10 shows the Properties subfolder for the TextField class.

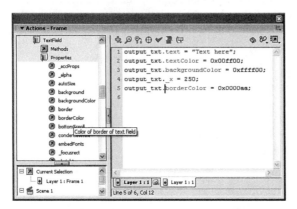

FIGURE 3.10   Built-in class properties.

In the preceding script, you may have noticed that the instance name has the extension or suffix _txt. This extension is important because it triggers the code hints for all the class elements, including properties, methods, events, and listeners. Several classes have these special suffixes, as shown in Table 3.4.

TABLE 3.4

Suffixes Used to Automatically Trigger Code Hints

CLASS NAME	EXTENSION	CLASS NAME	EXTENSION
Array	_array	PrintJob	_pj
Button	_btn	NetConnection	_nc
Camera	_cam	NetStream	_ns
Color	_color	SharedObject	_so
ContextMenu	_cm	Sound	_sound
ContextMenuItem	_cmi	String	_str
Date	_date	TextField	_txt
Error	_err	TextFormat	_fmt
LoadVars	_lv	Video	_video
LocalConnection	_lc	XML	_xml
Microphone	_mic	XMLNode	_xmlnode
MovieClip	_mc	XMLSocket	_xmlsocket
MovieClipLoader	_mcl		

Using the class suffixes makes learning and applying properties, classes, events, listeners, and other class elements much easier.

Constants

Constants associated with classes work differently than properties. Constants are invariable, and they must be assigned to a variable as part of a class and not an instance of the class. For example, the following script shows the correct way to assign the value of pi to a variable:

```
var circleBuild:Number = Math.PI;
var radius:Number = 20;
var circleArea:Number = circleBuild*(radius*radius);
trace(circleArea);
```

However, if you attempt to first create a Math object and assign the constant to the object, the attempt fails. For example, the following does *not* work:

```
var circleBuild:Math = new Math;
var radius:Number = 20;
var circleArea:Number = circleBuild.PI*(radius*radius);
trace(circleArea);
```

Keep in mind that constants associated with classes need to be passed to variables using the actual class name and constant, and not instance names of the class.

Methods

Depending on the class and method, you'll encounter many different settings and parameters. Methods associated with a class work very much like properties, but methods tend to require values assigned for arguments rather than assignments of values. For example, the following script works with two instances of the MovieClip class, called arrow_mc and target_mc, created on the Stage using the hitTest method:

```
for (x=20; x<500; x += 10) {
    _level0.arrow_mc._x = x;
    if (_level0.arrow_mc.hitTest(target_mc)) {
        _level0.target_mc._alpha = 20;
    }
}
```

Using the dot (.) syntax, the method is simply attached to the object (instance name) with the necessary parameters filled in. Thus, the line segment

```
arrow_mc.hitTest(target_mc)
```

provides all the necessary information for the hitTest method to be implemented.

Events

Events associated with a class are unique to that class, and although some classes may have the same method names, they may behave very differently. An event is accessed in the same way as methods and properties, using the dot syntax. For example, using a button object created on the Stage, the following script shows a halted playhead awaiting an event to go to and stop at a frame labeled *products*:

```
stop();
products_btn.onPress = function() {
    gotoAndStop("products");
};
```

Most events are triggered by a user action, such as a mouse event. However, other events are triggered by events that occur within the system, such as an external file loading. For instance, one of the LoadVars() class's events is onLoad. The following script illustrates how to use this event:

```
textHere = new LoadVars();
textHere.onLoad=function() {
    output_txt.text=myExternalStuff;
};
textHere.load("ExternalFile.txt");
```

The LoadVars.load method starts the process, and once the file has been loaded, the onLoad event is triggered along with the unnamed function to place the text into a dynamic text field named output_txt.

Listeners

Listeners are more important in Flash MX Professional 2004 than in previous versions of Flash because they're used with components. In Flash MX, change handlers were employed, but now listeners have replaced the change handlers to report an event. If you look at the classes in the Actions toolbox, you'll notice that some classes include listeners. For example, the Key class has two listeners: onKeyDown and onKeyUp.

To use these listeners, you first need to construct an object that can be used to hold them. Then, using the addListener() method, you use the object as an argument. For example, the following script uses the onKeyDown listener:

```
var hearKey:Object = new Object();
//onKeyDown is Key class listener
hearKey.onKeyDown = function() {
    if (Key.isDown(Key.SPACE)) {
        trace("Space bar pressed");
    }
};
Key.addListener(hearKey)
```

Other classes have different listeners, and all class-related listeners require an Object class instance for you to use them.

Objects

As noted in the discussion of OOP near the beginning of this chapter, objects are made up of properties and methods, but they can contain other objects as well. One class that contains objects is the System class. Two objects are in the System class: capabilities and security.

The reference to an object within an object is simple and straightforward. The object within the object follows the class name. For example,

```
System.security.allowDomain("http://www.sandlight.com");
```

uses the System class and the security object, which contains the allowDomain() method. In the same way that dot syntax is used to reference an object's properties and methods, it is used to reference an object within a class instance in its place in the hierarchy. When there's a direct reference to a method, the method follows the class. For example, the line

```
System.showSettings(2);
```

displays the Flash Player Settings panel for the microphone settings. The line doesn't reference the security object.

Basic Procedural Structures

This section examines the basic procedural structures used in ActionScript 2.0. All these structures are employed in creating the different OOP structures and represent the most basic fundamentals of program structures. They closely resemble similar structures in other languages.

Sequence

The sequence structure in ActionScript 2.0 is simply the code that executes in order, one after another. In its most elementary form, the sequence is simply a list of statements. For example, the following sequence places text in different instances of text fields:

```
name.text = "Joe Smith";
address.text = "123 Elm Street";
city.text = "Taft";
state.text = "CT";
```

A more important use of sequences is where one set of events needs to precede another. For example, in creating an instance of a built-in class, the sequence doesn't include first creating an external AS file, but to use a class's methods and properties, the construction sequence requires that an instance of that class be constructed first before any of its methods or properties can be used. Consider the following example:

```
//Construct instance of String class
var tracker:String = new String("Chance favors the prepared mind.");
//Employ Class property length
var howLong:Number = tracker.length;
trace(tracker+" has "+howLong+" characters.");
```

Here, a string object first needs to be created. Then the `length` property can be used in the next line. Finally, both the new object and the variable holding its length can be employed in a third line. The sequence requires that order, and if a step in a sequence is missing, the script either will not execute or won't execute as intended.

Loop

Loop structures in Flash are similar to most other languages (see Statements, Conditions/Loops in the Actions toolbox). Loops in Flash can be divided into two classes: `for` loops and `while` loops. The `for` loop has two types: `for` and `for..in`. The `while` loop also has two types: `while` and `do while`.

The basic `for` loop has the following structure:

```
for(counter=N; end condition; increment/decrement counter) {
    //statements
}
```

The counter represents a variable used to set a beginning value, a flag to set the termination of the loop, and an operator and value (if needed) to increase or decrease the value of the counter. For example, the following loop generates the output of an array:

```
var playOffs:Array = new Array();
playOffs.push("Marlins", "Cubs", "Yankees", "Red Sox");
for (x=0; x<playOffs.length; x++) {
    trace(playOffs[x]);
}
```

The `for..in` loop iterates through an object's properties or, in the case of an array, its elements. In using the preceding example, the `for..in` loop is substituted for the `for` loop:

```
var playOffs:Array = new Array();
playOffs.push("Marlins", "Cubs", "Yankees", "Red Sox");
for (teams in playOffs) {
    trace(playOffs[teams]);
}
```

The `teams` variable acts as an iterant (that is, it counts iterations through the loop). No matter how short or long, the iterant variable always stops after the last property or element.

The `while` loop keeps running until a quit condition has been met, using the following format:

```
while(condition) {
    //Do something
}
```

For example, the following while loop waits until the end of an array before it stops sending out the array elements:

```
var counter:Number = 0;
var roster:Array = new Array();
roster.push("Tom", "Mary", "Dick", "Suzy", "Harry", "Kim");
while (counter<roster.length) {
    trace(roster[counter]);
    counter++;
}
```

A second type of while loop, the do..while loop, places its conditional statement at the end of the loop rather than at the beginning. In a while loop, if the condition to stop the loop is met immediately, none of the statements within the loop are executed. However, a do..while loop executes at least one iteration before stopping, even if the termination condition is immediately satisfied. As you can see in its structure, do..while is clearly different from the while loop:

```
do {
    //Do something
} while (condition)
```

For example, the following do..while loop executes the trace statement even though the stop condition is met in the first iteration:

```
var counter:Number = 0;
do {
    trace("This is an iteration");
} while (counter != 0);
```

One of the problems you may encounter is an infinite loop. If you make a small mistake in your termination condition, the loop may never be able to exit and will crash Flash.

Conditional

The final basic structure is the conditional statement, which in Flash Pro is fairly standard and comparable to that of conditional statements in other languages.

The simple if statement tests a condition using the following format:

```
if(condition) {
    //execute this
}
```

For example, the following looks at a response in an input text field to provide the user with more information about a product by sending him or her to a different URL:

```
choose_btn.onPress = function() {
    var checkIt:String = new String();
    checkIt = decide_txt.text;
    checkIt.toLowerCase();
    if (checkIt == "yes") {
        getURL("http://www.sandlight.com", _blank);
    }
};
```

Forcing a Case

When you're using conditional statements where you have user input, because you have no way of knowing whether the user will use the correct case, changing the input to a single case makes testing the condition easier. Strings can be transformed to all lowercase, as in the previous example, or to uppercase.

A second type of if statement is if..else. This statement has the following format:

```
if(condition) {
    //execute this
} else {
    //do something else
}
```

So when you have a single alternative, the else statement is handy. For instance, you could change the previous if code example by adding an else statement to make two options now available, as the following shows:

```
choose_btn.onPress = function() {
    var checkIt:String = new String();
    checkIt = decide_txt.text;
    checkIt.toLowerCase();
    if (checkIt == "yes") {
        getURL("http://www.sandlight.com", _blank);
    } else {
        getURL("http://www.room99.co.uk", _blank);
    }
};
```

As a reminder from the "Miscellaneous Operators" section earlier in this chapter, you can use the ternary (?:) operator instead of the if..else statement. Using the ternary operator, the conditional statement from the preceding code would be the following:

```
checkIt=="yes" ? getURL("http://www.sandlight.com", _blank) :
➥getURL("http://www.room99.co.uk", _blank);
```

With several different conditions, you will need to use either the else if statement or the switch and case statements. The following script looks to see where the position of a movie clip is and, depending on its location, has different feedback:

```
moveMe_mc.onPress = function() {
    this.startDrag();
};
moveMe_mc.onRelease = function() {
    stopDrag();
};
if (moveMe_mc._x<100) {
    trace("Move right");
} else if (moveMe_mc._x>300) {
    trace("Move left");
} else if (moveMe_mc._y<100) {
    trace("Move down");
} else if (moveMe_mc._y>300) {
    trace("Move up");
}
```

Sometimes, rather than using a series of else if statements, you'll want to use the switch/case combination. The general format for the switch/case statement, when employing both the break and default optional statements, is the following:

```
switch(exp) {
    case 'state1' :
        //do something
        break;
    case 'state2' :
        //do something else
        break;
    default :
        //do default
}
```

The following example takes information from an input text field, places it into a String object, and then uses that string ("tool") as the expression within the switch parameter. After each of the case statements is a statement to execute if the case is strictly true in that its contents match that of the switch parameter (strict equality, ===). For example, if the user puts in PHP as a choice, "PHP" is changed to lowercase ("php") by the `tool` object. If the `case` strictly equates "php", it gets the appropriate URL and then breaks out of the `switch` statement using the `break` statement. If none of the `case` statements finds a strict equality, the `default` statement executes.

```
choose_btn.onPress = function() {
    var tool:String = new String();
    tool = decide_txt.text;
    tool = tool.toLowerCase();
    switch (tool) {
    case 'flash' :
        getURL("http://www.macromedia.com");
        break;
    case 'php' :
        getURL("http://www.php.net");
        break;
    case 'mysql' :
        getURL("http://www.mysql.org");
        break;
    case 'apache' :
        getURL("http://www.apache.org");
        break;
    default :
        trace("No luck");
    }
};
```

Although both the `else if` statement and `switch` and `case` statements can generate similar results, the choice of one or the other depends on the nature of the coding problem being solved or the developer's personal preferences.

Functions

The built-in functions in Flash MX Professional 2004 are either in the Global Functions folder or part of the Deprecated folder, both in the Actions toolbox. Those in the latter folder have been replaced by methods in the built-in classes. Therefore, this section will focus on the global functions and the user functions.

Like all functions and methods, the global functions create some action, many of which are unique to Flash. They have been organized into the following folders in the Actions toolbox:

- Timeline Control
- Browser/Network
- Movie Clip Control
- Printing Functions
- Miscellaneous Functions
- Mathematical Functions
- Conversion Functions

As you use any of these functions, you'll find a good deal of overlap with the methods associated with built-in classes. For example, a global function is gotoAndPlay(). Likewise, you will find that one of the methods associated with the MovieClip object is gotoAndPlay(). As a global function, gotoAndPlay() can be used in just about any script independent of a movie clip. A button script like the following is typical of how a global function would be used:

```
on(release) {
    gotoAndPlay(5);
}
```

The same function, used as a MovieClip class instance method, would have to be associated with a specific movie clip. For example, the script

```
myMovieClip_mc.gotoAndPlay(5);
```

instructs the movie clip myMovieClip_mc to play Frame 5 *on its own Timeline.*

Some of the more common global functions include the stop() and play() functions, often found in frame scripts. Subsequent chapters include various uses of these functions, and depending on the context of their use, you should be able to tell whether they're methods or functions.

User-Defined Functions

User-defined functions are used both in a program proper and in the Script Editor in creating classes and their methods. Here's the basic format for creating a user function:

```
function FunctionName(arguments) {
    //actions
}
```

The arguments (or parameters) are optional in a function. For example, the following is a perfectly good user function:

```
checkFuel function() {
    gotoAndStop("fuel");
    if(fuelLevel < 2) {
        warning=true;
    }
}
```

The function is invoked by the following simple line:

```
checkFuel();
```

By adding an argument to a function definition, you can add a good deal of flexibility to the function. The following function has hor and vert arguments that are used in the function to specify the horizontal and vertical position of a movie clip:

```
function McPlace(hor, vert) {
    moveMe_mc._x = hor;
    moveMe_mc._y = vert;
}
```

To invoke the function, the developer places values in argument positions. For example, the following would place the movie clip at the horizontal position 250 and vertical position 150:

```
McPlace(250,150);
```

When functions are used in class definitions, they can become methods of the class. For example, a handy class would be to convert the dollar and cent formatter used with the modulo (%) operator discussed earlier in the section on operators. By casting the sequence as a function inside of a class definition, the function becomes a method of that class. For example, the two files shown in Listings 3.4 and 3.5 are, respectively, an AS file defining the class and a sample FLA file that uses the class to show how the function becomes a method. The function convert() in the class definition is used as the method convert() in the FLA script.

LISTING 3.4 A Cent Formatter for Virtually Any Business Use (CentFormat.as)

```
class CentFormat {
    function convert(amount:Number) {
        var dollars:Number = Math.floor(amount);
        var cents:Number = Math.round(amount*100)%100;
        var zero:Boolean = cents<10;
        var zerozero:Boolean = cents == 0;
        if (zero) {
            var cents:String = "0"+String(cents);
        } else if (zerozero) {
            var cents:String = "00"+String(cents);
        }
        return "$"+dollars+"."+cents;
    }
}
```

Once you save the CentFormat.as file, create a new Flash Pro document with a button (go_btn), an input text field (purchase_txt), and a dynamic text field (output_txt). The instance names are in parentheses.

LISTING 3.5   An Easy Way to Format Cents Using the `CentFormat` Class (`functionClass.fla`)

```
var purchase:CentFormat = new CentFormat();
go_btn.onPress = function() {
    var myPurchase = Number(purchase_txt.text);
    output_txt.text = purchase.convert(myPurchase);
};
```

After saving the files to the same folder, you can use the `convert` method with an object created from the `CentFormat` class. Any value placed in the input text field is reformatted and placed into the output text field when the button is clicked.

Unnamed Functions

A final fundamental feature of ActionScript 2.0 functions can be found in the use of unnamed functions. Throughout the examples, you have seen several unnamed functions. They're very useful when placing object control scripts in frames rather than attaching them directly to the objects themselves. For example, instead of using the button script

```
on(release) {
    gotoAndPlay(5);
}
```

you can use an unnamed function to do the same thing:

```
someButton_btn.onRelease = function() {
    gotoAndPlay(5);
};
```

A recommended practice is keeping all your scripts in one place—ideally in a single frame. By using unnamed (or anonymous) functions, you can address an object anywhere in a document. When it comes time to debug a script, you'll be glad you did.

What's Next?

This chapter's purpose is to give you a hefty dose of ActionScript 2.0 early in this book so that in later examples of using Flash Pro, you'll have a good foundation for understanding what the scripts mean and how to use them. As more ActionScript is introduced, you'll get additional information.

In the next chapter, you'll learn how to create animations, including using movie clips as part of the animation process. Although a good deal of animation is accomplished using tweens, organizing an animation often requires judicious use of ActionScript 2.0.

In Brief

- ActionScript 2.0 offers a range of structures for object-oriented programming.

- Classes can be created as separate AS files using the new Script Editor.

- AS files can be placed anywhere and are automatically found by the ActionScript created in the Actions panel through a user-defined path.

- You can create simple and sophisticated scripts using the Behaviors panel without having to write a program in the Actions panel.

- The Actions panel has a single scripting mode with code hints that appear automatically when suffixes are used with variable and object names.

- ActionScript 2.0 is case sensitive and uses strong typing of variables.

- ActionScript 2.0 has adapted the ECMA v.4 standards and performs very much like JavaScript 2.0, but ActionScript 2.0 still maintains its unique Flash-related terms.

PART II

Creating Flash Sites

Animations and Interactions

Animations in Flash MX Professional 2004 serve the same functions as in past versions of Flash. This chapter reviews the fundamentals of tweening and using animations in conjunction with shapes and objects.

Quick Review of Animation Basics

Before we discuss the techniques of animation using Flash tools, you need to understand something about the model of animation on which Flash is based, which will help you both in understanding animation and how to use the Flash tools to achieve animation.

Studies in animal and human locomotion led to an understanding of the movement and position of limbs. By reproducing the sequence of these positions, it became possible to reproduce the animated movement. All that was required was some method of rapidly showing one image after another.

Prior to the invention of motion picture technology, Eadweard Muybridge experimented with multiple image action shots by having people and animals pass by a battery of 12 cameras. As they moved in front of each camera, it was triggered so that the motion would be caught in different positions. The immediate impact of Muybridge's experiment, beginning in 1878, was to change the conceptions of how people and animals actually positioned their bodies and limbs during motion.

Using 12 images from Muybridge's work formatted as JPEG images, you can reproduce the motions of the people and animals that predate motion pictures. Using sequential filenames, beginning with `horse1.jpg` and ending with `horse12.jpg`, I was able to use the same images from over 100 years ago and create a smooth animated moving horse in Flash. (The images are available at `www.sandlight.com` if you want to use them.) The following steps are used:

FIGURE 4.1   The sequence of images is placed into 12 keyframes.

1. Open a new document and select File, Import, Import to Stage.

2. Select the folder where you have the horse images stored and select `horse1.jpg`. As soon as you make that selection, a message box appears and asks whether you want to import all the images to be part of a sequence. Click Yes.

That's it. Flash Pro automatically creates keyframes and sequentially places the images in individual frames, as shown in Figure 4.1.

Looking at the images from left to right and top to bottom in Figure 4.2, you can see the different positions of the horse as it walks in front of Muybridge's battery of cameras. They don't appear to be especially sequential, but when they're placed into the Flash Timeline panel and played, the amount and quality of the animation is truly remarkable.

FIGURE 4.2   The 12 images of a moving horse from Muybridge's battery of cameras.

Although technology today is light years ahead of the battery of cameras used to record animal and human locomotion in Muybridge's day, the principles of animation haven't really changed. By creating a sequence of images that displays the correct relative positions of torso, head, arms, legs, and feet, the animation appears to move in a realistic manner. The section "Coordinating Animated Parts" at the end of this chapter examines the animator's art of re-creating natural movement. First, though, we need to review the main built-in Flash Pro animation tools and processes.

Vector Graphics Versus Bitmap Graphics

Bitmapped graphics can be imported from various sources, ranging from digital photos to user-created graphics developed on drawing applications. As noted in Chapter 1, "Getting to Know Flash Pro," bitmapped graphics are "weightier" (have larger file sizes) than vector graphics in most cases, and Flash has an option for transforming bitmapped graphics into vector graphics (select Modify, Bitmap, Trace Bitmap). Depending on the settings used to convert a bitmapped graphic into a vector graphic, the weight differs significantly. When you're using digital photographs in JPEG format, a good-quality picture will actually result in a much higher weight for a vector graphic than a bitmapped graphic. To reduce the graphic weight, the original JPEG graphic is distorted when it's transformed into a vector graphic, as shown in Figures 4.3 and 4.4.

FIGURE 4.3 The original graphic in JPEG format created with a screenshot.

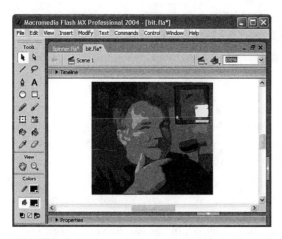

FIGURE 4.4 Once a bitmapped graphic has been changed to a vector graphic, reduction to a smaller file size can distort the graphic.

Tracing vector graphics from bitmapped graphics has an inverse relationship between quality and size. The graphic in Figure 4.4 only resolved to a SWF file of about 12KB. However, when the bitmap tracing used higher-quality settings, the SWF file with the vector image was

193KB. The bitmapped image in the SWF file was only 12KB as well, so other than blurring the picture and gaining the ability to change the size of the image without pixel distortion, nothing is gained by changing the image from bitmapped to vector graphics. The weight of the SWF files for both the vector graphic and bitmapped graphic are the same.

Starting with the Right Tools

When you need to change the size of a bitmapped graphic, rather than changing it into a vector graphic and making it larger or smaller, it's generally a better idea to change the bitmapped graphic in an application such as Macromedia Fireworks or Adobe Photoshop and then import it into Flash.

Table 4.1 provides an overview of the unique settings in the Trace Bitmap dialog box. Compare the file sizes in the last line of the table to see how the settings have an impact on the file sizes of the bitmap.

TABLE 4.1
Trace Bitmap Parameters and Settings

PARAMETER	SETTINGS	SAMPLE 1	SAMPLE 2
Color Threshold	1–500. The lower the setting, the more unique colors that are included.	100	10
Minimum Area	1–1000. Takes into account the number of pixels to consider when assigning color values.	10	1
Curve Fit	The Pixels setting is more exacting than the Normal setting, which gives you a smoother fit and therefore takes more memory.	Normal	Pixels
Corner Threshold	Many Corners, Normal, or Few Corners. The more corners, the more exact the fit.	Normal	Many Corners
SWF File Size	Single graphic in SWF file.	12KB	193KB

The best practice in using the Trace Bitmap dialog box depends on meeting the needs of your project. Ideally, if you can create your graphics in Flash, you won't have to worry about the weight and limitations of bitmapped graphics in your applications.

When imported into Flash, complex vector graphics, especially those created with a program such as Macromedia FreeHand or Adobe Illustrator, can be very heavy. A 50KB FreeHand illustration imported into Flash will not be lighter than a 50KB bitmapped graphic, and although it retains the ability to be changed without distortion, such an image can be very heavy. For example, a 25KB vector graphic image imported from FreeHand will compile into about a 45KB SWF file.

Often a bitmapped graphic may be more appropriate for a Flash movie for nondynamic content such as backgrounds. Also, because certain graphic images such as digital photographs are very heavy when converted to vector graphics, they, too, are best left in bitmapped format.

However, vector graphics can be created in Flash and other applications and used effectively in a Flash movie. The point to keep in mind is that complex and heavy vector graphics won't become less heavy if imported into Flash and compiled into a SWF file.

Working the Timeline

The Timeline in Flash Pro is best envisioned as a strip of movie film. On that strip of film you can see individual frames, and as the playhead moves across the frames they're shown sequentially so that images appear to move. As noted in Chapter 1, the frames can be keyframes (including blank keyframes) or regular frames (simply called *frames*). The keyframes contain images, and the frames between the keyframes have the in-between images to fill in the changes in object position, thus creating smooth animation.

Animation Is Always an Option

Of course, you're not *required* to have animated objects in the keyframes; Flash Pro can be employed as a tool for developing general Web pages or sites. For example, you can use keyframes to place different pages in a menu-driven application. However, the main purpose of using the Timeline is animation, and this chapter focuses on creating different types of animation.

Shape Tweens

You create shape tweens by placing a drawing in one keyframe and a different drawing in another keyframe. The differences in the drawings are automatically filled in by the intervening frames when the first keyframe (the one on the left) is set as a shape tween. To set a keyframe, simply select the keyframe and select Shape from the Tween pop-up menu in the Property Inspector.

You can use shape tweens for changing shape colors and positions on the Stage. If two identical shapes are used in different positions, the shape simply moves from one position to another. You can create interesting effects using shape tweens by changing solids into linear or radial color gradients, without changing the shape of the drawing.

Morphs

A morph is rooted in the term *metamorphosis*, where one object morphs into another. Perhaps the best known such transformation is that of a caterpillar into a butterfly. Getting a good morph in Flash Pro is a matter of what changes occur in a drawing as well as having solid single colors versus many colors. For example, Figure 4.5 shows a drawing of a pheasant on the ground. By creating another drawing of a pheasant in flight (see Figure 4.6), an attempt was made to transition the standing bird to the flying one using a simple shape tween.

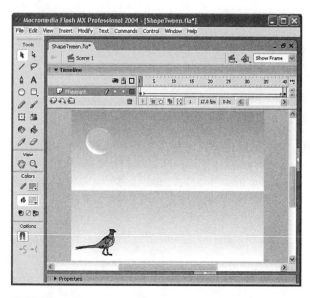

FIGURE 4.5   Original drawing in Frame 1.

FIGURE 4.6   Second drawing in Frame 40.

Using 40 frames for the transition, the bird appears to fall apart and then be reconstructed. Figures 4.7 and 4.8 show the tweened frames created between the keyframes.

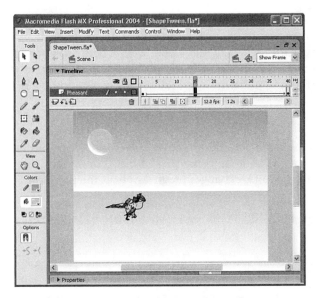

FIGURE 4.7 In Frame 15, the bird appears in disjointed pieces.

FIGURE 4.8 By Frame 30, the bird is coming back together as the bird in flight, but it's still disjointed.

One solution to remove the in-between frames that display unwanted disjointed elements is to have fewer frames between the original drawing (bird standing) and the final drawing (bird in flight). A quick change generates what could be taken as the flapping effect of a bird taking off. For example, if you change the number of frames from 40 to 5, the in-between frames are not as noticeable as being drawings in the process of morphing. However, such half-measures, although sometimes convincing, generally don't work well. A better solution is to use more keyframes and less morphing. Morphing works best with solid, mono-colored objects, and for professional-looking results, more drawings and judicious use of morphing is in order.

Using Shape Hints to Morph Fonts

One option available to create better morphing in Flash Pro is to use *shape hints*. Shape hints serve as guides for morphing from one shape to another. Using shape hints, a drawing is less likely to display outlines or irregular changes while it changes progressively as the playhead moves along the Timeline.

The following simple example shows how to use shape hints and what differences they can make in creating transitions:

You Need Rulers to Get Guides

In this next example, you'll find it useful to use the rulers and guides. Select View, Rulers. Then, once the rulers appear at the top and left sides of the Stage, you can drag guides onto the Stage from the bottom and sides of the rulers to help precisely position your drawings.

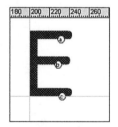

FIGURE 4.9 Frame 1 with shape hints.

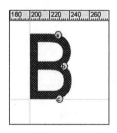

FIGURE 4.10 Frame 30 with shape hints.

1. Open a new document and add a keyframe to Frame 30. In Frame 1, type the letter **E** in a 96-point black Verdana font. Select the letter and press Ctrl+B to change it into a drawing.

2. In Frame 30, type the letter **B** in a 96-point black Verdana font. Select the letter and press Ctrl+B to change it into a drawing. Use your guides and rulers to position the second letter so that it's exactly where the letter E has been placed in Frame 1.

3. Move the playhead to Frame 1, select the E drawing, and then select Modify, Shape, Add Shape Hint from the menu. Create a total of three shape hints and place them as shown in Figure 4.9.

4. Move the playhead to Frame 30, select the B drawing, and position the shape hints as shown in Figure 4.10. (Initially you'll see only a single shape hint because the other two are beneath the one that's visible.)

5. Click Frame 1. In the Property Inspector, select Shape from the Tween pop-up menu.

By examining the tween images created midway in the 30-frame movie, you can see the differences. Figure 4.11 shows how the mid-frame appears with no shape hints.

FIGURE 4.11 Frame 15 of a morph with no shape hints.

FIGURE 4.12 Frame 15 of a morph with shape hints.

Using the shape hints, as shown in Figure 4.12, you can see that the image doesn't break up into outlines and irregular shapes. The mid-frame image shows a solid image that "grows" into a B.

For the hobbyist, morphs are a lot of fun, but for professional work, they must be used with care. Large amorphous dynamic images such as clouds and liquid motion can be created effectively using shape tweens and morphing techniques. However, they tend to be a special-case use in most applications. Although they're interesting, you should use them only where they do the best job. As you'll see in the next section, motion tweens are a better choice in most cases.

Motion Tweens

Motion tweens are the primary type used in animation. Rather than tweening shapes or creating morphs, motion tweens have a more complex array of tweens, as shown in Table 4.2.

No matter what type of format is used, none of the changes have the morphing characteristics seen in shape tweens. When the size of any of the formats changes, the change is continuous. For example, if you tween an instance of a movie clip so that in the first keyframe the instance is small and in the second it's large, the effect is a smooth change in size with no outlines or other morphing effects.

TABLE 4.2

Motion Tweens

FORMAT/PROPERTY	INSTANCE	TYPE	GROUP
Position	Y	Y	Y
Size	Y	Y	Y
Rotation	Y	Y	Y
Skew	Y	Y	Y
Color	Y	I*	I*

* Reformatted as instance.

Tweening a Point Size Change

The changes to be tweened need to be done in certain ways, especially with groups and type. For example, if you want to change the size of type and then tween the changes using a motion tween, you can't use the Text tool to change the size from, say, 24 to 48 points in the second frame. If you do, the change won't be a gradual tween. Instead, it will jump to the larger size when the playhead reaches the second frame. To effect a tween change, you can use either the Transform panel or the Free Transform tool. Try the following:

1. Open a new document and add 30 frames. Using a 24-point Arial font, type **Resize This** in Frame 1.

2. Insert a keyframe in Frame 30. Select the type block in Frame 30. In the Transform panel, check the Constrain check box and type **200%** in either of the top text windows.

3. Click the first frame. In the Property Inspector, select Motion in the Tween pop-up menu. Test the movie, and you'll see the text change progressively from 24 to 48 points.

If you try to achieve the same effect by changing the font size in the second keyframe to 48 using the Text tool, the size change will be abrupt as the playhead enters the second keyframe.

Tweening Imported Vector Graphics

The advantages of vector graphics should be incorporated whenever possible. However, given the limited tool set for creating vector graphics in Flash Pro, designers typically prefer to create vector graphics in a program such as Adobe Illustrator or Macromedia FreeHand. The designer can use any favored application to create images with vector graphics and then import these graphics into Flash easily using File, Import, Import to Stage (or import to a library) from the menu. However, once a vector graphic arrives in Flash Pro, the format is unlikely to be one for optimal use in a motion tween.

SHOP TALK

Making Motion Tweens Tween Correctly

In tweening changes, you'll find that the Free Transform tool and Transform panel are pretty safe to use in changing the size, rotation, or skew of the instance, type, or group. By the same token, the tools that created the instance, group, or type initially are usually not the tools to use when making changes in the target image you're tweening to. Unlike shape tweens, where the same tools are used to create the initial and changed images, the opposite is true with motion-tweened objects. Therefore, if a grouped object is initially created using the Paintbrush and Fill Bucket tools, if those same tools are used to change the image in a second keyframe, the changes won't tween but instead will be abrupt as the playhead moves to the second keyframe in a motion tween.

You may find thinking about motion tweens as movement rather than shapes helpful. For example, if you use the Transform panel to change a graphic symbol instance from 100% size to 400% size, the symbol appears to be moving closer to the viewer. That is, the effect is *motion*, not shape, even though the shape has indeed changed. Likewise, rotation is a movement change, even though the object looks different depending on its rotation angle.

Exceptions to this concept abound, however. You can use a motion tween to change an object's tint, color, and transparency level. For example, if you want to use a movie clip to act as a fade-in screen by tweening the alpha (transparency) level from 0% to 100%, the motion tween works fine, and there's absolutely no motion at all—just a change in its transparency. There's no movement or perception of movement. However, the changes in tint, color, or transparency are not made using tools from the Tool panel. Rather, you make such changes by selecting an object and changing its color, tint, or alpha setting in the Property Inspector.

Figure 4.13 shows an imported vector graphic on the Stage. The image consists of several blocks; instead of being a single image, it's actually several images. When Motion is selected in the Tween menu in the Property Inspector, a warning icon appears. The warning brings attention to the fact that only a single object can be tweened in a single layer.

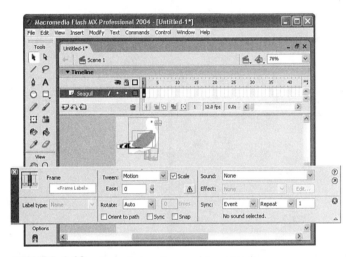

FIGURE 4.13   Imported vector graphic on Stage.

However, by selecting all the parts of the vector graphic and opening the Convert to Symbol dialog box (by pressing F8), you can maintain all the vectors in a single symbol. Figure 4.14 shows the conversion from a multipart vector image into a Graphic symbol.

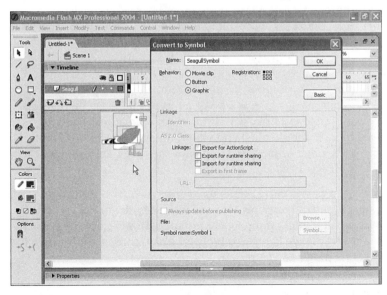

FIGURE 4.14   Transforming the multiple parts of a vector image into a Graphic symbol.

Then, when a size change is tweened, the entire image smoothly tweens from the original size to the large size. Using the file-size economy inherent in vector graphics, the SWF file, including the tweening, takes up only 2KB on the disk. Figure 4.15 shows the larger (220%) image that is tweened to.

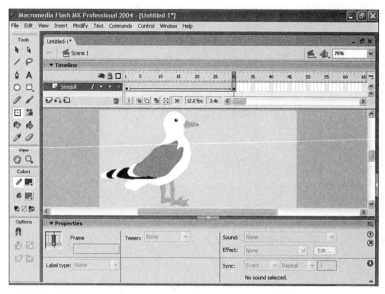

FIGURE 4.15 The instance at 220% in the second keyframe.

Using imported vector graphics created using another application such as Macromedia FreeHand or Adobe Illustrator or from clip art collections is an excellent way to take advantage of vector graphics. Other than using Flash's capability to transform the imported graphics into symbols, you can easily use them "as is" with little changes required.

Repositioning Center Points

One of the key animation structures in Flash Pro is the ability to move center points to achieve realistic animation. The *center point* serves as a pivot point so that when an object is rotated, it rotates where you want it. For example, when you create animation of an arm moving, the pivot points need to be at the shoulder and elbow, not at the default positions in the middle of the graphic. Any symbol instance selected with the Free Transform tool can have its center repositioned to wherever needed.

A simple example illustrates how to move center points to achieve maximum realism in animation. The following example shows both how to move instances of a unified object to different layers and how to move the center point of each instance. This example began with a drawing of a palm tree on a desert island. The tree is broken up into three graphic symbol instances, all on the same layer, as shown in Figure 4.16.

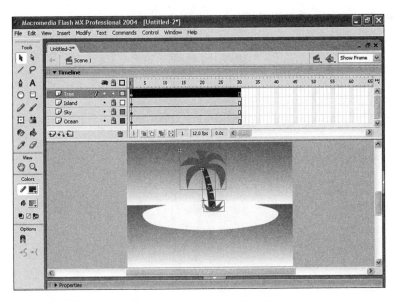

FIGURE 4.16   The initial figure broken into three instances.

Given the image shown in Figure 4.16 as the starting point, here's how you transform it into an animated movie using motion tween and pivot points:

1. Add two layers above the Tree layer, naming them Trunk and Leaves, as shown in Figure 4.17.

2. Click the top image (palm leaves) and cut the leaves. Click the first frame of the Leaves layer and select Edit, Paste in Place from the menu.

3. Don't move the center point in the Leaves instance; it's positioned where it needs to be. In the base object at the bottom on the tree, use the Free Transform tool to move the center point to the bottom of the base. Change the name of the Tree layer to Base.

4. At this point, the movie is ready for you to add motion tweens. After inserting keyframes at Frames 10, 20, and 30, you can rotate the tree's parts left and right in the keyframes so that the leaves, trunk, and base sway in a hefty breeze. Insert motion tweens in Frames 1, 10, and 20. Figure 4.18 shows the final movie with the sway to the left in Frame 10.

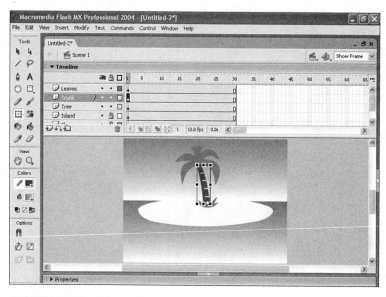

FIGURE 4.17   Moving the center point.

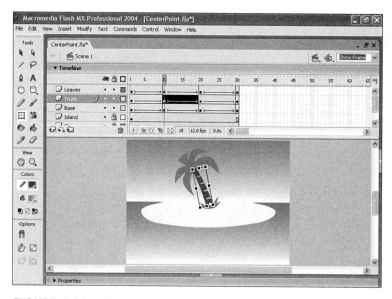

FIGURE 4.18   The palm tree's parts are rotated to the left.

In addition to rotation and moving the center point, the Free Transform tool can be used in skewing and resizing images.

Making and Using Guide Layers

The special layer in Flash used with motion tweens is the guide layer. Guide layers are used to draw a path for tweened objects to follow. In the first keyframe of a tween, the object is attached to the starting point of the guide, and in the second keyframe, it's attached to the ending point. When the movie plays, the guided object will follow the line used in the guide layer, no matter how circuitous. Imagine the flight of a bumblebee buzzing among the flowers and a line the bee might follow. If you draw such a line, using the Pencil, Bezier Pen, or Paintbrush tool, and then attach the bee object to that line, you'll see the kind of crazy path of a bee.

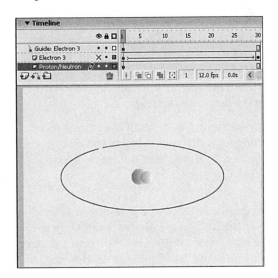

FIGURE 4.19   An oval-shaped guide path.

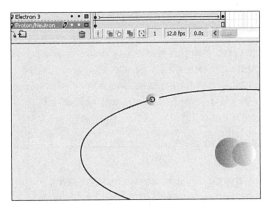

FIGURE 4.20   Placing the object at the beginning of the path.

Creating a guided path is simple, but many developers and designers have difficulty at first. So as a refresher or introduction, the following little project steps through the process of making and using guide layers:

1. Open a new document. Add 30 frames and a second layer. Name the bottom layer Proton/Neutron and the top layer Electron 3.

2. Click the Add Motion Guide icon, located below the bottom layer to the left. A guide layer appears above the Electron 3 layer, named Guide: Electron 3.

3. In the Proton/Neutron layer, draw two overlapping spheres to represent the proton and neutron of an atom. Lock the layer. Then in the Guide layer use the Oval tool to draw an oval with no fill around the proton and neutron image in the middle of the Stage. Finally, using the Eraser tool, erase a notch in the oval, as shown in Figure 4.19. Lock the guide layer.

4. In Frame 1 of the Electron 3 layer, create a small sphere using the Oval tool and a radial fill with no stroke line. (This will be the electron object.) Convert it into a Graphic symbol by pressing F8 and selecting Graphic.

5. Click Frame 30 and insert a keyframe. Click Frame 1 of the Electron 3 layer, select Motion in the Tween menu, and with the Snap to Objects condition invoked, drag the electron object to the left side of the gap in the guide line, as shown in Figure 4.20.

The Good and Evil of Snapping to Objects

After an unscientific survey, I discovered that Snap to Objects is turned on about 90% of the time when I don't need it and turned off 100% of the time when I do need it. The most important time for me to use Snap to Objects is when placing an object on a motion guide. Other times when I want objects to align with one another, I find the Snap option helpful.

However, having said that, I definitely find that placing objects where I want them on the Stage is easier with Snap off. Using the grid and guidelines helps more than Snap, and for the great bulk of the work I do, the Snap option is off.

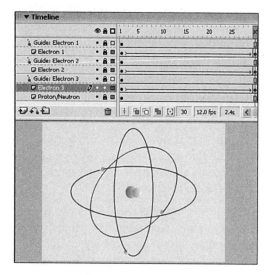

FIGURE 4.21   When the movie is complete, the three electrons have orbital paths around the neutron and proton.

6. Click Frame 30 and drag the electron object to the right side of the gap in the oval. Test the movie, and you should see the "electron" follow the path around the proton/electron in the center of the Stage.

7. Repeat steps 2–6, creating Electrons 2 and 1 along with their guide layers and oval orbits. Figure 4.21 shows how the movie appears when completed.

When the file is tested as a compiled file, you'll see that the motion guides disappear. Only a single guide path (and no other objects, text, or drawings) should ever be placed on the motion guide layers.

Tweening and Layers

As noted in Chapter 1, the layers in Flash represent the stacked layers of glass early animators used to create depth and easily move characters within that depth. Thus, using layers, moving a character behind a tree was simply a matter of placing the layer with the tree at a higher level than the character hiding behind the tree. The same is true in Flash Pro. With the exception of a masking or transparent object, an object on a higher layer blocks the view of objects on lower layers.

Lock and Snap

Once you have completed drawing the guide path on the guide layer, always lock the layer. As long as the layer with the object attached to the guide layer is unlocked, the object will still snap to the beginning or end of the guide line if the Snap option is on.

When it comes to movement on a layer, Flash Pro is different from movement and animation on the old glass layers. When tweening shapes, you can place multiple shapes on a single layer and have them tween, or you can have different shape tweens on multiple layers. For example, if you place a single shape in a keyframe and then have three shapes in another keyframe with a tween between them, the single shape will morph into three shapes. However, when you're using motion tweens, each tweened object must be on a separate layer.

Masking Layers

Like motion guides, the masking process requires two linked layers. The top layer is the mask, and any indented layers directly below the Mask layer are the masked layers. In Flash, the mask reveals a "mask hole" to the masked layers. Using a single object on the mask layer, the shape of the object shows a portion of the masked layer in the form of the mask shape. For example, if the object on the mask layer is in the shape of a star, all that is viewed on the layer below is the star-shaped portion of the masked layer.

To create a mask layer, right-click the layer above the layer you plan to mask to open a context menu. Select the Mask option in the context menu, and the selected layer and the layer below are transformed into a mask layer and masked layer, respectively. Place a single object on the mask layer and then lock both layers. With locked layers, the mask effect is invoked.

Project: Mask Parts of a Movie

The best way to see how masks work is with an example. The following document is developed over several subsections so that all nuances of masking can be examined. Here are the steps to follow:

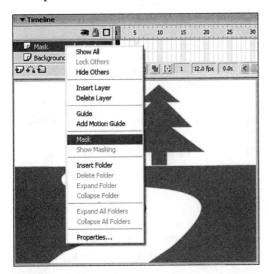

1. Open a new document and create two layers with the top one named Mask and the bottom one named Background.

2. In the Background layer, draw a scene to mask. In the example, the scene is composed of a river, a tree, and the surrounding earth.

3. Place the mouse pointer on the Mask layer and right-click to open the context menu (Control-click on the Mac). Select Mask, as shown in Figure 4.22.

   Once the mask layer is complete, the appearance of both the mask and masked layers changes, as shown in Figure 4.23.

FIGURE 4.22   Creating a mask layer.

FIGURE 4.23   The mask and masked layers.

FIGURE 4.24   The object on the Mask layer with layers unlocked.

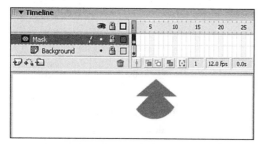

FIGURE 4.25   View of mask effect.

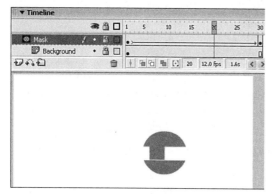

FIGURE 4.26   Animated mask.

4. Lock the Background layer, and in the Mask layer draw a circle and convert it to a Graphic symbol. Place the object directly over some discernable object on the Stage, such as the top of the tree, as shown in Figure 4.24.

5. Lock both layers, and everything disappears except for the area on the Background layer covered by the mask, as shown in Figure 4.25. In the SWF file, this is the kind of effect you can expect.

6. Finally, you can animate the mask so that it moves around the Stage revealing different parts of the masked layer. The Graphic instance is animated by using a motion tween. Figure 4.26 shows the mask over the background halfway through a motion tween.

If you test the movie, the results are not very interesting. All you see is the different parts of the background as the mask moves across the Stage. More interesting effects are possible using a revealed text message or some other background or mask shape. However, even with the current document, we can make it more interesting, as explored in the next subsection.

Echoing Layers

Layers below the mask layer that are not masked are fully visible. Although you may have several masked layers beneath a mask layer, none are blocked by or revealed by the mask layer unless they're indented beneath the mask layer or one of its masked layers.

If you duplicate the background layer and paste it below a darkening filter layer, when the mask passes over the masked layer, it appears to lighten. To see how this works, we'll expand the mask document from the preceding section. Use the following steps for the expansion:

1. Add three layers and drag them to the bottom of the layer column. Name the bottom layer Echo Background, the second from the bottom, 35% Dark Filter, and the third from the bottom, Sky.

2. Select the Sky layer and right-click the mouse to open the context menu. In the menu, select Properties and click the Masked option. The layer title will indent and change to a masked layer.

3. Select the Background layer, select everything, and copy the contents of the background. Click the Echo Background layer and select Edit, Paste in Place from the menu so that an identical background is beneath the original background image.

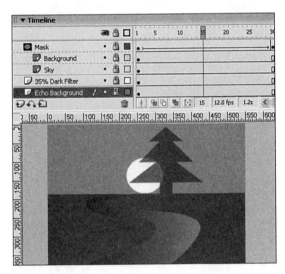

4. In the 35% Dark Filter layer, draw a black rectangle the same size as the Stage. Convert it to a Graphic symbol, and in the Property Inspector adjust the alpha level to 35%. Now the second background should appear darker than the original, and when all layers are locked, all you should see is the dark background layer and a circle where the mask covers.

5. In the Sky layer, insert a yellow linear gradient rectangle. Rotate the rectangle so that the lighter side is on the bottom. Size the rectangle so that it fills the Stage horizontally and from the top of the Stage to the horizon line. When the round mask goes over the yellow gradient sky, it appears to be the moon lighting up the dark. Figure 4.27 shows the revised document.

FIGURE 4.27 The mask lighting up the top background.

Using filters and echo layers, you can do much more with masks. Although you can have multiple masked layers, you can only have a single object serve as the mask. However, a document can have as many mask/masked combinations as you want.

Moving Masks with a Guide

One of the peculiarities of Flash is that a guide layer cannot be placed above a mask layer. Therefore, you cannot create a motion guide for a masking object. However, using a workaround and a little ActionScript 2.0, you'll find that setting up a motion path for a masking object is not difficult at all. Extending the previous example, the following steps show you how:

1. Add two layers above the Mask layer. Name the top one Actions and the bottom one Guide.

2. Select the Guide layer. Click the Add Motion Guide button to add a motion guide layer. Draw a guideline in the motion guide layer and then lock the layer. (See Figure 4.28 for an idea of how this looks.)

3. In the Guide layer (beneath the motion guide layer), draw a small circle and convert it to a movie clip. Give it the instance name guide_mc.

4. Add a keyframe to Frame 30 of the Guide layer, click Frame 1, and add a motion tween. Still in Frame 1, drag guide_mc to the beginning of the guide path. Then click Frame 30 and drag guide_mc to the end of the guide path. Test it to make sure that guide_mc follows the motion path.

5. Open the Library panel and change the circle object used for the mask from a Graphic symbol to a movie clip. To make the change, click the object in the Library panel, click the *i* icon at the bottom of the panel to open the Symbol Properties dialog box, and then select Movie Clip Behavior. Provide the instance name mask_mc for the movie clip.

6. In the Actions layer, Frame 1, add the following script:

```
guide_mc._visible = false;
guide_mc.onEnterFrame = function() {
    mask_mc._x = guide_mc._x;
    mask_mc._y = guide_mc._y;
};
```

Once you're finished, test the movie. Figure 4.28 how the Stage looks when complete.

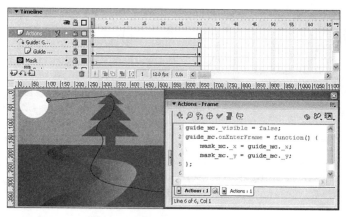

FIGURE 4.28   A guide path for the movie clip mask to track.

Basically, all you've done is to add an addressable object (guide_mc) to a motion path, add another addressable object to the Mask layer (mask_mc), and provide code that instructs the masking object to follow guide_mc. Because guide_mc shouldn't be visible at all, its _visible property is set to false.

> **Mask Uses Script to Follow Another Movie Clip's Guide Path**
>
> The motion tween was not removed from the Mask layer; however, it could have been. The moving mask object is not being tweened from one frame to the next, but instead it is being repositioned by the changes in its _x and _y properties, mimicking guide_mc. Therefore, you can remove both the motion tween and the keyframe in Frame 30 in the Mask layer.

Dragging a Mask

Before we end our discussion on masking, one more technique you may find useful is dragging the masking object. In this way, you can design documents where the user drags the mask to reveal different information. To see how this works, just remove Frames 2–30 (press Shift+F5 on all selected frames) in the sample mask movie, remove all motion tweens, and add the following code to the Actions layer frame:

```
mask_mc.onPress = function() {
    startDrag(this);
};
mask_mc.onRelease = function() {
    stopDrag();
};
```

Now the "moon" mask can be dragged anywhere the user wants. Although this is not especially useful in this movie, in designs where user interaction is encouraged, having the user drag an object is one way to get him or her involved.

Timeline Effects

A new feature of Flash MX Professional 2004 is Timeline Effects. You can quickly create the following effects and changes:

- Blur
- Drop shadow
- Expand
- Explode
- Transform
- Transition

To create a Timeline effect, all you have to do is create an object on the Stage, select it, and then select Insert, Timeline Effects, [Effect/Transition] from the menu. Some effects, such as a drop shadow, add no additional frames, but others, such as the blur effect, add several frames, creating a little movie. Figure 4.29 shows a star object subjected to the blur effect.

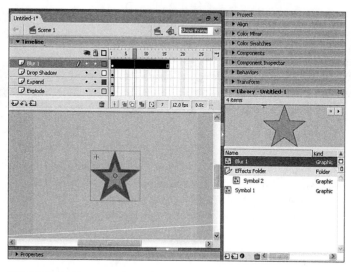

FIGURE 4.29   The blur effect.

When a Timeline effect is instantiated, an Effects folder and additional symbols are added to the Library panel. Note in Figure 4.29 that in addition to Symbol 1, the Library panel contains Blur 1, Effects Folder, and Symbol 2, which were automatically generated by applying the Timeline effect.

When an effect, transition, or transform option is selected, a Timeline Effects dialog box opens and, depending on the effect, provides different settings to adjust. For example, the explode effect shows a preview of the effect and parameters for the number of frames, direction of explosion, arc size, fragment rotation, fragment size change, and final alpha setting. Figure 4.30 shows the Explode dialog box with the fragments in mid-explosion.

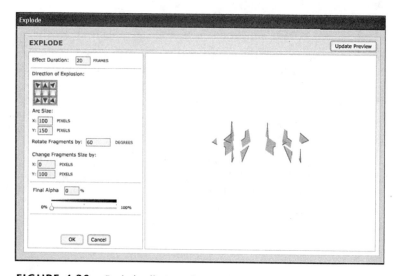

FIGURE 4.30   Explode effect preview.

Because a Timeline effect adds variable numbers of frames to a document, depending on both the effect and the user parameter settings, you can best control the effect by putting it on movie clip Timelines rather than on the main Timeline.

Dancing Baloney Made Easy

The Timeline effects can have definite uses for professionally developed applications. However, don't be tempted to add these effects simply because they're available, fun, and easy to add to a Flash Pro document. Early Flash developers and designers were accused of adding superfluous "dancing baloney" to their creations. Some of these early animated features were quite good as far as animations were concerned, but after viewing their effects once or twice, users found them to be annoying. Make sure that Timeline effects add to the site being developed and aren't just annoying distractions.

Coordinating Animated Parts

When you're working on animation, especially cartoon animation, planning is the key to good results. Likewise, understanding the entire cartooning process using Flash, including creating a story and animating it, is the only way to do more than simple animations. The best resource for this kind of cartooning is Mark Clarkson's *Flash 5 Cartooning*. Although it deals with an older version of Flash, it lays down the basic concepts of cartooning, including how to coordinate the different parts of a cartoon character. Likewise, Tony White's 1986 pre-Flash work, *The Animator's Workbook*, provides another good source for cartoon animation and how the professional animator sets up steps for successful cartoon animation. You'll find that the principles of cartooning that apply to drawn animation apply equally to Flash animation.

Planning the Animation

Even a simple animation, such as a walking motion, has to be planned. Using Flash you can create a surprisingly realistic walk using three positions, but even three positions have to have all the body parts coordinated. The first thing to plan is the organization of parts on separate layers. Using layer folders helps organize this process. Each part has to be a Graphic symbol so that none of the parts would morph when tweened. Moreover, each part needs its own layer because only a single object on a layer can be tweened. The organization plan is to place each limb in a folder containing the parts of the limb. This proves to be very simple because the left limb parts can be used for the right limb parts as well. The torso is a single part that serves to hold the more animated parts, and the head simply sits atop the torso. So, the most animated parts of the leg are the following:

- Thigh
- Calf
- Foot

And here are the most animated parts of the arm:

- Upper arm

- Forearm

- Hand

The arms and legs are divided into left and right folders, and identical graphic symbols are employed in the left and right portions of the figure. You can create a folder by clicking the New Folder icon. As you drag each layer you want into the folder, it indents beneath the folder, as shown in Figure 4.31. Using this setup, coordinating all the parts is much simpler. Figure 4.31 also shows how the Timeline and layers appear once all the parts have been organized and tweened.

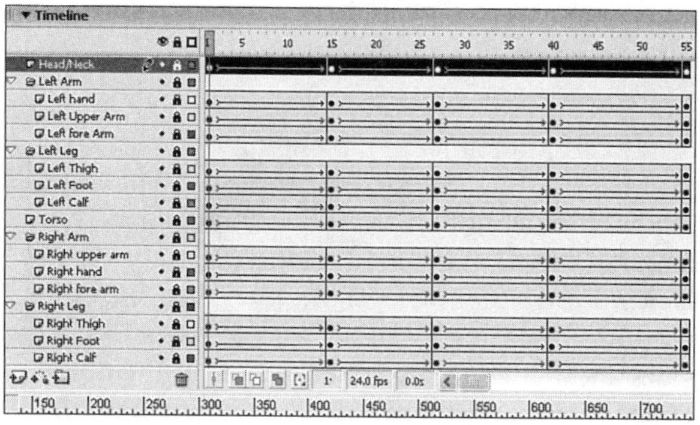

FIGURE 4.31 Completed Timeline, folders, and layers.

When all the parts are complete, you can move the pivot points to their appropriate positions on the different graphic symbols representing the arm and leg parts. Whenever an instance is dragged to the Stage, the pivot points are all set and consistent.

Choosing Positions for a Figure

A simple set of drawings is employed to test the animation. Like the proverb stating that a journey of a thousand miles begins with a single step, animating starts with a walk. A step has three parts. The first keyframe has the beginning position, the next keyframe is the "crossover" frame where one leg crosses over the other, and the third is the ending position where the step has been completed. Figure 4.32 shows the three basic positions.

The next step simply reverses the two ending positions, and the crossover frame shows the opposite leg crossing over.

When doing multiple positioning of different parts, use the guides and rulers to help keep the parts where they belong. Then, as the figure is tweened from one set of positions to another, it keeps a coherent appearance. The walking movements don't move the body—only the limbs.

Therefore, a vertical guide helps to keep the head and torso horizontally aligned regardless of the angle at which the limbs have been positioned. Likewise, the horizontal guideline assists in positioning the arms and legs in different keyframes. Figure 4.33 shows the figure in the initial position with the guidelines in place. (Also note the different body parts with their center points positioned at the joints and the symbols in the Library panel.)

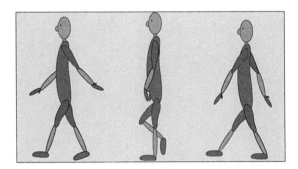

FIGURE 4.32 A single step.

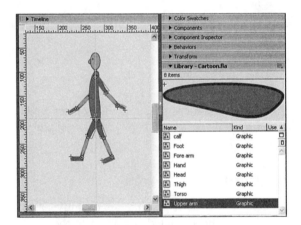

FIGURE 4.33 Guides around the figure.

Copying and Pasting Frames

One of the timesaving features of Flash Pro is the ability to copy frames and paste them in another set of frames. A full step, for example, begins and ends with the figure in the same position. Rather than repositioning all the parts, you can copy and paste one set of positions in a different set of blank keyframes.

To copy and paste frames, follow these steps:

1. Select the frames and, with the pointer in one of the selected frames, right-click (Control-click on the Mac) the mouse to open the context menu.

2. Select Copy Frames from the menu.

3. To paste the frames and their contents, place the mouse pointer in a set of blank keyframes equivalent to the frames copied. (If you have 11 keyframes copied, you'll need 11 blank keyframes to paste the copied frames.) Figure 4.34 shows the keyframes in the first frame being copied.

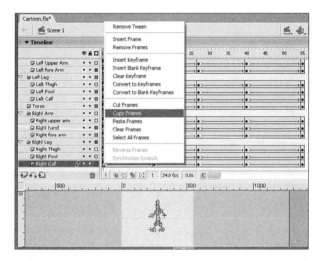

FIGURE 4.34   Copying frames.

You can use the copy/paste frames method to save time when creating a moving object made up of several coordinated parts. In the next section, you'll see how to copy frames to place the contents of the main Timeline into a movie clip.

Project: Animating an Advertisement

The following Flash banner ad begins with the premise that static graphics are primitive, and using styles from cave drawings, that point is displayed. The animated characters in the banner are a hunter, drawn in the petroglyph style, and a buffalo, rendered after a cave drawing. Both could have been drawn using the rectangular torso common in petroglyphs. However, both cave drawings and outdoor petroglyphs seem to provide far better detail to the animals than to humans, so the buffalo looks a lot more like a primitive bison than the spearman looks human. Nevertheless, both are primitive enough to get across the initial point that something in the banner, including the Smudger LET font, is primitive.

The scene shows a man with a spear facing a big buffalo, with the top line

Primitive Static Graphics?

presented in 32-point font. Then, at the bottom in a clear 10-point message in parentheses is the invitation:

```
(Click the buffalo for some action)
```

The bottom message uses Verdana font for its clarity on the Web. When the user clicks the buffalo movie clip, its legs begin moving as it runs toward the hunter, who then throws a spear at the buffalo. The buffalo collides with the hunter, who is then thrown in the air and off the Stage. The buffalo then stops near the edge of the banner. The final message at the top of the banner is

```
Next time, try Sandlight!
```

in the same 32-point Smudger LET font as the initial banner message. Slightly below the center is the Sandlight Productions URL using all-lowercase Smudger LET 32-point font. The URL is set to the _blank option in the Target drop-down menu next to the link window where the URL goes. Remember that the user has come to the site to see its goods and services. Through the use of the _blank option, the client's site in the banner ad comes up as a separate page, making it easy for the user to get back to his or her site of interest.

If the user clicks the buffalo again, the original banner appears. However, nothing in the banner animates unless the user wants it to. In this way, the user/potential client has at the very worst a neutral opinion of the services offered. If the user chooses to click the buffalo to start the animation process or the URL, he or she is never taken away from the site he or she came to visit in the first place.

SHOP TALK

How to Drive Viewers Nuts Using Bad Banners

Before starting on an animated banner ad for the Web, you should be aware that creating banner ads must be done judiciously with an eye to not alienating the user. A banner ad can be as annoying as a telemarketer at dinnertime. Therefore, before creating one for a client, you need to think it through. This often involves discussing effective online ads with your client. If your client wants a leaping, pouncing ad that will drive the viewer to a click off the page, you have to provide the client with alternatives and explanations why a wiser course of action would achieve the desired effect.

First, no matter how clever your banner ad, after people have seen it do its dance once or twice, they don't care to see it again. Second, motion, even a small motion, draws the user's eye to the advertisement. Because users visit pages for the content they contain, banner ads are always treated as uninvited guests unless they deal with the specific content at the site. Any distracting (or attention-getting) movement should be subtle and then quit. Better yet, movement should be controlled by the user. Then if you pique the user's interest, you can let him or her decide to fire off your little show.

Because multiple animated characters are to be used in the banner ad, two movie clips will be used to prevent having a maze of layers on the main Timeline. So, to begin, both animated characters are created as movie clips. As with the example of the animated walk, the animations need to be broken down into basic parts. Using photographs from Muybridge, the basic shapes are planned. Figure 4.35 shows the petroglyph-like spearman's key positions above the corresponding positions of a man throwing a spear for Muybridge's movement studies.

FIGURE 4.35   The animated character and photos of the spear throw.

FIGURE 4.36   The buffalo's running positions.

The animation requires four positions (in the five images, the first and third are the same).

The buffalo requires positioning as well. Figure 4.36 shows the three positions for the running (or trotting) buffalo. Again, Muybridge's photo studies provide the position guide.

Animating the Spearman
To begin, create all the parts of the spearman. Each part should be transformed into a Graphic symbol. Given the simplicity of the character, the upper arms double as the thighs, and the forearms are used as the calves. The following inventory is a guide:

- Torso and head
- Spear
- Thigh/upper arm
- Forearm/calf

Okay Now, In Together and Out Together

An important positioning tip to remember about the movement of four-legged animals is that the legs on each side are opposite one another and of the legs on the opposite side. That is, when the left foreleg is outward away from the center of the body, the hind leg is also outward. At the time that the two left legs are outward, the right legs are inward. (In the second and third photographs in the bottom row in Figure 4.4 near the beginning of the chapter, you can see this clearly.) This phenomenon varies with the speed that the animal is moving, and although you can clearly see the positions of the buffalo's legs in the drawings in Figure 4.36, the buffalo in Muybridge's photos is not quite as cooperative in positioning his legs.

A simple trick is to use a 4-point line for the thigh/upper arm and a 3-point line for the calf/forearm. After turning all the drawings into Graphic symbols, use the Free Transform tool to position the center points at the joint locations.

Once all the body parts and the spear are made, use the layers and folders in the order shown in Figure 4.37.

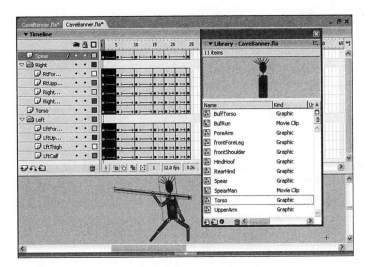

FIGURE 4.37   The layers, folders, and tweens for the spearman.

Note the center points of the spearman character in Figure 4.37. The only center point not used is the spear, which retains its original position in the center of the spear line.

Use the following steps to complete the spearman animated character:

1. Add 24 frames to all the layers so that each layer has a total of 25 frames.

2. Beginning in Frame 1, use Figure 4.35 as a guide to position the parts. Only a single part is placed in each layer. Once the character is positioned in Frame 1, add keyframes in Frames 25, 18, 15, 10, and 5, in that order. In this way, you will have the beginning figure in all the frames.

3. Frames 1, 10, and 25 use the same positions for the body, so you can leave those alone except for Frame 25, where you place the spear about 300 pixels from the spearman character at about a 45-degree angle in the "ground." (No buffaloes were harmed in the production of this movie.)

4. In the other frames, use the sequence shown in Figure 4.35, remembering that the first and third positions are identical.

5. Add motion tweens to all layers in Frames 1, 5, 10, 15, and 18.

Once you have completed placing the character parts where they belong and set motion tweens in their places, test the movie by following these steps:

1. To create a movie clip for this character, select all the layers and frames and then right-click (Control-click on the Mac) any of the selected frames to bring up the context menu. Select Copy Frames.

2. Select Insert, New Symbol from the main menu and then select Movie Clip for the behavior and SpearMan for the name in the Symbol dialog box.

3. In the symbol-editing Timeline, click the first frame and then right-click (Control-click on the Mac) the frame to bring up the context menu. Select Paste Frames. All the frames, folders, and positioned elements will appear in the movie clip's Timeline.

4. Exit the Symbol Editor and open a new document. Open the Library panel and drag a copy of the SpearMan movie clip to the Stage. Test the movie to see if it works correctly. If it does, save the movie and prepare to create the buffalo movie clip.

It's Only an Illustration: Don't Do This Without an Adult Present

The preceding process is a little convoluted, and it's included simply to show you how to copy and paste frames and layers into another Timeline.

Animating the Buffalo

Creating the parts is a little different for the buffalo. You will use the same document in which the SpearMan movie clip has been placed on the Stage. First, use the following parts inventory to get started:

- Torso, head, and tail
- Front shoulder
- Front foreleg
- Upper hind and leg
- Hind hoof and foreleg

Unlike the simple petroglyph character of spearman, creating the buffalo takes a different tack:

1. First draw or trace the buffalo. Then use the Oval tool with no fill to draw circles in the front shoulder area and rear hind area. The center of these circles come to be the pivot points for the legs.

2. Divide the buffalo drawing into the parts detailed in the preceding bulleted list and turn all the drawings into Graphic symbols.

3. Because the buffalo is to be made as a movie clip, press Ctrl+F8 (Cmd+F8 on the Mac) to open the Create New Symbol dialog box, select Movie Clip for the behavior, and name it BufRun.

4. Using Figure 4.38 as a guide, create the folders and layers. Each layer should only contain a single buffalo part, with the layer name indicating which part belongs in the layer.

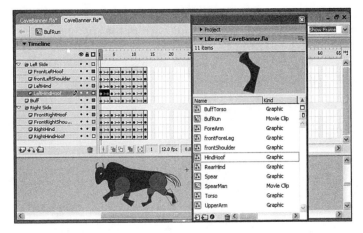

FIGURE 4.38 The BufRun movie clip layers.

Now complete the buffalo movie clip:

1. Add 12 frames to all the layers so that each layer has a total of 13 frames.

2. Beginning in Frame 1, refer to Figure 4.39 as a guide to position the buffalo parts. Only a single part is placed in each layer. Once the character is positioned in Frame 1, add keyframes in Frames 13, 10, 7, and 4, in that order. This way, you will have the beginning figure in all the frames.

FIGURE 4.39 The buffalo's running positions.

3. Frames 1 and 13 use the same positions for the body, so you do not need to change the positions in Frame 13. Likewise, Frames 5 and 10 are identical. When you've completed Frame 5, copy and paste all the layers in Frame 5 to Frame 10.

4. Once all the positions are set in the keyframes, place motion tweens in all the keyframes except the last one (Frame 13).

The buffalo is easier to animate than spearman because its body is in fewer positions. Also, the keyframes are closer together to move the buffalo's legs faster, giving it a more urgent trot.

Bringing the Parts Together

The rest of the movie is pretty simple once you have the two main movie clips built. Here are the steps to follow:

1. First, set the Stage size to 600×200, which is a bit big for a banner ad, but given the size and resolution of contemporary monitors, it's not overwhelming.

2. As shown in Figure 4.40, use four layers, named Actions, Text, Spear Man, and Buffalo. Drag an instance of each movie clip onto the Stage, placing each in the appropriately labeled layer. Use the positions shown in Figure 4.40 as a guide.

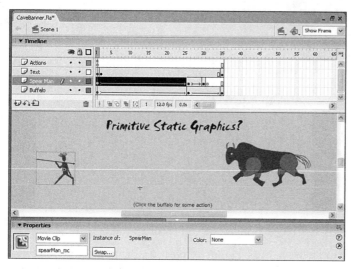

FIGURE 4.40   Initial positions of the movie clips.

3. Once you have the initial Stage set up and the layers inserted, create frames out to Frame 35 for all layers.

Now use the following steps to finish up the movie:

1. Give the spearman movie clip the instance name spearMan_mc, and give the buffalo movie clip the instance name buf_mc.

2. Click the first frame of the Actions panel and place the following script in the Actions panel:

```
stop();
spearMan_mc.stop();
buf_mc.stop();
buf_mc.onPress = function() {
    this.play();
    spearMan_mc.play();
 play();
};
buf_mc.onEnterFrame = function() {
    if (this.buf_mc._x<200) {
            this.stop();
            _level0.stop();
    }
};
```

Buffalo Size *Does* Matter!

The script stops the movie when buf_mc moves to less than position 200 on the Stage. Results will vary depending on the size of the buffalo movie clip. If the movie doesn't stop, try adjusting the value to 200.

The script addresses both the movie clips and the main Timeline, and to completely stop a movie, each movie clip must be addressed separately.

3. In the Text layer, place a 32-point message using a static text field. (Use any message you like.) At the bottom of the banner, tell the user to click the buffalo to start the action.

4. Add a keyframe to Frame 2 of the Text layer. Select the keyframe and delete the instructions at the bottom of the banner. Add a keyframe to Frame 35. Remove the beginning message and add an ending message. (Use any message you want or the one shown later on, in Figure 4.42).

5. In the Spear Man layer, on which only the spearMan_mc instance should be placed, add a keyframe in Frame 30. Add another keyframe in Frame 26. Using the Free Transform tool, drag the center point of the movie clip to the middle of the spear thrower's body, and in Frame 30 place the spearMan_mc instance at the top of the banner and invert it, still using the Free Transform tool. Only a small portion of the top of the movie clip should be visible in the upper-left corner of the Stage. Add motion tweens in Frames 1 and 26. Finally, add a blank keyframe in Frame 31. This will make spearman disappear from the Stage. Figure 4.41 shows the position of spearman in mid-tween between Frames 26 and 30.

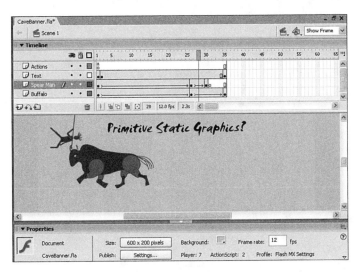

FIGURE 4.41 Spearman being tweened and rotated upward.

6. In the Buffalo layer, with the buf_mc instance on the Stage, add a keyframe in the last frame. Move the buffalo movie clip to the far right side of the Stage, as shown in Figure 4.42.

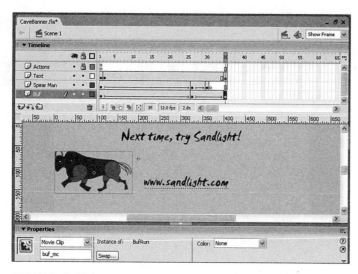

FIGURE 4.42   The final position of the buffalo movie clip.

In Figure 4.42, you'll see a keyframe in Frame 26. This was placed there while repositioning the spearman movie clip, but it's unnecessary.

At this point, your banner ad should be complete. Use the test movie to see whether it works as expected. If it doesn't, make adjustments to either the movie clips or the main Timeline. Figure 4.43 shows how the banner ad appears shortly after the spear has been thrown and just before the spearman gets bounced off the Stage.

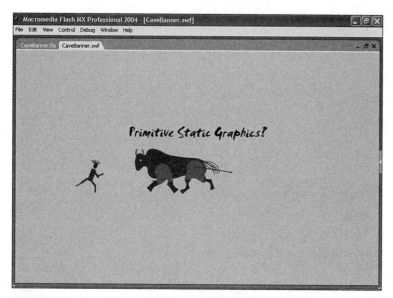

FIGURE 4.43   The banner ad in the middle of the animated action.

What's Next?

This chapter has shown one of the key features of Flash—the ability to create animations. The banner ad only took up a little over 13KB of memory (14KB on disk). The amount and quality of animation possible with Flash provides the designer and developer with more flexibility in creating Web pages and sites because it adds the dimension of interactivity and animation.

In the next chapter, this discussion is continued as the full power of movie clips is examined further. Among other topics is a full discussion of the new MovieClip class, along with its many properties and methods. Although this chapter has explored the many documents you can create using movie clips, the next chapter takes it to the next level of functionality in Flash Pro.

In Brief

- Flash uses the same basic concepts of animation as traditional animation created without computers.

- Vector graphics help to make smooth animation because they're not distorted when changed in size, as are bitmapped graphics.

- The Timeline in Flash can be treated exactly like the Timeline in a Film Editor.

- Masks are used to show the viewer-selected portions of underlying layers.

- The new Timeline effects make it very simple to create complex animations.

- All the traditional animation methods can be applied in Flash to create realistic animated motions of people, animals, and other things.

Movie Clip Control

Movie Clip Levels and Hierarchies

Chapter 4, "Animations and Interactions," covered the animation development process, using both the main Timeline and movie clips. This chapter brings out the true flexibility and power of movie clips as they can be used in Flash Pro.

Movie clips have their own Timelines, and a movie in the form of a SWF file or movie clip can be loaded into another movie or movie clip. Because of the different places where a movie clip can be located relative to the main Timeline, the initial level (_level0), and other movie clips, understanding Flash's movie and movie clip hierarchy needs to be a top priority for developers and designers.

The following key identifiers and properties make up the primary terms used to address a movie clip from the main Timeline or from another movie clip:

- _level
- _root
- _lockroot
- _parent

Using _root and _level

The _root property is often used (and misused) to address either the main Timeline or an object on the main Timeline. For example, the following two lines illustrate typical uses of _root:

```
_root.gotoAndStop(7);
_root.house_mc._alpha=88;
```

Depending on the circumstances, these lines of code may or may not do what the developer expects. If the commands are issued from an object on level 59, they will only affect the main Timeline of _level59. Assuming that the code is from level 59, the same code would be correctly written as follows:

```
_level59.gotoAndStop(7);
_level59.house_mc._alpha=88;
```

However, if the developer really meant to address the main Timeline of the zero level—what many consider to be the "bedrock" level of a movie—the script should be written as follows:

```
_level0.gotoAndStop(7);
_level0.house_mc._alpha=88;
```

To avoid confusion, a recommended practice is to use _levelN rather than _root in movies and movie clips. The _root property is relative, and the _levelN identifier is absolute.

The _parent Identifier

Another relative reference identifier is _parent. A reference from a movie clip to _parent directs the method or property to the movie clip (or main Timeline) containing the movie clip. For example, suppose you have a movie with the path

```
_level0.boat_mc.cabin_mc
```

with this statement:

```
_parent._alpha=20;
```

Depending on where you have the line, different events will transpire. If you place the line in boat_mc, all the objects on the main Timeline will become transparent with an alpha value of only 20. If the line is in cabin_mc, the boat object, including the cabin, will be reduced to an alpha value of 20—but no other objects on the main Timeline will be affected.

Depending on the number of embedded movie clips that reside within one another, you can "back out" to any level you want by using the relative reference of the _parent identifier. For example, from the cabin_mc level, the line

```
_parent._parent._rotation=90
```

will knock all the objects on the main Timeline on their side, including instances of symbols, text, and drawings. If you prefer relative addressing to absolute addressing, you can use the _parent identifier.

Who's the Daddy?

Although using multiple _parent identifiers will work to address a particular object, that practice is not recommended. One of the hallmarks of good coding is clarity. When you use the _parent reference to back into a higher-level object, the object's path is unclear. When you're referencing any object at a higher level, the reference should begin at the highest level for that object, which is the root level, and then you should name the identifiers downward to the desired object. Using a top-down method clarifies the path to the object, and debugging is far simpler.

Figure 5.1 shows an outline of the general hierarchies. Each rectangle represents an instance of a movie clip. Above the movie clips is each movie clip's parent. Below the delta1_mc instance are two different ways of expressing a path, but movie clips on the main Timeline can be addressed with no root reference by simply referencing each movie clip's instance name.

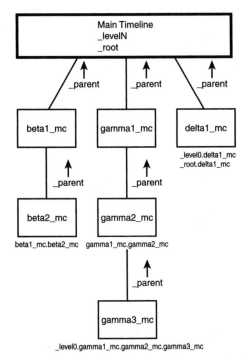

The _lockroot **Movie Clip Property**

Flash MX 2004 has a new movie clip property that can lock the root level within a movie clip. This property, _lockroot, establishes the root level in the movie clip that has designated itself as the root level. For example, if you have one SWF file named loadee.swf and a movie clip button named burst_mc with the script

```
stop();
this._lockroot=true;
burst_mc.onPress = function() {
    _root.gotoAndStop(8);
};
```

then the statement

```
this._lockroot=true;
```

FIGURE 5.1 Flash movie clip hierarchy.

establishes that movie as the root of any movie it loads into.

If you place the following code in a movie named loader.swf, it will load the loadee.swf movie into a movie clip instance called loader_mc (loader_mc is a movie clip used as a button):

```
var loadMyOtherMovie:MovieClipLoader = new MovieClipLoader();
loader_mc.onPress = function() {
    loadMyOtherMovie.loadClip("loadee.swf", this);
};
```

When the movie clip button burst_mc in the loadee.swf file is clicked, the movie plays the root Timeline of the loadee.swf file and not the loader.swf file into which it has been loaded.

In some applications, using the redirected root layer can be very handy. However, it must be used appropriately lest it add more confusion to the movie clip hierarchy reference system.

Loading Movie Clips

Movie clips, both as SWF files and movie clips, can be brought to the Stage. When I discuss the MovieClip class methods shortly, you'll see how to load a movie clip from the Library panel to the Stage. This section examines loading SWF files into current movies. First, we'll look at the older loadMovie and loadMovieNum functions.

loadMovie() **and** loadMovieNum()

Experienced Flash users will recognize the loadMovie() and loadMovieNum() functions. Both are being upstaged by the new MovieClipLoader class, but a quick review of these two veteran movie clip loaders is in order for those new to Flash.

The loadMovie() function loads a movie or JPEG file into a movie clip on the Stage using this format:

```
loadMovie("URL",target_mc,[optional POST or GET])
```

If the SWF or JPEG file to be loaded is in the same folder as the host movie, all you need to include is the filename. For example, here's a typical use of loadMovie():

```
loadMovie("automobile7.SWF", carShow_mc);
```

The SWF file named automobile7.SWF would be placed in the movie clip named carShow_mc. It represents a typical use of loadMovie(), in which several different SWF files are loaded and unloaded. As soon as another SWF file is loaded into a movie clip, the previous one is unloaded.

You can also use unloadMovie(mc) to remove a movie loaded into a movie clip. The only parameter required in the unloadMovie() function is the name of the movie clip instance name. The following script illustrates loading a movie into and unloading a movie out of a movie clip:

```
loadMovie("coolStuff.swf", loader_mc);
off_btn.onPress = function() {
    unloadMovie(loader_mc);
};
```

The button instance off_btn fires a function to unload the movie in the loader_mc, but you don't need to specify the name of the movie—only a single movie at a time can reside in the movie clip instance.

You can also load movies into the main Timeline. Because the main Timeline is considered a "movie clip," the following scripts work just fine:

```
loadMovie("coolStuff.swf", _root);
```

```
loadMovie("coolStuff.swf", _level0);
```

However, if you try using a level other than _level0, you must first have another movie loaded at that level.

Another extremely useful loading function is loadMovieNum(). This function has the following format:

```
loadMovieNum("url",level,[optional variables])
```

The advantage of loading external movies into levels rather than movie clips is that you don't need any movie clips to receive the movies loaded. A movie loaded into the same level as an existing movie replaces the movie only at that level.

Let's look at an example to see how loadMovieNum() and its unloading companion, unloadMovieNum(), work. Follow these steps:

1. Set up a movie with a single movie clip on the Stage, along with four buttons for loading and unloading the movies.

2. Create two other movies, positioning any images in such a way that they won't cover up any others on the Stage.

3. Name the movies to be loaded level1 and level22 (see Figure 5.2). The images at the bottom and at the right are movies loaded into different levels in the host movie.

FIGURE 5.2 Loading movies at different levels.

4. On the host movie, use the following instance names for the four buttons:

- load1_btn
- load22_btn
- unload1_btn
- unload22_btn

5. In the first frame of the host movie, place the following script:

```
load1_btn.onPress = function() {
    loadMovieNum("level1.swf", 1);
};
load22_btn.onPress = function() {
    loadMovieNum("level22.swf", 22);
};
unload1_btn.onPress = function() {
    unloadMovieNum(1)
};
unload22_btn.onPress = function() {
    unloadMovieNum(22);
};
```

6. Play the movie. As you click the load buttons, you'll see the different SWF files load; if you have any animations in the loaded movies, they'll animate.

The newer LoadVars class has replaced much of the functionality that used to be employed with loadVarNum() and its ability to post/get variables. In the later discussion of using the LoadVars class, you'll see how to send variables to and receive variables from external scripts.

MovieClipLoader

A major new addition in Flash Pro is the MovieClipLoader class. Not only can it be employed to load movie clips like the loadMovie() function, but it can load movies to levels like loadMovieNum() does. It can also "listen to" the progress of the load. Using a listener callback, the class has methods for determining different loading properties. Tables 5.1 through 5.3 summarize the methods, properties, and listener callback functions in the MovieClipLoader class.

TABLE 5.1

MovieClipLoader **Methods**

METHOD	ACTION
addListener(*obj*)	Connects an object that listens for callback
removeListener(*obj*)	Removes the Listener object
getProgress(*target_mc/level*)	Gets the number of bytes currently loaded and the total number of bytes
loadClip("*url*",*target_mc/levelN*)	Begins loading the SWF/JPEG file into *target_mc* or the specified level
unloadClip(*target_mc/levelN*)	Removes the loaded clip

TABLE 5.2

`MovieClipLoader` **Properties**

PROPERTY	CHARACTERISTIC
bytesLoaded	Returns the number of bytes currently loaded when the getProgress() method is invoked
bytesTotal	Returns the total number of bytes of the object being loaded when the getProgress() method is invoked

TABLE 5.3

`MovieClipLoader` **Listener Callback Functions**

LISTENER CALLBACK FUNCTIONS	EVENT
onLoadComplete(target_mc)	The download is complete.
onLoadInit(target_mc)	The download is complete *and* the actions in the first frame are complete.
onLoadError(target_mc, errorCode)	The download fails or is terminated by the unloadClip method.
onLoadProgress(target_mc,LB,TB)	An alternative to the getProgress method; this function can be used as a single function for tracking loaded bytes (LB) and progress indicators needing the total bytes (TB).
onLoadStart(target_mc)	The download initiates.

Here's the general format for both a movie clip and level:

```
var mcLoader:MovieClipLoader = new MovieClipLoader;
mcLoader.loadClip("myMov.swf",target_mc)
```

or

```
mcLoader.loadClip("myMov.swf",7)
```

The class is most useful when the callbacks are employed in a script to provide information about the progress of an upload or to fire a function using a callback.

The callback listener functions act something like events. The following generic example shows the format for listening to the completion of the loading process:

```
var MyListener:Object = new Object();
MyListener.onLoadComplete = function(obj) {
    _//Statements
};
```

The next simple project shows how the class can be used to load movie clips into another movie and provide information while doing so. More importantly, though, it offers a model for developing templates that you can use over and over without having to rewrite code or redesign modules. The two dummy modules loaded represent a registration module and a contact module. The main page is a generic one as well and serves as a platform to accept the loading movie clips. Here are the steps to follow:

1. Open a new Flash document and create six layers, named from top to bottom: Actions, MC, Buttons, Info text, Text bg, and Bottom BG. Set the size to 700×600 pixels. Set the background color to #99CC99.

2. Select the Bottom BG layer and use the Rectangle tool to create a rectangle with the width of the Stage and a height of 60, aligned to the bottom of the Stage. Use #FFF3CC for the fill color and a 2-point #CC0033 colored stroke. Lock the layer.

3. Using Figure 5.3 as a placement guide, select the Button layer and place two UI Button components over the rectangle at the bottom of the Stage. Use the Property Inspector to provide each button with instance names—register_btn for the one on the left and contact_btn for the right button. Add the label Register for the left button and Contact for the right one. Lock the layer.

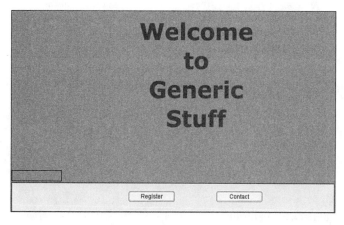

FIGURE 5.3   The Stage is set with a single movie clip, two buttons, and a dynamic text field.

4. Select the Text bg layer and draw a rectangle with the dimensions W=108 and H=21, with a 1-point black stroke line and no fill color, placing it on the left side of the Stage directly above the bottom rectangle. Lock the layer and then select the Info text layer. In the lower-left corner above the bottom rectangle, add a dynamic text field as shown in Figure 5.3, giving it the instance name loadInfo_txt.

5. Select the MC layer. Add a movie clip in the middle of the Stage. In the sample movie, the text is actually a movie clip (the text is broken into vector graphics that are then converted to a movie clip). Give it the instance name target_mc.

6. Once you have the Stage set, click the first frame, open the Actions panel, and add the following script (`MCLoader.fla`):

```
stop();
var loadEmUp:MovieClipLoader = new MovieClipLoader();
var loadEar:Object = new Object();
//Listen for Complete load
loadEar.onLoadComplete = function(movieClip) {
    _level0.loadInfo_txt.text = "Complete";
};
loadEmUp.addListener(loadEar);
//Button scripts
register_btn.onPress = function() {
    loadEmUp.loadClip("register.swf", target_mc);
};
contact_btn.onPress = function() {
    loadEmUp.loadClip("contact.swf", target_mc);
};
```

When you test the movie, you should see the original movie clip on the Stage, as shown earlier in Figure 5.3. At this point, it won't do anything because it still needs the SWF files to load.

Now you need two SWF files to load into the MCLoader movie. The two movies created to load into the initial movie represent two kinds of typical modules required by business applications. Rather than requiring the movie to jump to a different keyframe with the modules residing in the frames, both of these are brought in from external sources. The advantage of using external movies is that they don't take up bandwidth while the main movie loads. A typical document or set of documents for a business site might have several static features on the page. Rather than either movie bringing in all the static features, including graphics, and several modules on the initial loading of the movie, another tack is to bring in just the foundation module on the initial loading and then load the different modules as needed on top of the foundation module.

Rather than a Stage size of 700×600, the module is sized to a Stage of 250×200 pixels. The smaller Stage illustrates the utility of creating modules in separate documents and fitting them more exactly to their actual size. To make the registration module, use the following steps:

1. Open a new Flash document setting the Stage to 250×200 pixels. Add the following layers, from top to bottom: Actions, Text Fields, and Background.

2. Select the Text Fields layer and add two UI Button components. Label the buttons Register and Close, and use the instance names `reg_btn` and `close_btn`.

3. Using Figure 5.4 as a guide, add three input text fields with the instance names, from top to bottom, `fname_txt`, `lname_txt`, and `email_txt`.

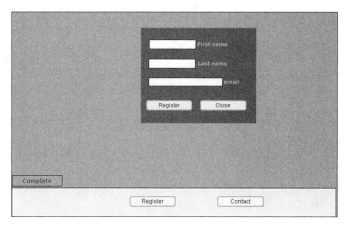

FIGURE 5.4   Registration module.

4. Select the Background layer and add the labels for the text fields.

5. Click the Actions layer and add the following script (register.fla). It only works when loaded into the MCLoader.swf file. (It doesn't do much other than demonstrate how a working movie clip can be loaded and closed.)

```
stop();
close_btn.onPress = function() {
    _level0.loadInfo_txt.text="Unloaded";
    _level0.loadEmUp.unloadClip(_level0.target_mc);
};
reg_btn.onPress = function() {
 //Clear
    fname_txt.text = "";
    lname_txt.text = "";
    email_txt.text = "Registered";
 //Pass variables to server side script
};
```

Interacting with the Mother Ship

The MCLoader.fla script first creates an instance of the MovieClipLoader class, loadEmUp, and the second two scripts use that object (instance of the class) to unload themselves from the movie. In other words, one SWF file can instantiate a class, and then movie clips loaded from external sources into the movie can use the instance of the class without defining it separately. The statement

```
_level0.loadEmUp.unloadClip(_level0.target_mc);
```

in the register.fla script uses the instance created in the MCLoader.fla document without first instantiating it in its own script.

The second movie clip to be loaded into the main movie is a contact module. It represents the kind of feature that allows the site visitor to make comments and send them to a site representative. The following steps explain how to put it together:

1. Open a new Flash document and set the Stage to 250×200 pixels. Add the following layers, from top to bottom: Actions, Text Fields, and Background.

2. Select the Text Fields layer and add two UI Button components. Label the buttons Send and Close, and use the instance names send_btn and close_btn.

3. Use Figure 5.5 as a guide and add two input text fields with the instance names, from top to bottom, email_txt and comments_txt.

4. Select the Background layer and add the labels email and Comments, as shown in Figure 5.5.

   Figure 5.5 shows the module loaded into the main movie.

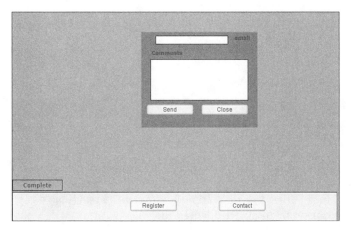

FIGURE 5.5   Contact module loaded into the MCLoader.swf file.

5. Select the Actions layer and add the following script (contact.fla). Like the registration module, this one is a dummy placeholder.

```
stop();
close_btn.onPress = function() {
    _level0.loadInfo_txt.text = "Unloaded";
    _level0.loadEmUp.unloadClip(_level0.target_mc);
};
send_btn.onPress = function() {
    //Clear
    comments_txt.text = "Thank you for contacting us. ";
    comments_txt.text += "We'll get back to you as soon as possible.";
    //Script to contact serverside
};
```

Seeing Through to the Main Movie

One trick to better integrate loaded SWF files with the main program is to add background layers using solid colors different from but complementary to the main module. However, you set the backgrounds to 50% transparency (alpha). By having transparent backgrounds, the modules more easily integrate with the main movie into which they've been loaded, yet at the same time they serve as a platform for their own text fields, labels, and buttons.

Both modules generate an "unloaded" message for the dynamic text field on the main Timeline. The scripts use a direct reference to the `loadInfo_text` instance rather than using the `loadEmUp` instance of the `MovieClipLoader` class. The reason is that although `MovieClipLoader` has a "load completed" event, it doesn't have an unload event.

SHOP TALK

Getting Organized: Movie Clips at the Core of the Flash Universe

Just about everything in Flash is a movie clip or part of a movie clip. The "main movie" is probably better understood as the "prime movie clip." For some, the creation of multiple movie clips and the accompanying multiple Timelines is a source of confusion rather than a valuable resource. Actually, movie clips are core objects in an object-oriented tool.

Like effective object-oriented programming, working with multiple movie clips requires good planning, organization, and above all thinking in terms of the objects needed to accomplish a task. Organizing ActionScript code in a single frame or layer helps keep track of where everything is located. Likewise, in more sophisticated and complex projects, scripts can be used to turn selected movie clips "on" and "off," usually in the form of starting or stopping a movie clip's play.

In the same fashion as a director of a movie, Flash developers not only need to think in terms of actions broken into discrete shots or scenes, but in terms of reusable objects. A walking character in a live-action movie is simply a matter of directing an actor to walk. In Flash, the director (designer or developer) directs the use of a certain movie clip that "does walking" (or running, jumping, or car crashing).

When looking at movie clips, developed on the Stage or dynamically in a class, remember that every movie clip is a self-contained work. (Also, you don't have movie clips that want a bigger trailer or have a problem with drugs.)

The MovieClip **Class**

Because so much of Flash is centered around the MovieClip class in one way or another, attempting to cover all the features of the MovieClip class here would be overwhelming and not too useful. Instead, representative materials from each class category—methods, properties, events, and drawing methods—have been provided in little projects in this chapter. In subsequent chapters, more key aspects of the MovieClip class are discussed where appropriate. For example, because Chapter 6, "Viewing and Entering Information with Text Fields," focuses on text fields, the getTextSnapshot() method is discussed in detail in that chapter instead of this one.

Each MovieClip subsection begins with a table that summarizes the methods, properties, drawing properties, or event handlers. Then a short sample project or reference to the chapter project shows how to use selected features. In this way, you can get a quick overview of MovieClip class features and see how to use them in practical applications.

MovieClip **Methods**

Like all methods associated with a class, MovieClip methods generate some kind of action with MovieClip class instances. Throughout the book, these instances are referenced as both class instances (or just instances) and objects. With this in mind, all table references are to I_mc, which points to the object/instance name of the movie clip. Table 5.4 shows the rich collection of methods in the MovieClip class.

TABLE 5.4

MovieClip **Class Methods**

METHOD	ACTION
I_mc.attachAudio(*src_ns*)	Assigns and plays streams generated in a microphone. Requires the NetStream source (*src_ns*) parameter.
I_mc.attachMovie(*id,nn,d*)	A SWF file from the library attached to a movie clip object with a linkage name (*id*), new name (*nn*), and depth (*d*).
I_mc.createEmptyMovieClip(*in,d*)	Similar to attachMovie() but doesn't require a link. Instance name (*in*) and depth (*d*) are its two parameters. (See the drawing methods in Table 5.7.)
I_mc.createTextField(*in,d,x,y,w,h*)	Creates an empty text field with instance name (*in*), depth (*d*), horizontal position (*x*), vertical position (*y*), and height (*h*).
I_mc.duplicateMovieClip(*nn,d,[io]*)	Makes a copy of a movie clip object with parameters requiring new name (*nn*) and depth (*d*). An optional parameter is initObject containing the properties to populate the movie clip.
I_mc.getBounds(*cs*)	Returns a SWF's minimum and maximum x and y coordinates in a coordinate space (*cs*).
I_mc.getBytesLoaded()	Returns a specified movie clip's bytes currently loaded.
I_mc.getBytesTotal()	Returns a specified movie clip's total bytes.
I_mc.getDepth()	Returns a specified movie clip's depth, ranging from -16384 to 1048575.

TABLE 5.4

Continued

METHOD	ACTION
I_mc.getInstanceAtDepth(*d*)	Returns an instance name of a movie clip at a specified depth (*d*).
I_mc.getNextHighestDepth()	Returns a nonnegative value that specifies the next depth higher than the highest depth of extant movie clips.
I_mc.getSWFVersion()	Returns the player version number of a movie clip.
I_mc.getTextSnapshot()	Creates a TextSnapshot object containing the text in the static text fields in the specified clip returned. (See Chapter 6 for details.)
I_mc.getURL(*url*, [*window*,GET/POST])	Works like a link in HTML. It retrieves the document at *url*, placing it in the optional window (for example, _blank).
I_mc.globalToLocal()	Changes the coordinates of point object to the movie clip's coordinates from Stage coordinates.
I_mc.gotoAndPlay(*n*)	Moves the playhead to the frame number (*n*) or label of the specified movie clip. The playhead then continues to the next frame.
I_mc.gotoAndStop(*n*)	Moves the playhead to the frame number (*n*) or label of the specified movie clip, and the playhead stops there.
I_mc.hitTest(*x*, *y*, *Boolean*) I_mc.hitTest(*target_mc*)	Returns true when the target movie clip (target_mc) or bounding box (*x*, *y*) intersects with the movie clip instance.
I_mc.loadMovie(*swf*)	Loads a SWF file into a movie clip. (Use of the MovieClipLoader class instead is recommended.)
I_mc.loadVariables(*url*,GET/POST)	Loads the extant variables in the movie clip into the specified URL. (Use of the LoadVars class instead is recommended.)
I_mc.localToGlobal()	Changes the coordinates of point object to Stage coordinates from the movie clip's coordinates.
I_mc.nextFrame()	Moves the playhead to the next frame and stops.
I_mc.play()	Starts the movie clip's playhead moving.
I_mc.prevFrame()	Moves the playhead to the previous frame and stops.
I_mc.removeI_mc()	Removes the movie clip if it is created with duplicateMovieClip(), I_mc.duplicateMovieClip(), or I_mc.attachMovie().
I_mc.setMask(*mask_mc*)	Establishes the movie clip (mask_mc) to mask the movie clip instance (I_mc).
I_mc.startDrag([lock,*l*,*t*,*r*,*b*])	Makes the move clip draggable, with optional parameters for locking to the center of the mouse (lock True/False) as well as left (*l*), top (*t*), right (*r*), and bottom (*b*) limits.
I_mc.stop()	Stops the movie clip's playhead moving.
I_mc.stopDrag()	Ceases the movie clip's draggable state.
I_mc.swapDepths(*target*) I_mc.swapDepths(*depth*)	Exchanges two SWF files' depth levels (makes them switch which one is on top).
I_mc.unloadMovie()	Unloads the SWF file loaded with loadMovie().

All movie clip methods are related to specified movie clip instances, including the main Timeline (for example, _level0). In addition to using specific instance names or root levels, you can also use the this identifier. Typically, this is used within an unnamed function, such as the following:

```
some_mc.onPress=function() {
    this.stop();
}
```

The playhead is stopped only in the instance some_mc, and none other.

In developing classes and methods within classes, often the this identifier is used as a general reference to the movie clip that uses these classes. For example, in the section "Linking User Classes to Movie Clips," later in this chapter, the class uses this in reference to any instance associated with the class.

The project at the end of this chapter provides several examples of these methods in action. The following short application shows how to use some of the methods associated with MovieClip to replace using mask and masked layers. It also illustrates using the drag methods associated with the MovieClip class. It's a handy little application for simulating the magnification process. Here are the steps to follow:

1. Create a new Flash document and set it up with five layers using the following names and in the following order: Actions, VisibleMag, Mask, Big Doc, Little Doc.

2. Select the VisibleMag layer and draw a magnifying glass, using vector graphics. Be sure that the circular area of the glass has no fill. Convert it to a movie clip and give it the instance name mag_mc. Lock the layer.

3. In the Mask layer, draw a circle that fits the "glass" area of the magnifying glass. Convert it to a movie clip and give it the instance name mask_mc. Lock the layer.

4. In the Little Doc layer, create a document that appears to be a sales contract in the center of the Stage. Use the graphic and text tools so that it looks like the image in Figure 5.6. Use the dimensions W=155, H=181. At the bottom of the document in 8-point font, type **Always read the fine print**. Convert it into a movie clip and give it the symbol name Contract. (Contract is the symbol name, not the instance name.) Lock the layer.

5. In the Big Doc layer, drag an instance of the Contract movie clip to the Stage. With the instance selected, open the Transform panel and enlarge it to 150%. Position it so that its lower-left corner is on top of the lower-left corner of the same symbol on the underlying layer. (It will help if you click the Outline icon on the Big Doc layer.) Name the instance contract_mc.

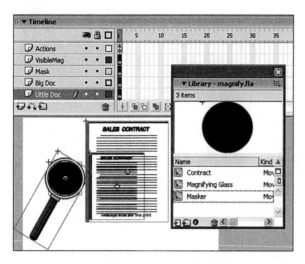

FIGURE 5.6 Setting up instances on the Stage.

6. With all the objects on the Stage with the appropriate instance names and positions, add the following script to the first frame of the Actions layer:

```
mag_mc.onPress = function() {
    this.startDrag();
};
mag_mc.onRelease = function() {
    stopDrag();
};
mag_mc.onMouseMove = function() {
    mask_mc._x = mag_mc._x-20;
    mask_mc._y = mag_mc._y+20;
};
contract_mc.setMask("mask_mc");
```

In this application, the masking work is done using the MovieClip.setMask() method. The mask is a movie clip as well as the masked object. Any other object on the Big Doc layer containing the contract_mc instance, which is masked, is fully visible, unlike using masked layers. Figure 5.7 shows how the page looks before the movie clip "magnifying glass" is dragged over the masked object.

FIGURE 5.7 The page before the magnifying glass is dragged over the masked object.

FIGURE 5.8 Dragging the magnifying glass over the masked object appears to magnify the smaller instance.

When the mask_mc movie clip, which follows the magnifying glass movie clip, moves over the larger (invisible) "contract" movie clip, it appears beneath the circular mask movie clip. Because the larger movie clip is simply a 150% version of the small movie clip, it gives the appearance of being magnified, as shown in Figure 5.8.

The other methods, briefly described in Table 5.4, work along the same principles. Throughout the book you'll find other examples and contexts for using most of the MovieClip class methods. As you've seen in other examples and projects in this and previous chapters, many of the methods have already been used.

MovieClip **Properties**

The MovieClip class properties, like other movie clip features, apply to either an instance of a movie clip or to the main Timeline. Table 5.5 provides an overview of the MovieClip class properties.

TABLE 5.5

MovieClip **Class Properties**

PROPERTY	CHARACTERISTICS
I_mc._alpha	The degree to which a movie clip is transparent (0–100). Lower the value for increased transparency.
I_mc._currentframe	The current frame where the movie clip's playhead is located.
I_mc._droptarget	Contains the slash syntax path to the target object on the Stage on which a draggable movie clip is released (/my_mc). The slash syntax is an older path reference preceding the dot syntax (for example, level0.my_mc).
I_mc.enabled	A Boolean value indicating whether a button movie clip is enabled.
I_mc.focusEnabled	Sets the movie clip to receive focus even if it's not a button movie clip.
I_mc._focusrect	If the value is set to true, the focused or button movie clip has a yellow rectangle surrounding it when the user tabs to it.
I_mc._framesloaded	Indicates how many frames of a streaming SWF file have been loaded.
I_mc._height	The number of pixels in a movie clip's height. Height is measured from the lowest point to the highest on the Stage for irregular shapes.
I_mc.hitArea	Another movie clip assigned as the hit area for a button movie clip. Uses the assignment operator (=).
I_mc.menu	Used to assign a ContextMenu object to a movie clip. Uses the assignment operator (=).
I_mc._name	A movie clip's instance name.
I_mc._parent	The instance name of a movie clip that encloses the movie clip. If this movie clip is on the main Timeline, the parent is _level0.
I_mc._rotation	The rotation degree (0°–360°) of the movie clip.
I_mc._soundbuftime	Specifies the number of seconds to buffer before a sound starts to stream.

TABLE 5.5

Continued

PROPERTY	CHARACTERISTICS
I_mc.tabChildren	A Boolean value determines whether the movie clip's children receive automatic tab ordering. An undefined or `true` value indicates ordering, and a `false` value disables the children's automatic tabbing order.
I_mc.tabEnabled	Defaults to undefined, but can be set to `true` or `false`. If the setting is `true` or undefined, automatic tabbing is enabled. A `false` setting disables tabbing.
I_mc.tabIndex	Integers assigned to indicate tab order.
I_mc._target	Returns the path to a movie clip in slash syntax.
I_mc._totalframes	A movie clip's total number of frames. May be used with the movie clip or main Timeline (for example, `level0`).
I_mc.trackAsMenu	Used when a movie clip or buttons are used in a menu. A Boolean setting of `true` means that other buttons or movie clips respond to "mouse release" events.
I_mc._url	A SWF file's originating URL that has been downloaded.
I_mc.useHandCursor	The default setting is `true`, which means a hand appears over a button movie clip. This can be set to `false` to leave the pointer unchanged as it passes over a "hot spot."
I_mc._visible	The default value of `true` can be changed to `false` to hide the movie clip.
I_mc._width	The number of pixels in a movie clip's width. Width is measured from the leftmost point to the rightmost point on the Stage for irregular shapes.
I_mc._x	The movie clip instance's horizontal position on the Stage.
I_mc._xmouse	The mouse pointer's horizontal position in a movie clip.
I_mc._xscale	The movie clip instance's horizontal scale as a percentage.
I_mc._y	The movie clip instance's vertical position on the Stage.
I_mc._ymouse	The mouse pointer's vertical position in a movie clip.
I_mc._yscale	The movie clip instance's vertical scale as a percentage.

To get a good mix of MovieClip class properties, this next application shows one way to create a movie clip preloader. The purpose of a preloader is to inform the user and perhaps distract him from the fact that he has to wait for the movie to load. Generally, you should try to avoid creating documents so large that they require preloaders, but given the ubiquity of phone modem connections on the Internet, preloaders are often a necessity.

The PreLoader class in Listing 5.1 uses several different properties to change the position and scale of the movie clip acting as a "preshow." It grows along with the percentage of the loading movie clip. The primary function contains three parameters:

- The name of the movie clip that the movie will be loaded into

- The preloader clip's name

- The name of the text field where the percentage of loaded materials goes

LISTING 5.1   All-Purpose Preloader Class (`PreLoader.as`)

```
class PreLoader {
    function PreLoader(loading_mc:MovieClip, target_mc:MovieClip,output_txt:TextField) {

        var output:String;
        var loaded:Number = loading_mc.getBytesLoaded();
        var percent:Number = Number((loaded/loading_mc.getBytesTotal())*100);
        target_mc._x = (100-percent);
        target_mc._y = (100-percent);
        target_mc._xscale = percent;
        target_mc._yscale = percent;
        output = Math.floor(percent)+"%";
        output_txt.text=output;

    }
}
```

The movie clip (preloader) that incorporates the `PreLoader` class needs only a single frame for the following script:

```
onEnterFrame = function () {
    var bearIt:PreLoader = new PreLoader(_level0.dummy_mc, bear_mc,load_txt);
};
```

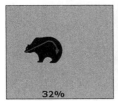 

The preloader movie in this case has a Native American bear fetish movie clip with the instance name `bear_mc` and a single dynamic text field with the instance name `load_txt`. It's saved as `Preloader.fla` and generates the compiled file `Preloader.swf`. Figure 5.9 shows what the image looks like while the movie clip is loading and after the movie clip is fully loaded.

FIGURE 5.9   The preloader image changes as the movie clip loads.

The preloader can be used with virtually any application, and the following example shows how to do so. The preloader is loaded into an unused level so that when its work is finished, it can be removed from the screen. The movie to be loaded (anyMovie.swf) is loaded into the movie clip `dummy_mc`. Using the `_framesloaded` and `_totalframes` properties, as soon as the movie is loaded, the preloader, which has been loaded into `_level1`, is unloaded and the movie is all set to view. The following script uses a button to begin the loading process, which involves loading the preloader as well as the purposely loaded movie clip:

```
fire_btn.onPress = function() {
    loadMovieNum("PreLoader.swf", 1);
    loadMovie("anyMovie.swf", dummy_mc);
};
```

```
_level0.onEnterFrame = function() {
    if (_level0.dummy_mc._framesloaded == _level0.dummy_mc._totalframes) {
        unloadMovieNum(1);
    }
};
```

The preloader SWF *must* compile to a small size. The one used in this example is only 1KB, so it does not compound the problem with its own size.

MovieClip **Event Handlers**

The movie clip event handlers capture several different events. Many of the events are associated with buttons, such as onPress and onRelease, and movie clips that incorporate those event handlers are referred to as "movie clip buttons." From previous examples throughout this book, you have seen different examples of movie clip buttons using this format:

```
MovieClip.onPress=function() {
    //some actions
}
```

However, the MovieClip class contains far more event handlers, as you can see in Table 5.6.

TABLE 5.6

MovieClip **Class Event Handlers**

HANDLER	EVENT
I_mc.onData	Fires as soon as all the data is loaded into a movie clip.
I_mc.onDragOut	Fires after the mouse button is pressed inside a movie clip button, the mouse is dragged out of the movie clip's area, and the mouse button is released.
I_mc.onDragOver	Fires when the mouse button is pressed as the mouse moves over the instance's area.
I_mc.onEnterFrame	Fired each time the playhead moves into a new frame, with ActionScript preceding other actions attached to the frame.
I_mc.onKeyDown	An event used in conjunction with the Key.getCode() and Key.getAscii() methods. This event occurs as soon as a key is pressed.
I_mc.onKeyUp	Fires when a key is released.
I_mc.onKillFocus	Fires as focus leaves the button.
I_mc.onLoad	Fires as soon as a movie clip from the library is instantiated on the Timeline.
I_mc.onMouseDown	Fires when the left mouse button is pressed.
I_mc.onMouseMove	Fires when the mouse is moved.
I_mc.onMouseUp	Fires when the left mouse button is released.
I_mc.onPress	Fires when the left mouse button is pressed over a movie clip button.

TABLE 5.6

Continued

HANDLER	EVENT
I_mc.onRelease	Fires when the left mouse button is released over a movie clip button.
I_mc.onReleaseOutside	Fires after the mouse button is pressed inside a movie clip button and then the mouse button is released outside of the movie clip button area.
I_mc.onRollOut	Fires when the mouse pointer rolls over and out of a button area.
I_mc.onRollOver	Fires when the mouse pointer rolls over a button area.
I_mc.onSetFocus	Fires as a key is released when the button has input focus.
I_mc.onUnload	Fires after the movie clip has been removed. Any movie clip instance subject to the unloadMovie() method affects this method.

Several of the events have been used in this chapter and previous chapters; however, an important distinction in mouse events concerns those events that can occur anywhere on the Stage and those events that must occur when the pointer is over the movie clip. For example, the following code will render the movie clip to 50% transparency no matter where on the Stage the mouse is pressed:

```
box_mx.onMouseDown=function() {
    this._alpha=50;
}
```

However, if the code is written as follows, the transparency property is changed only if the mouse pointer is directly over the movie clip:

```
box_mx.onPress=function() {
    this._alpha=50;
}
```

When you're using onMouseDown, onMouseUp, or onMouseMove events, keep in mind that these events can occur anywhere, whereas most of the other mouse-related actions require being on or near the associated movie clip.

MovieClip **Drawing Methods**

The drawing methods give developers and designers a dynamic environment for creating and changing graphic elements without employing any of the drawing tools. With practice, a good designer can program any shape that can be created with the drawing tools in the Tools panel. Table 5.7 shows the different drawing methods available for use with movie clips.

TABLE 5.7

MovieClip Class Drawing Methods

METHOD	ACTION
`I_mc.beginFill(colorHex,alpha)`	Starts a solid-color fill action in a drawn object. You must specify the hex color (`colorHex`) and alpha value (`alpha`).
`I_mc.beginGradientFill(t,c,a,r,m))`	Starts a gradient color fill action in a drawn object. You must specify the fill type (`t`), hex color (`c`), alpha value (`a`), ratios (`r`), and matrix (`m`).
`I_mc.clear())`	Deletes all drawing method actions associated with a movie clip instance.
`I_mc.curveTo(cX,cY,aX,aY))`	Draws a curved line using the current line style.
`I_mc.endFill())`	Terminates the fill started by `beginFill()` or `beginGradientFill()`.
`I_mc.lineStyle(th,colorHex,alpha)`	Establishes the stroke of lines drawn with the `lineTo()` and `curveTo()` methods. You must specify the thickness (`th`), hex color (`colorHex`), and alpha value (`alpha`).
`I_mc.lineTo(x,y))`	Draws a line to x,y coordinates using the defined line style.
`I_mc.moveTo(x,y))`	"Lifts" the pencil and moves to the x,y coordinates.

The matrix used for creating the gradient is referred to as a *transformation matrix*. This matrix has nine points laid out as a 3×3 matrix:

$$\begin{matrix} a & b & c \\ d & e & f \\ g & h & i \end{matrix}$$

The values placed in the matrix determine the shape of the gradient. The moveTo and lineTo methods are fairly straightforward. The moveTo method is like lifting the pen off the paper and moving it to a new location, whereas lineTo is a line drawn from one x,y coordinate to another. For instance, to draw a square, you could use the following:

```
moveTo(300,300);
lineTo(400,300);
lineTo(400,400);
lineTo(300,400);
lineTo(300,300);
```

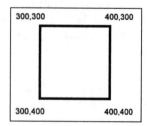

FIGURE 5.10 Lines move from one x,y coordinate to another.

Figure 5.10 shows the square figure with the directions of the drawing. It's a simple figure, but with some planning and a grid, any number of shapes are possible.

Curved lines are similar in construction to straight lines, except they include a second set of x,y coordinates to curve to before the line ends. The line begins at the coordinates of the previous command, curve to the first set of coordinates in the curveTo() method, and end at the second set of coordinates.

For example, the following script draws a line beginning at 300,300, curving up to 350,200, and then moving back down to 400,300:

```
_level0.createEmptyMovieClip("curve_mc", 0);
with (curve_mc) {
    lineStyle(2, 0x000000, 100);
    moveTo(300, 300);
    curveTo(350, 200, 400, 300);
}
```

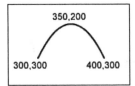

FIGURE 5.11 Two coordinate sets provide a curve point for drawings.

Figure 5.11 shows the curved line the script generates:

Using a combination of straight and curved lines, along with the grid background, you can create just about any image you want. With especially complex drawings, you can save the script as a class and reuse it with any program you want. For example, a logo created using a script could be used again and again once the initial work has been completed.

Linking User Classes to Movie Clips

In some instances you may want to create a new class or the extension of a movie class and connect the script directly to your symbol. For example, if you have a task you're likely to use again and again, creating a user class and linking that class directly to a movie clip can save a lot of time.

Suppose you want to have several movie clips on the Stage that can be dragged wherever the user wants them. You might want to develop a fish tank movie that allows children to drag any number of fish movie clips around the "tank" (Stage). Rather than writing a separate drag script for each of the fish instances, you can extend the MovieClip class in a dynamic class and link *all instances* of the symbol to the class.

The following steps provide a quick, simple example:

1. Draw a fish on the Stage and convert it to a symbol, giving it the symbol name Fish.

FIGURE 5.12 The Linkage Properties dialog box.

2. Select the Fish symbol in the Library panel and use the Library panel's drop-down menu to open the Linkage Properties dialog box.

3. Click the Export for ActionScript check box. Enter the identifier name **Fish** and the AS 2.0 class name **DragMe**. When listing the class, don't include the .as filename extension. Figure 5.12 shows how the dialog box appears filled out correctly.

4. Open a new ActionScript file and enter the following script, saving it as `DragMe.as`:

```
dynamic class DragMe extends MovieClip {
    function onPress() {
        this.startDrag();
    }
    function onRelease() {
        stopDrag();
    }
}
```

FIGURE 5.13   All instances of linked symbols are subject to a class script.

5. On the Stage, drag a couple more instances of the Fish symbol. Enlarge one and reduce one, flipping it horizontally so that your Stage looks something like Figure 5.13.

You should now have three instances of the fish, none having instance names, and no code has been written in the Actions panel. When you test the movie, all three fish can be dragged. This feature of Flash MX 2004 allows you to write different classes for commonly used functions and attach them directly to the symbols and all the instances of those symbols.

What's Next?

Understanding movie clips is the key to using Flash MX Professional 2004 optimally. Although a great deal can be done with movie clips without using ActionScript, using the movie clips in conjunction with code increases their functionality and the control a developer or designer has over the actions that can be generated.

Getting used to movie clips with ActionScript, especially using object-oriented programming techniques, can be a daunting task, especially for designers. However, rather than looking at ActionScript and OOP as barriers to successfully achieving a goal, they should look at them as aids toward goal achievement. For nonprogrammers, ActionScript need not be absorbed all at once. Likewise, for procedural programmers, OOP need not be applied all at once. Rather, when faced with a problem to solve that cannot be done using noncoding techniques in Flash, you should look at the different methods (including drawing methods), properties, and event handlers associated with movie clips and see if they can help solve the problem. Likewise, if you spend a lot of time creating the code for a complex problem, think about using OOP techniques to make that code available for similar challenges. By working code into little classes, you can begin developing a code library of useful code modules.

The next chapter employs movie clips with text fields. As in this chapter, you'll see that much can be done with text fields without employing the more advanced techniques used with ActionScript. However, also like this chapter, you can do a great deal more—and your options are far broader—when you use ActionScript to aid you in the development process.

In Brief

- A central feature of using Flash optimally is to use movie clips effectively within a hierarchy.

- Loading movie clips from external sources reduces the size of the main movie and encourages the use of modular applications.

- Preloader movie clips can be used for both a main movie and smaller movie clips.

- Movie clips can be called dynamically from the library using linkages.

- Drawing methods in the `MovieClip` class allow developers to create different drawings dynamically, based on planned data or user events.

Viewing and Entering Information with Text Fields

Understanding Flash Text Fields

Text fields are an important key to interactive Flash movies. They provide a place for both user input and site output. Moreover, text fields are a primary source of content for any site, and they serve as labels for graphic content. Navigation systems can make use of dynamic text as context-sensitive text field content changes, depending on current options. For example, a text field's content could explain various options available depending on what other events are occurring, such as an FLV file being streamed.

Flash Pro text fields still consist of the same three stalwart types—static, input, and dynamic—as in previous versions of Flash. However, some important changes have occurred in the latest version. Static text fields can now be used in conjunction with the `TextSnapshot` class, and input and dynamic text fields can embed graphics.

This section will cover some familiar ground for veteran Flash users, but it includes some of the newer features as well. Those who are new to Flash can quickly see what options are available in the Property Inspector when it's in text mode.

Working with the Property Inspector in Text Mode

No matter what type of text field is selected, the Property Inspector changes into text mode, providing the options for the various types of text (see Figure 6.1).

Text field type

FIGURE 6.1   Text mode in the Property Inspector.

Most of the options in the text version of the Property Inspector are fairly self-explanatory, but some could use a little more elaboration—or in the case of pop-up menus, revelation. Table 6.1 clarifies the more obtuse options.

TABLE 6.1

Options in the Text Version of the Property Inspector

OPTION	DESCRIPTION
Constrain Lock	This option is new to Flash MX 2004. To keep the proportions in a text field (or any object on the Stage), click the lock so that it's closed. To change text field proportions, click the lock again to open it.
Edit Format Options	This pop-up menu contains four options: indent, line spacing, left margin, and right margin.
Edit Character Options	This pop-up menu allows embedded font outlines for a series of characters and languages (for example, Uppercase, Numerals, Japanese Kana, Hangul, and Hebrew). Two radio buttons provide options for No Characters and Specify Ranges. If you select Specify Ranges, first select the language or set of characters you want to specify ranges for and then type in the character and click Auto Fill. (This option is used only with input and dynamic text.)
Maximum Characters	The Maximum Characters box is not shown in Figure 6.1. It appears only if the input type is selected. It restricts the number of characters that the user can enter.
Line Type	This pop-up menu provides options for single line, multiline, multiline no wrap, and password (input only). It is inoperable with static text.
Variable	This option is a residue from earlier versions of Flash. When it's used, the contents of either dynamic or input text fields are considered the data in text format of the variable name. No instance name is required. Generally, the use of a text field with an instance name is preferable because then all the `TextField` class methods, properties, and event handlers are available. In essence, using a variable name is the same as `TextField.text`. (The use of this field is not recommended.)
Character Position	In static mode only, the options are Normal, Superscript, and Subscript.

Static Text Fields

The static mode offers nonscrollable text used for labeling or short messages on the Stage or on objects. The text can't be changed once this mode has been set in the editor. Two unique characteristics of the static mode include the ability to select and break apart the text and the use of the new TextSnapshot class.

Converting Text to Vector Graphics

All static text can be selected and converted to vector graphics with a two-step process. Each word or phrase contains separate text characters. To convert the individual characters to vector graphics, first you must break them from the word block and then from the individual characters. The easiest way to make the conversion from text to vector graphics is to select the text box and press Ctrl+B twice (Cmd+B on the Mac). Once the text has been broken into vector graphics, it can be treated like any other graphic on the Stage. The following example shows how to make the conversion:

1. Open a new Flash document and in 24-point text type **Everyone loves Flash**.

2. Select the text block and then select Modify, Break Apart from the menu, as shown in Figure 6.2.

FIGURE 6.2   Select the text and then select the Break Apart option.

3. If necessary, select all the individual letters in the broken-apart word and repeat step 2, as shown in Figure 6.3.

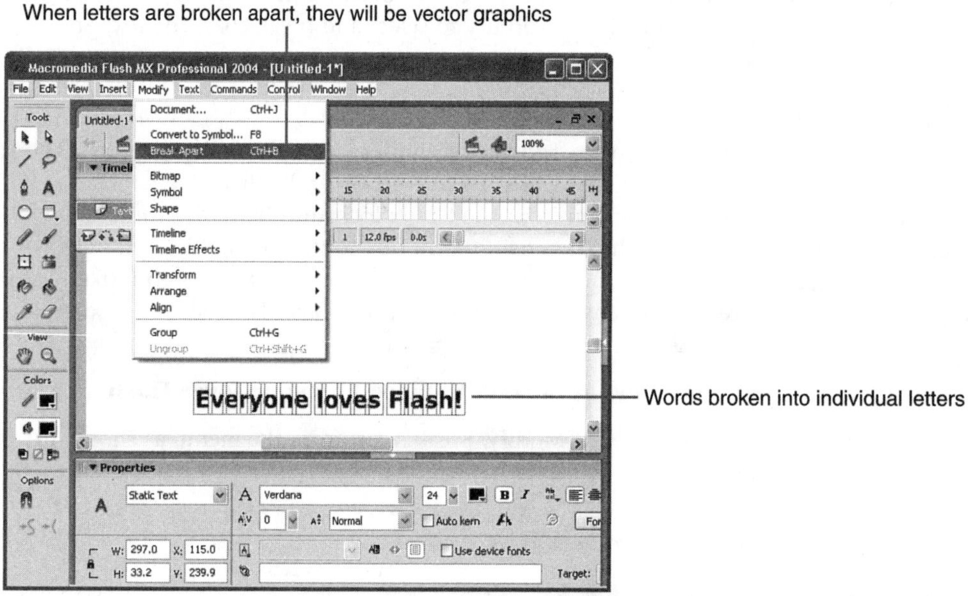

When letters are broken apart, they will be vector graphics

Words broken into individual letters

FIGURE 6.3 Broken-apart text has to be selected and broken apart a second time.

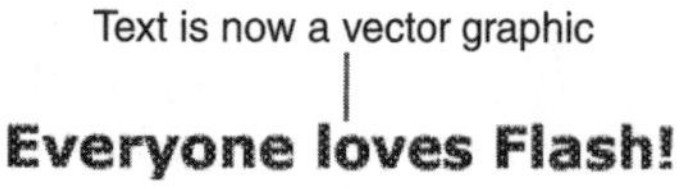

Text is now a vector graphic

Everyone loves Flash!

FIGURE 6.4 Text that has been converted to graphics appears just like any selected graphic.

After the text has been broken apart the second time, it's in vector graphic format. Now when you select the text, it appears as individual graphic elements, as shown in Figure 6.4.

Static Text Font Outlines

Because static text in Flash carries with it font outlines, the user doesn't need to have the font on his or her system to see the font's shape. Therefore, it's generally unnecessary to convert static text into graphics so that all viewers can see the intended font. Not all fonts, though, can be exported as outlines. If you select View, Preview Mode, Antialias Text from the menu and then view the font when you preview your movie, a jagged appearance indicates that no outline is available for that particular font.

The TextSnapshot **Class and Static Text**

The TextSnapshot class in Flash MX 2004 allows some dynamic use of static fonts. Using the TextSnapshot class and its methods, you can find the number of text characters in static text fields, find specific characters, and then use the information to employ the text characters dynamically. Table 6.2 summarizes the class methods for TextSnapshot.

TABLE 6.2

TextSnapshot **Methods**

METHOD	ACTION
TS_instance.findText(b,txt,Boolean)	Returns an integer specifying the zero-based position of the text (txt). The options specify where to begin the search (b) and whether the search should be case sensitive (Boolean).
TS_instance.getCount()	Gets the number of characters in all the static text on the Stage.
TS_instance.getSelected(b,e)	Returns a Boolean value of true if any characters in the specified range, beginning (b) to end (e), are selected in TS_instance.setSelected().
TS_instance.getSelectedText()	Returns a string that contains all the characters specified by TS_instance.setSelected().
TS_instance.getText()	Returns a string containing the characters in the specified range.
TS_instance.hitTestTextNearPos(x,y[,m])	Lets you determine which character within the object is on or near the specified coordinates (x,y) at an optional maximum distance (m).
TS_instance.setSelectColor(0xrrggbb)	Sets the border color (0xrrggbb) of the text selected with the TS_instance.setSelected() method.
TS_instance.setSelected(b,e,Boolean)	Sets the range of text to be selected, beginning at b and ending at e. (Specify the Boolean value of true to select or false to deselect.)

Using the various methods is fairly straightforward. The constructor requires an instance (variable) name and data typing. As long as static text is on the Stage, the instance will recognize it and use it. For example, type **Flash to the rescue.** on the Stage using static text. Enter the following script in the first frame:

```
var snappy:TextSnapshot = _level0.getTextSnapshot();
trace(snappy.findText(0, "rescue", true));
```

The findText() method specifies the zero-based beginning position as the beginning of all static text. In this case, the value in the output window is 13, because, beginning with 0, the first letter of the word *rescue* is in position 13 of the sentence (remember to count the spaces).

Project: Use `TextSnapshot` to Get a Set of Characters
This project shows you how to get a set of characters using the `TextSnapshot` class with
multiple text blocks and dynamic output:

1. Open a new Flash document and create layers labeled (from top to bottom) Actions,
   Text Fields, and Graphics.

2. In the Graphics layer, add three graphic images. This example uses Native American
   fetishes—a bison, a scorpion, and a bird—but any three graphics will do. To the right of
   the second image (the scorpion, in this example), draw a rectangle (W=112, H=41)
   using a contrasting color with the background. Lock the layer.

3. In the Text Field layer, using static text, add labels for the images (Bison, Scorpion, and
   Bird, in this example).

> **Watch the Order!**
>
> Be careful here: The `TextSnapshot` class uses character-position values based on the order in
> which the characters are placed on the Stage—not the position of the text block. In other
> words, if you type the text labels in any order and then rearrange the text blocks next to the
> graphics, you won't have rearranged the order that the `TextSnapshot` class uses to sequence
> the characters.

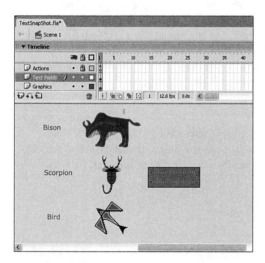

FIGURE 6.5　Static text labels and their placement on the Stage.

4. Place a dynamic text field on the Stage to
   the right of the scorpion image and give it the
   instance name `showTS_txt`. Figure 6.5 shows
   the initial setup on the Stage and the placement
   of the objects.

5. Once the Stage is set up, click the first frame of
   the Actions layer and enter the following script
   in the first frame of the document:

```
var snappy:TextSnapshot = _
➥level0.getTextSnapshot();
var total:Number = snappy.getCount();
var scorpion:String = "Scorpion";
var bird:String = "Bird";
var startHere:Number =
➥scorpion.length+bird.length;
snappy.setSelected(total-startHere, total-
➥bird.length, true);
showTS_txt.text = snappy.getSelectedText();
```

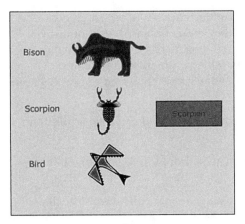

FIGURE 6.6   The `TextSnapshot` class can be used to identify specific static text characters and use them dynamically.

6. Test the movie (see Figure 6.6). The word *Scorpion* appears in the dynamic text field. The word was selected out of the `TextSnapshot` instance by first getting the full number of characters in the object using the `TextSnapshot.getCount` method. The length of the last word *(Bird)* and the length of the selected word *(Scorpion)* were subtracted from the character count to determine the beginning point for the selected text. Then the last word was subtracted to determine the ending point.

Input Text Fields

The input text field is used for user data entry. The input area can be anything from a small window for single words (such as a username and password), to large, multiline windows for extended comments by users. A unique line type for input text fields is the password line. All data entered into a password input field is encoded as asterisks. For example, if a user enters

```
Smith
```

the field shows this:

```
*****
```

However, when the `text` property is used in a conditional statement, the encoded text is read just as though all the characters were visible. Here's an example:

```
if(input_txt.text=="Smith") {
    //allow entry
}
```

In this way, the user can enter information without others seeing what's being typed. At the same time, the developer can create a script and not have to compare nonsensical encoded characters in conditional statements.

Dynamic Text Fields

The main purpose of dynamic text fields is to hold text that changes or text loaded from external sources. Changing text provides users with feedback, informing them of a page's current status. Dynamic text fields can be placed directly on the Stage or created using ActionScript.

One use of dynamic text fields is to provide a window of information in which users can view different types of information based on choices they make. Because blocks of text can flow beyond the bounds of a text field, some kind of scrolling mechanism may be required. Flash Pro has the TextField component with a built-in scrollbar (discussed in the next chapter). However, using buttons and a few scrolling ActionScript terms, you can easily create scrolling text.

This next example loads an external text file into a dynamic text field and then scrolls it up and down using two buttons:

1. Create a new Flash document with three layers named, from top to bottom, Actions, Text Field, and Buttons.

2. In the Text Field layer, use the Text tool to create a dynamic text field with the dimensions W=325, H=140. Give it the instance name kate_txt.

3. Open the Buttons common library and drag two circle button-next instances to the Stage.(The menu path to the buttons is Window, Other Panels, Common Libraries, Buttons.) Rotate one button –90 degrees and the other 90 degrees so that one points straight up and the other points straight down. Place them on the right side of the text field. Provide the up-pointing button with the instance name up_btn, and the down-pointing button the instance name down_btn. Figure 6.7 shows the initial setup on the Stage.

SHOP TALK

There's More to Security Than a Password

In just about every aspect of professional Web site development using Flash, security is an issue. If you simply create password protection using the password option for input text fields, the security is minimal. Anyone with a Flash decompiler can easily look into your code. (Decompilers reveal the code in compiled files, such as SWF files. To get an idea of how easy it is to get your hands on a Flash decompiler, type **Flash decompiler** in your favorite search engine, and you'll find that many are available.)

To make life more difficult for hackers who use decompilers, you can place your security code in an AS file with returns embedded in the methods. However, that just makes hacker snooping more difficult—it doesn't ensure good security. Many of the good practices associated with OOP are designed to enhance security, but even good OOP is not enough.

If you're creating sites for clients who need secure money transfers, you should work with companies who have secure credit card interfaces or with companies such as PayPal that set up accounts with individual users to transfer funds between buyer and seller. Likewise, valuable information transferred to databases can be at risk as well. Flash is an excellent front end for database entry and retrieval. With all the problems out there, from identity theft to international terrorists funding their operations through online fraud, you shouldn't trust security to a few passwords. In fact, I recommend downloading a Flash decompiler and using it for the trial period just so you can see how easy it is for someone to view all your code.

Text field type

Instance name

FIGURE 6.7 Only the text field and scroll buttons are added in the FLA file.

4. Copy the following excerpt from Shakespeare's *Taming of the Shrew* into a text editor such as Notepad and then save it as `kate.txt`:

```
--Taming of the Shrew--
No shame but mine: I must, forsooth, be forced
To give my hand opposed against my heart
Unto a mad-brain rudesby full of spleen;
Who woo'd in haste and means to wed at leisure.
I told you, I, he was a frantic fool,
Hiding his bitter jests in blunt behavior:
And, to be noted for a merry man,
He'll woo a thousand, 'point the day of marriage,
Make feasts, invite friends, and proclaim the banns;
Yet never means to wed where he hath woo'd.
Now must the world point at poor Katharina,
And say, 'Lo, there is mad Petruchio's wife,
If it would please him come and marry her!'


William Shakespeare
```

5. Open the Actions panel and enter the following script:

```
//Load text into dynamic text field
var kateUp:LoadVars = new LoadVars();
kateUp.onData = function(contents) {
    //Remove extra linefeeds
    if (contents.indexOf("\n") != -1) {
        contents = contents.split("\n").join("");
    }
    //Place text into dynamic text field
    kate_txt.text = contents;
};
kateUp.load("kate.txt");
//Scroll text
up_btn.onPress = function() {
```

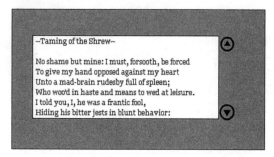

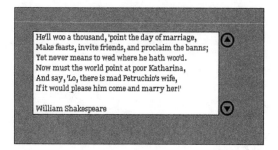

FIGURE 6.8 The dynamic text field with text at the top of the scroll.

FIGURE 6.9 The dynamic text field with text at the bottom of the scroll.

```
    kate_txt.scroll -= 1;
};
down_btn.onPress = function() {
    kate_txt.scroll += 1;
};
```

6. Save the document in the same folder as the kate.txt file using the name textScroll.fla.

7. When you test the movie, you should see the text field with the text flowing beyond the bottom of the text window, as shown in Figure 6.8.

8. After clicking the down button several times, you'll arrive at the bottom of the text, as shown in Figure 6.9.

The key part of the script uses the scroll property of the TextField class. Increasing the scroll value pushes the text in the field downward, whereas decreasing the scroll value pushes it up. (In Chapter 12, "Dealing with External Data and Objects," you'll learn more about the LoadVars() class used at the beginning of the script to place the text into the dynamic text field.)

Project: Embedding Movie Clips from the Library
Using HTML graphic and text formatting in Flash may seem to be regressing to an awkward format. However, one of the useful formats in HTML is text flow around a graphic image. Using HTML text formatting in Flash Pro, you can take advantage of graphics in a dynamic text field. The following steps show how to create a simple example:

1. Open a new Flash document and create two layers: Actions and Text Field.

2. Create or import an elaborate graphic text letter *T*. In this example, the graphic text is one similar to those used in Medieval illuminated manuscripts. Convert the graphic text to a Graphic symbol.

3. Open the Library panel by pressing Ctrl+L (Control+L on the Mac) and then select the graphic letter symbol. Click the Library drop-down menu and select Linkage. In the Linkage Properties dialog box, select the Export for ActionScript option and then type the Linkage name **BigT**, as shown in Figure 6.10.

FIGURE 6.10 Linkage name for the symbol.

4. Select the first frame of the Text Field layer and place a dynamic text field in the middle of the Stage with the dimensions W=280, H=225. In the Property Inspector, select Multiline Line Type and Render Text as HTML. Give the text field the instance name story_txt.(If you forget to select Render Text as HTML in the Property Inspector, the text field won't accept HTML tags!)

5. Click the first frame of the Actions layer, and enter the following script:

```
//Render Text Field as HTML
story_txt.htmlText = "<p><img src='BigT'><br>his story begins a long, long time ago
➥in the dawn of the Internet age around the early 1990's.";
story_txt.htmlText+="   Before the browser there was the Gopher.
➥With Gopher you could read web sites that contained text fields (only)
➥formatted for Gopher reading. (Early HTML). While it was not as dramatic
➥as the later browsers, it was a way to get out a message over the Internet."
```

Sorry About Those Line Breaks

When you use htmlText instead of the text property of text fields, using compound operators (+=) places unwanted new paragraphs, so the preceding script wraps around here. The single compound operator is placed where a paragraph is desired.

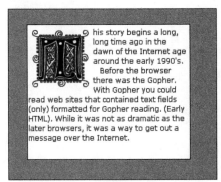

FIGURE 6.11 Text flows around the decorative font.

When you test the movie, you'll see the text flowed around the large graphic cap, as shown in Figure 6.11.

Project: Embedding JPEG and SWF files

In addition to embedding linked symbols in dynamic text fields, you can do the same thing with JPEG and SWF files. If the dynamic text field is set to render text as HTML, all that needs to be done is to create the script to place the SWF or JPEG file into the text field. For example, the following line of code brings in a JPEG file:

```
fast_txt.htmlText = "<p><img src='fastF.jpg'> Here is
a fast mover";
```

Using the identical format, you can bring an external SWF file into a dynamic text field. The only difference is that the extension is .swf instead of .jpg:

```
fast_txt.htmlText = "<p><img src='fastF.swf'> Here is a fast mover";
```

Working with different sets of JPEG and SWF files along with HTML tags, you can make the interior of a dynamic text field into a small HTML page. The following project places an animated rocket inside a dynamic text field (while the text field remains static, the rocket inside moves up and down):

1. Open a new document and create a 150×200 Stage with a movie that tweens a rocket ship movie clip up and down and has a little animated flame out the back. Save the document as **rocket** and publish the `rocket.swf` file.

2. Create another document using the default Stage size. Add a single dynamic text field with the dimensions W=320, W=210. Give it the instance name `fast_txt`.

3. Click the first frame and add the following script (note that the third line of the script dynamically sets the text field to one that renders HTML, so you don't have to set it in the Property Inspector):

```
fast_txt.background=true;
fast_txt.backgroundColor=0xABDFD2;
fast_txt.html = true;
fast_txt.htmlText = "<img src='rocket.swf'>Here is a fast mover.";
fast_txt.htmlText += "<br>The rocket is inside the text field.";
```

4. Test the movie. The rocket moves up and down within the text field, as shown in Figure 6.12.

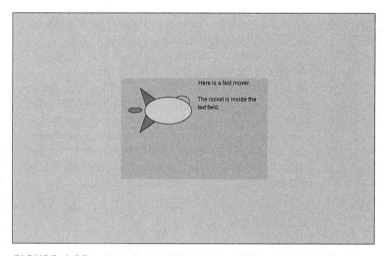

FIGURE 6.12   The animated SWF file moves inside the dynamic text field.

Working with the TextField Class

The TextField class contains methods, properties, events, and listeners for working with a wide variety of text applications. Although the class contains relatively few methods, events, and listeners, there's a long list of properties. The key to working effectively with the TextField class is using the properties effectively and in conjunction with text formatting.

Before beginning to look at the details of the class, let's take a quick look at creating and formatting text fields dynamically from MovieClip objects. The MovieClip.createTextField() method allows for dynamic creation of a text field, and the TextFormat class can fully establish a format. For example, the following small script generates a text field, provides some minimal formatting, and adds text:

```
_level0.createTextField("test_txt", 0, 100, 100, 200, 100);
test_txt.multiline = true;
test_txt.wordWrap = true;
test_txt.background = true;
test_txt.backgroundColor = 0xaa0000;
testFormat_fmt = new TextFormat();
testFormat_fmt.font = "Georgia";
testFormat_fmt.color = 0x00dd00;
test_txt.setNewTextFormat(testFormat_fmt);
_level0.test_txt.text = "This text field has been created dynamically ";
_level0.test_txt.text += "and did not exist on the stage before the ";
_level0.test_txt.text += "ActionScript made it so.";
```

The example shows a dynamic text field created on the main Timeline. The text field is formatted using both the TextField and TextFormat properties.

Differentiating Between TextField and TextFormat Properties

The line of demarcation showing which properties belong to which class is not obvious. For example, background color is a TextField property, but font color is a TextFormat property. Rather than looking too closely for the reasoning behind using one or another class's properties, simply use the class property tables in this chapter to determine which class property handles a given characteristic.

Later in this chapter, I show how text styling can be handled by Cascading Style Sheets (CSS). When you use CSS, many of the properties found either in the `TextField` or `TextFormat` class are defined within the same context. Therefore, both CSS `background-color` (`TextField.backgroundColor`) and `color` (`TextFormat.color`) are defined using the same formatting environment.

The rest of this section is a brief overview of the key methods, properties, events, and listeners associated with the `TextField` class.

`TextField` Methods

As with previous tables in this book, rather than using the class name preceding the method (or other attribute), a generic instance name with the `TextField` suffix (`_txt`) is employed. Where the `TextField` class name is listed, the method actually uses the class name rather than the instance name. Table 6.3 provides a quick overview of the `TextField` class methods.

TABLE 6.3

`TextField` **Methods**

METHOD	ACTION
`TF_txt.addListener()`	Establishes a listener with the text field object that will "hear" the invocation of either the `onChanged` or `onScroller` event handler.
`TextField.getFontList()`	Returns a list of the user's system fonts stored in array. Note that you use the generic `TextField` name rather than the instance name.
`TF_txt.getDepth()`	Returns the current depth of the text field instance.
`TF_txt.getNewTextFormat()`	Returns the format of the text inserted into a field.

`TF_txt.getTextFormat()`
`TF_txt.getTextFormat(i)`
`TF_txt.getTextFormat(b,e)`
	Returns a `TextFormat` object with format data about the text in a field. Optional parameters are available for index (i) or beginning and ending points in the text span (b,e).

`TF_txt.removeListener()`	Removes a listener.
`TF_txt.removeTextField()`	Removes a text field instantiated with `MovieClip.createTextField()`.
`TF_txt.replaceSel(s)`	Replaces the currently selected text with the text in the parameter (s). The text must first be focused using the `Selection.setFocus()` method. (See "Using the `Selection` Class with the `TextField` Class" in Chapter 7, "Tools for Use with Text and Text Components.")
`TF_txt.setNewTextFormat(tf)`	Establishes the `TextFormat` object instance to be used to format all materials in the text field or to be added by users.

`TF_txt.setTextFormat(tf)`
`TF_txt.setTextFormat(i,tf)`
`TF_txt.setTextFormat(b,e,tf)`
	Formats a specific subset of text in a text field. Requires the text field instance name (tf) and can include index (i) or beginning index (b) and ending index (e).

One of the methods that may cause confusion is `setTextFormat`. Basically, this method can be used to format a range of text within a formatted text field. For example, the following script first creates a text field and then uses the `setNewTextFormat` method to establish a format. Once that's established and text is placed in the text field, the `setTextFormat` method is employed to format only the word *is* in the sentence "This is a test."

```
_level0.createTextField("test_txt", 0, 50, 50, 100, 100);
var test_fmt:TextFormat = new TextFormat();
test_fmt.color = 0xaa0000;
var test2_fmt:TextFormat = new TextFormat();
test2_fmt.color = 0x0000aa;
test2_fmt.bold=true;
test_txt.setNewTextFormat(test_fmt);
test_txt.text = "This is a test";
test_txt.setTextFormat(5, 7, test2_fmt);
```

Note that although `setNewTextFormat` is established in the script before the text is added, the `setTextFormat` method must be placed after the text has been placed in the text field. Moreover, the text field can be established directly on the Stage as well as while unchanged formats from the Stage settings (in the Property Inspector) persist. Any changes established by the text formats applied using either of the two `TextField` methods that set the text format override those established in the Property Inspector. However, if the text is placed in the text field on the Stage, only the `setTextFormat` method will affect the text. When you use `setNewTextFormat`, the text in the field must be added after establishing the new text format.

The text format setting methods as well as the methods for setting up listeners are examined further in Chapter 4, "Animations and Interactions."

`TextField` Properties

The multitude of `TextField` class properties allows the designer and developer to establish templates that provide precision configuration and placement of text fields for use and reuse. For designers, the visual environment of the Stage is essential for setting up the right combination of objects on the Stage. Once these objects are placed on the Stage, all the placement information is available in the Property Inspector and can be used to create classes that will automatically place all the required text fields where needed. For example, a registration form is a typical form made up of different text fields that have a standard arrangement. Using the `TextField` properties, you can create a class to generate the fields you need.

Many of the `TextField` properties in Table 6.4 are used in the example in the section "Printing Text with the `PrintJob` Class" in Chapter 7, including how to associate context menus with text fields. The mouse wheel property is automatically included as a working property unless the `TextField.mouseWheel` property is set as `false`. Also, you'll find further examples and information about using the selection-related properties in "Using the `Selection` Class with the `TextField` Class" in Chapter 7.

TABLE 6.4

TextField **Properties**

PROPERTY	CHARACTERISTICS
TF_txt._alpha	Establishes the percentage of opaqueness in an object. Fully transparent is 0, and fully opaque is 100.
TF_txt.autoSize	The text field automatically sizes to the amount and format of text in the field.
TF_txt.background	A Boolean value that establishes whether the text field has a background. When this property is set to true, the text field has a background.
TF_txt.backgroundColor	A color value (in the format 0xrrggbb) is assigned to the background color of the text field. You must assign a color to see a background. If you assign the value 0xFFFFFF, for example, you'll see a white background, just as though you have set the background in the Property Inspector.
TF_txt.border	A Boolean value that establishes whether the text field has a border. A true value establishes a border around the text field.
TF_txt.borderColor	Establishes the border color (in 0xrrggbb format). The border property must be set to true for this to work.
TF_txt.bottomScroll	A read-only integer of the bottom visible line of the text field. The value is the line number of the last visible line of the text, and not the last line of the text that may be beneath the visible limits of the text field.
TF_txt.embedFonts	A Boolean value that returns true if the text field uses embedded font outlines or device fonts.
TF_txt._height	The height of the text field's bounding box.
TF_txt.hscroll	The text field's horizontal scroll. An integer sets the horizontal scroll position.
TF_txt.html	A Boolean value (read-only) indicating whether the text field is HTML. A true value allows rendering of HTML text.
TF_txt.htmlText	Used in conjunction with an HTML text field for entering a tagged string. Some HTML tags will be read and applied to text.
TF_txt.length	An integer reflecting the number of characters in the text property of the text field. This value changes with the number of characters in the text property, and not with the dimensions of the text field.
TF_txt.maxChars	The text field's maximum capacity for the number of characters a user may enter. A null reading means that it has no limits. The maximum character limit is set in the Property Inspector or using this property.
TF_txt.maxhscroll	A read-only integer reflecting the maximum value of the text field's hscroll property.
TF_txt.maxscroll	A read-only integer reflecting the maximum value of the text field's scroll property.
TF_txt.menu	The text field connects a ContextMenu with itself. The context menu area is inside the text field's boundaries.
TF_txt.mouseWheelEnabled	The default condition of mouse wheel scrolling is true. Setting this property to false has the effect of "locking" text so that it doesn't scroll when the mouse wheel is moved.
TF_txt.multiline	A Boolean setting for the text field to have multiple lines.
TF_txt._name	Contains the text field's instance's name.
TF_txt._parent	A reference to either the Button or MovieClip class parent. A reference to the instance that is the parent of this instance (of type Button or MovieClip).

TABLE 6.4

Continued

PROPERTY	CHARACTERISTICS
TF_txt.password	A Boolean true turns all text characters in the field into asterisks. This feature is typically used with coded passwords and input fields, but it also changes dynamic text field characters into asterisks.
TF_txt.restrict	Places limitations on the character set a user is able to type in a text field. Characters can be individual or a range (for example, A-F). Excluded characters are preceded by a caret (^). The value "^0-9", for example, accepts all characters except 0–9.
TF_txt._rotation	The rotation angle of a text field in degrees (values are 0 to 360).
TF_txt.scroll	The scrolling position point in text. Setting the value beyond 1 begins moving the text upward in the text field.
TF_txt.selectable	A Boolean value that sets whether text is selectable. A true value sets all entered text as selectable.
TF_txt.tabEnabled	Undefined or true means that the text instance is included in automatic tab ordering; a value of false indicates it's not included.
TF_txt.tabIndex	A positive integer used to set the tab index of a text field. This setting is most useful when ordering user input text fields (read/write).
TF_txt._target	A read-only slash syntax path to the text field (the slash syntax is not read by ActionScript 2.0).
TF_txt.text	Used to assign text to and read text from the text field.
TF_txt.textColor	Sets the text color using the 0xrrggbb format. Returns the text color value in decimal format.
TF_txt.textHeight	The text field's bounding box height.
TF_txt.textWidth	The text field's bounding box width.
TF_txt.type	Sets or returns the type (dynamic or input) of the text field. In setting this property, use "dynamic" or "input" set as a string.
TF_txt._url	A read-only URL of the SWF file that created the text field instance.
TF_txt.variable	Sets or stores the variable name of the text field (if any). The variable contains the contents of the text property.
TF_txt._visible	Default is visible; false hides the text field.
TF_txt._width	The width of the text field's bounding box.
TF_txt.wordWrap	A Boolean value of true indicates that word wrapping for the text field is in effect.
TF_txt._x	The horizontal position (x coordinate) of a text field.
TF_txt._xmouse	The relative position of the x coordinate of the mouse pointer to the text field.
TF_txt._xscale	A percentage specifying horizontal scale of the text field relative to its original size.
TF_txt._y	The vertical position (y coordinate) of a text field.
TF_txt._ymouse	The relative position of the y coordinate of the mouse pointer to the text field.
TF_txt._yscale	A percentage specifying the vertical scale of the text field relative to its original size.

When you're designing with text fields, using the right properties is as important as getting the text fields positioned where they can be found easily by users. The following example shows how to create a class that can be used with different color combinations to set up a registration input set of text fields.

Using the Script window (accessed by selecting File, New, ActionScript File), create and save the class shown in Listing 6.1.

LISTING 6.1   The Class for Generating Registration Information (`Register.as`)

```
class Register {
  //Method
  function buildReg(rFont:String, rFColor:Number, rBColor:Number, rBGColor:Number) {
    //Array for initial labels in the text fields
    var interiorLabels:Array = new Array("First Name", "Last Name");
    interiorLabels.push("Address","Email", "Phone", "City");
    interiorLabels.push("ST", "Zip");
    //Text Format that user sets with parameter values
    var reg_fmt:TextFormat = new TextFormat();
    reg_fmt.font = rFont;
    reg_fmt.color = rFColor;
    var count:Number;
    //Generate text fields and apply format
    for (count=1; count<9; count++) {
      var vert:Number = 25*count;
      _level0.createTextField("reg"+count+"_txt", count, 50, vert, 100, 20);
      _level0["reg"+count+"_txt"].setNewTextFormat(reg_fmt);
      _level0["reg"+count+"_txt"].type = "input";
      _level0["reg"+count+"_txt"].border = true;
      _level0["reg"+count+"_txt"].borderColor = rBColor;
      _level0["reg"+count+"_txt"].background = true;
      _level0["reg"+count+"_txt"].backgroundColor = rBGColor;
      _level0["reg"+count+"_txt"].text = interiorLabels[count-1];
            _level0["reg"+count+"_txt"].onSetFocus = function(null) {
          this.text = "";
        };
      if (count == 7) {
        _level0["reg"+count+"_txt"]._width = 24;
        _level0["reg"+count+"_txt"].maxChars = 2;
      } else if (count == 8) {
        _level0["reg"+count+"_txt"]._width = 56;
        _level0["reg"+count+"_txt"].maxChars = 5;
      }
    }
  }
}
```

Because this script is a bit complex, stepping through the key parts will help you better understand it. First, the buildReg method establishes the following four parameters:

```
rFont:String, rFColor:Number, rBColor:Number, rBGColor:Number
```

These parameters allow the user to include a font family (rFont) and a hexadecimal value for the color (rFColor), border color (rBcolor), and background color (rBGcolor). In the class, these parameters will be part of a value assignment to the statements that determine those properties.

The array is simply a place to store the values that will be used as default text field values (name, address, and so forth). Next, a new TextFormat object (reg_fmt) is created:

```
var reg_fmt:TextFormat = new TextFormat();
      reg_fmt.font = rFont;
      reg_fmt.color = rFColor;
```

Importantly, two of the properties of the TextFormat object, font and color, are assigned values from the parameters established at the beginning of the script.

The heart of the script is creating all the text fields. Using the MovieClip.createTextField() method, parameters for the instance name, depth, horizontal position, vertical position, width, and height are established. In the script, these parameters are a combination of variables and literals:

- **Instance name**—"reg"+count+"_txt"

- **Depth**—count

- **Horizontal position (x)**—50

- **Vertical position (y)**—vert

- **Width**—100

- **Height**—20

The loop generates the value of the count variable sequentially. As the loop generates each new text field instance, the script adds property values, including the border and background colors. The background and border colors (rBColor and rBGColor) are among the four parameters established at the top of the script.

Two conditional statements check to see whether the text fields will be State or ZIP Code values. If so, it sets them to a special smaller size and sets the maximum number of characters that can be placed in each.

The one other piece of script that needs a little explanation is the following:

```
_level0["reg"+count+"_txt"].onSetFocus = function(null) {
            this.text = "";
      };
```

The purpose of this script segment is to remove automatically any text in the field as soon as the user clicks it. Using the onSetFocus event handler along with an unnamed function that changes the text property to "" (blank) does the trick.

The Register class generates a set of input text fields that can be used for registering users new to a site. By using the different properties of the TextField class, you can precisely generate not only a set of identical standard-size input text fields, but in the case with the State and ZIP Code entries, you can use special sizes and control the maximum number of characters the user can enter.

The Register.buildReg method has four parameters that are used to designate the font, font color, border color, and background color of the text fields. The script in Listing 6.2 uses the Register class.

LISTING 6.2   Using the Register Class in a FLA File (useRegister.fla)

```
//Register Class
var warmStyle:Register = new Register();
warmStyle.buildReg("Verdana", 0x79252e, 0x000000, 0xe2dfee);
```

FIGURE 6.13
Configured text fields from the Register class.

Figure 6.13 shows what the class and script generate.

With the hex color 0x836556 as the background color of the Stage, the other colors provide a warm palette for the input of data. If you want a different color scheme, all that's required is a different set of colors used in the Register.buildReg method's parameters.

TextField Events and Listeners

The TextField listeners listen for TextField events. However, some events are handled by the event occurring without a listener object involved, responding directly to the event. For example, in the user class created in the previous section (Register.as), the lines

```
_level0["reg"+count+"_txt"].onSetFocus = function(null) {
    this.text = "";
};
```

use the onSetFocus event to clear the labels when the user clicks the input text field. In this way, the user can see what goes in the field but doesn't have to select and erase it. That job is done automatically as soon as the user clicks (sets the focus) on the text field.

Tables 6.5 and 6.6 describe the event handlers and listeners used with the TextField class.

TABLE 6.5

`TextField` **Events Handlers**

EVENT HANDLER	ACTION
`TF_txt.onChanged`	Invoked when the text field is changed
`TF_txt.onKillFocus`	Invoked when the text field loses focus
`TF_txt.onScroller`	Invoked when one of the text field `scroll` properties changes
`TF_txt.onSetFocus`	Invoked when the text field receives focus

TABLE 6.6

`TextField` **Listeners**

LISTENER	NOTIFICATION
`TF_txt.onChanged`	Notified when the text field is changed
`TF_txt.onScroller`	Notified when the `scroll` or `maxscroll` property of a text field changes

Using the events and event handlers involves constructing a function that fires when an event occurs. The general format used has been the following:

```
TF_instance.onEvent=function() {
    //statements
};
```

When you use an event function, the function fires when the associated text field is subject to the event. That is, if `TextField_A` is associated with an event function, only when that event happens to `TextField_A` does the function fire.

Project: Using `TextField` **Listeners**

When you use a listener, the specified event can happen to any text field listening for the event. To see how this works, put together the following little movie:

1. Create a new document with three layers, named Actions, Text Fields, and Background.

2. On the Text Fields layer, add two input text fields with the instance names `entry_txt` and `entry2_txt`. Add one dynamic text field named `dyno_txt`. In the `entry_txt` text field, type **<Label>**. When the movie is tested, you should see <Label> in only one input text field.

3. In the Background layer, add the labels **Input 1** over the `entry_txt` instance and **Input 2** over the `entry2_txt` text field. Over the `dyno_txt` instance, add the label **Dynamic**. Add backdrops to the three text fields, as shown in Figures 6.14 and 6.15.

4. Click the first frame of the Actions layer and add the following script in the Actions panel:

```
textListener = new Object();
textListener.onChanged = function() {
    dyno_txt.text = entry_txt.text;
};
entry_txt.addListener(textListener);
entry2_txt.addListener(textListener);
```

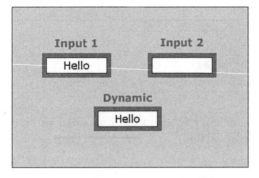

FIGURE 6.14   The dynamic text field changes as the Input 1 field changes.

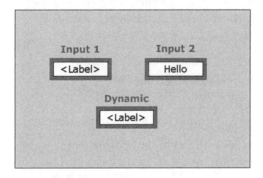

FIGURE 6.15   The dynamic text field getting text from the Input 1 field.

5. Test the movie by typing **Hello** in the Input 1 text field, as shown in Figure 6.14.

6. When you start typing in the first input text field, the typing changes the contents of that field, invoking the change (onChanged) event. When a change occurs, the function fires, and the dynamic text field is filled with the same text as that in the entry_txt instance.

7. Test the movie a second time, but instead of typing anything in the Input 1 text field, type **Hello** in the Input 2 text field. Figure 6.15 shows the result.

In this second trial, the text in the dynamic text field is the <Label> message from the Input 1 text field, because no matter what text field was subject to the event, the listener object invokes the unnamed textListener function. That function, in turn, duplicates the text property in the entry_txt instance to the dyno_txt instance.

One way of understanding how the events and listeners work is to think of an event as triggering a callback. As long as the listener "subscribes" to that event, it will trigger the callback as well. In the example, the callback is the unnamed function invoked by the onChange event, and both of the input text fields have such a "subscription."

Using the Stylesheet Class

In previous examples in this chapter, the formatting has been done by using either the TextField or TextFormat properties. A new class in Flash MX 2004 is TextField.StyleSheet. Because the StyleSheet folder is a subfolder of the TextField class, it doesn't look like a separate class, but it is. TextField.StyleSheet has a single event: onLoad signals that the StyleSheet.load() operation is complete. Table 6.7 shows the methods of TextField.StyleSheet.

TABLE 6.7

TextField.StyleSheet **Methods**

METHOD	DESCRIPTION
clear()	Clears the style sheet of all declarations
getStyle(sn)	Gets the named style defined and its property names and values
getStyleNames()	Gets the array containing the style names
load()	Begins loading a CSS file into StyleSheet
parseCSS(cssSheet)	Parses CSS in cssSheet and loads the style sheet
setStyle(name, style)	Inserts a new style with name and the given characteristics (style)
transform(cssSelector)	Transforms CSSselector into TextFormat

To work with the TextField.StyleSheet class, you first need to understand working with Cascading Style Sheets (CSS). This next section provides a quick review of using CSS and the subset of CSS available in Flash MX 2004.

CSS Flash Subset

Flash has a small subset of CSS. However, as a step in meeting ECMA standards and lining up ActionScript with other ECMA 4 languages, using CSS is important. Before we look at formatting styles with CSS, look at Table 6.8 to see what style attributes can be applied.

TABLE 6.8

CSS Attributes Available for Flash

CSS ATTRIBUTE	ALLOWED VALUES
text-align	left, center, right.
font-size	numeric value (px/pt equivalent).
text-decoration	none, underline.
margin-left	numeric value (px/pt equivalent).
margin-right	numeric value (px/pt equivalent).
font-weight	normal, bold.
font-style	normal, italic.
text-indent	numeric value (px/pt equivalent).

TABLE 6.8
Continued

CSS ATTRIBUTE	ALLOWED VALUES
font-family	mono, sans-serif, serif.
color	Use #rrggbb hexadecimal values only. Names such as "red" or "blue" are not allowed.
display	inline, block, none.

CSS has two basic style definitions. First, you can restyle certain tags. For example, the <p> tag tag> can be changed so that when it is used, everything between <p> and </p> adopts the defined style. The following defines the <p> tag style so that its font size is 13, the font color is red, and the font weight is normal:

```
p {
color: #ff0000;
font-size: 13;
font-weight: normal;
}
```

When the style is applied to a block of text, whenever the <p> tag is used, instead of the default style, it will have the new style. A very limited number of tags can be styled with CSS for use with Flash. Table 6.9 shows the tags subject to styling.

TABLE 6.9
Tags Subject to CSS Styling for Flash

TAG	TAGS AFFECTED
p	<p>.
body	<body>.
li	<li>.
a	<a>.
a:link	<a> (compound tag).
a:hover	<a> (compound tag). Applied after the <a> or a:link tag styles.
a:active	<a> (compound tag). Applied after the <a> or a:link tag styles.

When you're working with compound tags such as a:hover, the definitions are formatted a little differently. For example, the following would generate a blue color for link hot spots and then a green color when the mouse passes over the hot spot:

```
a {
   color: #0000bb;
}
a:hover {
   color: #00bb00;
}
```

Within a string, the applied style would look like the following:

```
var message:String='Link <a href=\"http://www.sandlight.com\">Sandlight</a>'
```

The word *Sandlight* will appear in blue, and when the mouse pointer passes over it, it changes to green.

The other type of styling is defining a style class using a *dot definition*, where you define an identifier by placing a period (dot) in front of it and then applying the style class as part of a <body>, <p>, or <span> tag. For example, the following generates orange, 24-point, bold, sans-serif text when applied:

```
.orangeBall {
    color: #ff6600;
    font-size: 24;
    font-family: sans-serif;
}
```

To apply a class to a block of text, you use an application tag to assign the class name within the tag. For example, the following assigns the orangeBall class to a text block:

```
This is regular text, and this: <p class="orangeBall">is Big Orange Text</p>.
This is regular text again.
```

When a dot-defined class is applied to a block of text, the dot (period) is not part of the class identifier.

Besides a truncated number of style features that can be added using CSS and Flash, units of measure are not used. For example, the line

```
font-size: 24;
```

although legal in a Flash CSS style sheet, is an illegal line in creating a regular CSS style sheet because no unit of measure accompanies the size. The standard CSS line would be

```
font-size: 24pt;
```

or

```
font-size: 24px;
```

However, in using CSS with Flash, no unit of measure is expected.

Applying CSS with Flash

Styling text within a text field can be very handy with dynamic text used with variables or simply assigned to a text field as a block. To see how to apply a text block with CSS to Flash, follow these steps:

1. Use the Script Editor to create a CSS style sheet. Save the following as `ford.css`.

```
.title {
    color: #aa0000;
    font-family: sans-serif;
    font-weight: bold;
    font-size: 24;
    text-align: center;
}

.bodStyle {
    color: #6b4301;
    font-family: serif;
    font-size: 12;
    text-indent: 10;
    margin-left: 20;
    margin-right: 12;
}

.showOff {
    color: #ff6600;
    font-weight: bold;
    font-family: mono;
    margin-left: 15;
}
```

2. Once the external CSS style sheet has been saved, all you need to do is to load it into the Flash style sheet object created and then assign the style sheet to the text field that will be using it. The general format is as follows:

```
var myStyleSheet=new TextField.StyleSheet();
myTxtField_txt.styleSheet=myStyleSheet;
myStyleSheet.load("mySheet.css");
```

3. Using HTML text, you can style the text within the text field you have assigned the style sheet. Using the `ford.css` file as a CSS style sheet, open a new Flash document and enter the following ActionScript:

```
//Create text fields
_level0.createTextField("ford_txt", 0, 115, 75, 380, 275);
_level0.ford_txt.multiline = true;
_level0.ford_txt.wordWrap = true;
_level0.ford_txt.border = true;
_level0.ford_txt.html = true;
_level0.createTextField("loadInfo_txt", 1, 115, 360, 104, 18.5);
//Instantiate new style sheet
var justMyStyle = new TextField.StyleSheet();
//Show that external css loaded or error occurred
justMyStyle.onLoad = function(cssLoaded) {
    if (cssLoaded) {
        _level0.loadInfo_txt.text = "CSS Loaded";
    } else {
        _level0.loadInfo_txt.text = "Load Boo Boo";
    }
};
ford_txt.styleSheet = justMyStyle;
//Text in variable with HTML formatting for CSS
var sword:String = '<p class=\"title\">Crossing at a Ford</p><br>';
sword += '<p class=\"bodStyle\">Crossing at a ford means, for example,';
sword += 'crossing the sea at a strait, or crossing over a hundred miles ';
sword += 'of broad sea at a crossing place. I believe this crossing at a ';
sword += 'ford occurs often in a man\'s lifetime. It means setting ';
sword += 'sail even though your friends stay in harbor, knowing the ';
sword += 'route, knowing the soundness of your ship and the favor of ';
sword += 'the day. When all the conditions are met, and a favorable ';
sword += 'wind blows, or a tailwind, then set sail. If the wind changes ';
sword += 'within a few miles of your destination, you must row across ';
sword += 'the remaining distance without sail.<br></p>';
sword += '<span class=\"showOff\"><br>Go Rin No Sho ';
sword += '--Miyamoto Musashi-- 1645</span>';

//Place text in text field
ford_txt.htmlText = sword;
//Load external style sheet
justMyStyle.load("ford.css");
```

The script generates one large and one small dynamic text field. When the external CSS file is successfully loaded, the small text field displays a message informing the user that the load is complete. A string variable named sword contains text with a collection of HTML tags, some of which are used to apply the styles in the ford.css file. Figure 6.16 shows the output when the document is test run.

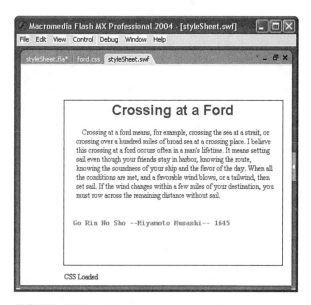

FIGURE 6.16   CSS styles have been applied to the text.

In the script, note that the <span> tag has been employed to assign a style to the text at the bottom of the large text field. You can use the <span> tag to introduce a style within a text block without causing line breaks, as when using the <p> tag.

Inline CSS Styling with Flash

Besides using external style sheets with CSS, Flash Pro has 11 inline CSS terms you can use to add inline styles:

- color
- display
- fontFamily
- fontSize
- fontStyle
- fontWeight
- marginLeft
- marginRight
- textAlign
- textDecoration
- textIndent

Using the inline CSS, you have a few more options, but the application is a little awkward. Rather than having only three font families, using the inline `fontFamily` (instead of `font-family`), you can enter the name of any font you want rather than just `mono`, `serif`, or `sans-serif`. However, most of the other options are pretty similar. The style is set using this format:

```
var myStyleSheet = new TextField.StyleSheet();
myStylesheet.setStyle(".dotDef", {attribute1: 'value', attribute2: 'value'})
```

So you can get an idea of how this works, this next application uses one text field and three buttons. Each of the buttons generates a different style presented in the text field. Figure 6.17 will give you an idea of what needs to be on the Stage, and the script in Listing 6.3, created in the Actions panel, provides the instance names.

LISTING 6.3   Dynamically Changing Text Styles with Inline CSS

```
var choiceSheet = new TextField.StyleSheet();
var message:String = new String();
var message:String = new String();
message = '<p class="nowStyle">The truth is, Socrates, that these '
message += 'regrets, and also the complaints about relations, are to '
message += 'be attributed to the same cause, which is not old age, '
message += 'but men\'s characters and tempers; for he who is of a '
message += 'calm and happy nature will hardly feel the pressure of age, '
message += 'but to him who is of an opposite disposition youth and age '
message += 'are equally a burden.';style1_btn.onPress = function() {
    choiceSheet.setStyle(".nowStyle", {fontFamily:'Verdana', fontSize:11,
    ➥marginLeft:10, color:'#983803'});
    doStyle();
};
style2_btn.onPress = function() {
    choiceSheet.setStyle(".nowStyle", {fontFamily:'Georgia', fontSize:12,
    ➥marginLeft:10, color:'#E39102'});
    doStyle();
};
style3_btn.onPress = function() {
    choiceSheet.setStyle(".nowStyle", {fontFamily:'Arial', fontSize:10,
    ➥marginLeft:15, marginRight:5,color:'#0000000'});
    doStyle();
};
function doStyle() {
    inlineField_txt.styleSheet = choiceSheet;
    inlineField_txt.htmlText = message;
}
```

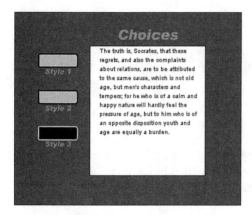

When you click each of the different buttons, you should see a different style. The purpose is to demonstrate how different styles can be generated on the fly and, depending on the circumstance (such as the event or selection), a different style appears. Figure 6.17 shows the style generated when the third button is clicked.

Styling with the
TextFormat Class

FIGURE 6.17   Dynamic styles applied.

Earlier examples of the TextField class showed the TextFormat class in action. TextFormat has just one method, TF_fmt.getTextExtent(), which provides text string measurement information. Most of the properties of the TextFormat class are fairly self-explanatory, as shown in Table 6.10.

TABLE 6.10
TextFormat **Properties**

PROPERTY	CHARACTERISTICS
TF_fmt.align	Indicates the alignment of a paragraph (left, center, or right).
TF_fmt.blockIndent	The point measurement of the indent of a text block. This sets how much the indent will be.
TF_fmt.bold	A Boolean value for boldface setting. When this property is set to true, the text will be boldfaced.
TF_fmt.bullet	A Boolean value for bullet font. When this property is set to true, the text will be in bullet format.
TF_fmt.color	The format text color value, written as 0xrrggbb. Even through the property is called color, it's actually the text color.
TF_fmt.font	A string with a font name (for example, "Verdana"). Sets the font family for the text.
TF_fmt.indent	The number of points paragraph is indented. This is a number only, without a unit of measure.
TF_fmt.italic	A Boolean value for italic setting. When this property is set to true, the text is italicized.
TF_fmt.leading	A vertical blank space between lines. *Leading* is a typesetting term left over from the old "hot type" days when different amounts of lead were added between lines for spacing.
TF_fmt.leftMargin	The number of points the left margin is from the side of the text field border. This property sets the entire text block.
TF_fmt.rightMargin	The number of points the right margin is from the side of the text field border.

TABLE 6.10

Continued

PROPERTY	CHARACTERISTICS
TF_fmt.size	The font size in points. In the latest version of Flash, smaller text sizes are visible, but sizes smaller than 6 points may be difficult to read. (Even 6 points is difficult to read!)
TF_fmt.tabStops	The number of points each tab stop moves (defaults to 4).
TF_fmt.target	The target window in the page that the hyperlink addresses. The window can be a named window in a frameset or _blank, _parent, _top, or _self.
TF_fmt.underline	A Boolean value for underline setting. When this property is set to true, the text will be underlined.
TF_fmt.url	The text link target URL. This works in a similar manner to the getURL() function.

As noted in the section on TextField methods, all text formatting is set using either TextField.setTextFormat or TextField.setNewTextFormat. The text format suffix is _fmt, which, when used, will invoke the auto code hints for the methods and properties of the class. Here's the general format for instantiating a TextFormat class and assigning property values:

```
var TF_fmt:TextFormat = new TextFormat();
TF_fmt.property = value;
```

Many of the TextFormat properties, such as bold and italic, are set using a Boolean value. Others receive values, mostly in points. The margin values, font size, leading, tab stops, block indent, and indent all use the same unit of measure (points).

Perhaps the most important part of using the TextFormat object is applying the format to a TextField object. Because the TextFormat object has no method for associating itself with a TextField object, either TextField.SetNewTextFormat or TextField.SetTextFormat must be used. If you use the TextField.SetNewTextFormat method, place the TextField.Text *before* selecting the format. For example, enter the following script into the Actions panel and test the movie:

```
_level0.createTextField("message_txt", 0, 50, 50, 400, 400);
message_txt.border = true;
message_txt.borderColor = 0xaa0000;
message_txt.background = true;
message_txt.backgroundColor = 0xcccccc;
var focusFormat_fmt:TextFormat = new TextFormat();
focusFormat_fmt.color = 0xaa0000;
focusFormat_fmt.size = 24;
focusFormat_fmt.align = "center";
focusFormat_fmt.font = "Verdana";
focusFormat_fmt.bold = true;
message_txt.setNewTextFormat(focusFormat_fmt);
message_txt.text = "Before and after....";
```

It should work fine. Now, swap the last two lines so they're like this:

```
message_txt.text = "Before and after....";
message_txt.setNewTextFormat(focusFormat_fmt);
```

None of the text formatting has been applied. That's because, when `setNewTextFormat` is used, the text must appear *after* the style is set. Finally, make the following adjustment by changing `setNewTextFormat` to `setTextFormat` so that it looks like this:

```
message_txt.text = "Before and after....";
message_txt.setTextFormat(focusFormat_fmt);
```

When you test the movie again, it works fine. That's because `setTextFormat` is applied to the text only *after* it has been placed in the text field.

In Brief

- Text fields can be static, input, or dynamic. Text can change dynamically in dynamic and input text fields, but not in static fields. Static text can be read dynamically using the new `TextSnapshot` class.

- The Property panel contextually sets the parameters for all text fields.

- The default state of all text in static text fields supplies the font outline so that any text can be viewed with the correct font on user computers, regardless of their system font set.

- Dynamic text field and font styling is accomplished using either CSS and the `TextStyle` class or the methods and properties of the `TextFormat` classes.

- Graphic elements can be added to text fields using HTML text settings.

Tools for Use with Text and Text Components

Using the `Selection` Class with the `TextField` Class

Whenever you click an object on the Stage, including a text field, you can use the `Selection` class to learn about what has been selected and act on that information. For example, if you're using input text fields with inline labels (for example, <name>, <address>), you can use the `Selection` class to find out exactly which input field the user has selected. Knowing that information, you can then provide further details in a dynamic text field to help guide the user through the data-entry process.

To help a user fill in the appropriate information in a field, you can use prompt information. Sometimes, a field may need lots of detail explaining to the user what needs to be typed into it. However, given the limited amount of space on the screen, only so much room is available. Rather than placing input instructions in static text and using a good deal of screen space, you can use the same information space for all the input fields. As the user clicks each field, different instructions appear in the same place, allowing for simple or expanded information. Because all the input field information is provided in the same place, the user has a single focal point for input and input instructions.

The `Selection` class allows the developer to respond to any object selected in a movie. Using `TextField.onFocus`, only the instance of the selected text field initiates an event. However, using a listener, any text field or other object can elicit a response.

Project: Building Changeable Text Fields

So that you can see one application of the Selection class, the following project begins with four input text fields and one dynamic text field. The four input text fields have instance names in the form of inputX_txt, where X is a numeric value, beginning with input1_txt. Using the information in Selection.getFocus() method, the script is able to identify which of the input text fields the user has selected. Depending on which text field is selected, a different message is sent to the dynamic text field to help the user understand what he or she is supposed to do. Here are the steps to follow:

1. Open a new Flash document and create three layers named, from top to bottom, Actions, Dynamic Text Field, and Input Text Fields.

2. Click the Input Text Fields layer and place four input text fields on the Stage. Then click the Dynamic Text Field layer and add a single dynamic text field. Use the relative positions shown in Figure 7.1. The output dynamic text field uses the instance name instruct_txt. The input text fields have the inline labels <Name>, <Email>, <Company>, and <Contact>, and the instance names input1_txt, input2_txt, input3_txt, and input4_txt, respectively, from top to bottom. Also add a static text label, **Welcome to Sandlight**, at the top of the Stage. (Actually, you can put in any text label you want.)

FIGURE 7.1 Four input text fields with inline labels and a single dynamic text field make up the Stage.

3. Click the first frame of the Actions layer and enter the following script:

```
//Create an object instance
var selectListen:Object = new Object();
var message:String;
//Create tab order
var tabPos:Number;
for (tabPos=1; tabPos<5; tabPos++) {
    _level0["input"+tabPos+"_txt"].tabIndex = tabPos;
}
//Set up a function invoked by focus on particular field
selectListen.onSetFocus = function() {
    var locus:String = Selection.getFocus();
    var setter:String = locus.charAt(13);
    _level0["input"+setter+"_txt"].text = "";
    if (setter == "1") {
        message = " Please enter your first and last name.";
```

```
        } else if (setter == "2") {
            message = " What email address is most convenient for you?";
        } else if (setter == "3") {
            message = " Enter your company name.";
        } else {
            message = " If you know the name of your Sandlight contact, ";
            message += "please enter his or her name. If you don't know ";
            message += "your contact's name, leave it blank.";
        }
        instruct_txt.text = message;
    };
    Selection.addListener(selectListen);
```

For you to understand and appreciate the use of the `Selection` class, we need to unravel
some of the script. First, the line

```
var locus:String = Selection.getFocus();
```

places `Selection.getFocus()` into a string. Because only a single focus point can exist at one
time, the class doesn't have a constructor for separate instances. Rather, the method can be
placed into a string. Then, using string properties, it can find which field is currently selected.

Next, the line

```
var setter:String = locus.charAt(13);
```

creates a string, `setter`, that identifies the character in position 13 of the instance name of
the input text field identified in `locus.charAt(13)`. Keeping in mind that the instance names
of the input text fields are sequentially named, `input1_txt` to `input4_txt`, the character at
position 13 may seem to you to be in the vapor beyond the string's length. However, each
text field is identified by its full path, beginning with position 0 as the first character in the
name. Therefore, looking at the line

```
_level0.input1_txt
```

you begin counting with the first underscore in `_level0`. When you get to the character 1,
you'll see that it's the 13th character in the full path name (you even have to count the dot
[.]). Therefore, using this technique, the variable `setter` is able to store which input text
field the user is currently selecting. Then, using conditional statements with the `setter` variable, the script determines which message should appear in the message box.

Figure 7.2 shows a partially completed set of input forms. The top three fields have been
completed, and the fourth one has been selected. As each is selected, its tag-like inline label
(<name>, <email>, and so on) disappears so that the user can enter data. At the same time,
information about what to fill in the field is posted to help the user complete the form.

FIGURE 7.2   Selections generate different responses.

Note that no `Selection` instance (or object) is created. Always use the root, `Selection`, with the different methods associated with the class, as you can see in `Selection.addListener()` and `Selection.getFocus()` in the script.

Printing Text with the `PrintJob` Class

When generating text content for the screen in Flash Pro, you may have a feature that allows the user to print out the contents of a text field. Using the new `PrintJob` class, you can print selected sections of a movie clip or text field. Tables 7.1 and 7.2 list the methods and properties of the `PrintJob` class.

TABLE 7.1

`PrintJob` **Methods**

METHOD	DESCRIPTION
`In_pj.addPage()`	Specifies the print target and optional print area, a bitmap Boolean, and frame number.
`In_pj.send()`	Spooled pages are sent to the printer.
`In_pj.start()`	Opens the operating system's print window and initiates spooling.

TABLE 7.2

`PrintJob` **Properties**

PROPERTY	CHARACTERISTICS (READ ONLY)
`PrintJob.paperHeight`	Overall paper height.
`PrintJob.paperWidth`	Overall paper width.
`PrintJob.pageHeight`	Height of the actual printable area on the page; any user-set margins are ignored.
`PrintJob.pageWidth`	Width of the actual printable area on the page; any user-set margins are ignored.
`PrintJob.orientation`	"Portrait" or "landscape."

The properties of the PrintJob class rely on the system's printer settings. The main work with PrintJob is in setting the PrintJob.addPage() method. To effectively use PrintJob where you want to print out only a segment of a movie clip or text field, you need to include the area of the movie clip to print in the PrintJob.addPage() parameters.

For example, suppose you have a text field in your movie with the x,y coordinates 50,50. If the width and height of the text field are W=300, H=200, the text field can be said to be contained within the area bounded by the following coordinates:

```
50,50,350,250
```

The print area in the PrintJob.addPage() method is constructed as follows:

- **xMin**—The x value for the top-left coordinate

- **xMax**—The x value for the bottom-right coordinate

- **yMin**—The y value for the top-left coordinate

- **yMax**—The y value for the bottom-right coordinate

Therefore, a text field bounded by the coordinates 50,50,350,250 would be placed in the PrintJob.addPage() method as follows:

```
{xMin:50, xMax:350, yMin:50, yMax:250}
```

The full set of parameters for PrintJob.addPage() are as follows:

```
PrintJob.addPage(level, {xMin:n, xMax:n, yMin:n, yMax:n},
➥{printAsBitmap:Boolean}, frame #)
```

Here, *level* refers to the target level or instance name of the movie clip to be printed. The following script shows how to have dynamic text content that can be printed to the user's printer. The example uses a "coupon" that takes up only a portion of the movie clip but can be printed by itself using PrintJob. Here are the steps to follow to re-create the movie:

1. Add a dynamic text field to the Stage with the instance name coupon_txt, and two buttons with the instance names thurs_btn and friday_btn.

2. Using Figure 7.3 as a guide, place the buttons and text field on the Stage.

3. Add the following script in the Actions panel:

```
//Text message for Thursday button
thurs_btn.onPress = function() {
    var cr = newline;
    var thursday:String = "THURSDAY: $5 Discount Coupon to the ";
    thursday += "D-Street Garage Band";
```

```
        thursday += cr+"Cameras, Audio Recorders, and Video Recorders Welcomed;";
        thursday += cr+"Back-stage pass for all coupon holders.";
        coupon_txt.text = thursday;
    };
    //Text message for Friday button
    friday_btn.onPress = function() {
        var cr = newline;
        var friday:String = "FRIDAY: $2 Discount Coupon to the ";
        friday += "D-Street Garage Band";
        friday += cr+"Cameras, Audio Recorders, and Video Recorders Welcomed;";
        friday += cr+"Back-stage pass for all coupon holders.";
        coupon_txt.text = friday;
    };
    //Set up ContextMenu for printing
    var textPrint_cm:ContextMenu = new ContextMenu();
    var coupon_mci:ContextMenuItem = new ContextMenuItem("Print Coupon", jobPrint);
    textPrint_cm.customItems.push(coupon_mci);
    textPrint_cm.hideBuiltInItems();
    //Specify portion of screen to be printed using PrintJob class
    function jobPrint() {
        var printField_pj:PrintJob = new PrintJob();
        var xMinV:Number = coupon_txt._x;
        var yMinV:Number = coupon_txt._y;
        var xMaxV:Number = xMinV+coupon_txt._width;
        var yMaxV:Number = yMinV+coupon_txt._height;
        var getCoupon = printField_pj.start();
        if (getCoupon) {
            getCoupon = printField_pj.addPage(0, {xMin:xMinV, xMax:xMaxV, yMin:yMinV,
            ➡yMax:yMaxV});
            printField_pj.send();
        }
        delete printField_pj;
    }
    //Display text to be printed in dynamic text field
    coupon_txt.menu = textPrint_cm;
```

As Figure 7.3 shows, the Thursday button has been clicked, and a context menu is used to set the print job in motion.

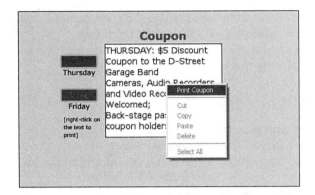

FIGURE 7.3   The context menu used to launch printing.

When a PrintJob instance is launched, the user sees the system's printer selections and options. At that time, the user can elect to use the default options or any others available on the system.

Using the ContextMenu **Class**

The ContextMenu class is not inherently associated with the PrintJob class or any of the text field classes, but it is introduced here because using it with PrintJob is one of the effective ways to employ it. The nice thing about the context menu is that you can add a control without having to add a button or other controller to the Stage. Instances of the TextField class are the ideal place for adding context menus because they represent one of the ways you can use the text area as a launching site for actions relating to a text field. Printing is one such action the designer or developer may want to add to a text field.

Basic Format

Here is the basic format for working with the ContextMenu class and TextField classes:

```
var contextMen_cm:ContextMenu = new ContextMenu();
var contextMenIt_cmi:ContextMenuItem = new ContextMenutem("Label", callback)
contextMen_cm.customItems.push(contextMenIt_cmi);
function callback() {
    //actions
}
someTextField_txt.menu = contextMen_cm;
```

You associate a text field instance with the context menu by assigning the context menu instance to the text field using the `TextField.menu` property. Keeping in mind that `ContextMenu.customItems` is an array property, you associate the items for the context menu (`ContextMenuItems` instance) with the menu using the `Array.push` method.

`ContextMenu` and `ContextMenuItem`

In using context menus, you typically work with two classes. In addition to the `ContextMenu` class, the `ContextMenuItem` class is employed as well. Using the `ContextMenuItem` class, you can add new labels and associated actions to the context menu. In the `PrintJob` example, an item is added to the context menu that calls the function where the `PrintJob` instance formats and sends printing information to the printer. By using the format

```
label1_cmi=new ContextMenuItem("Label 1", callback1)
label2_cmi=new ContextMenuItem("Label 2", callback2)
label3_cmi=new ContextMenuItem("Label 3", callback3)
contextMen_cm.customItems.push(label1_cmi, label2_cmi, label3_cmi);
```

you can add any number of labels and callbacks to a given context menu instance.

Tables 7.3 through 7.6 summarize the various methods, properties, and event handlers of the `ContextMenu` and `ContextMenuItem` classes.

TABLE 7.3

`ContextMenu` **Methods**

METHOD	DESCRIPTION
`ContextMenu.copy()`	Returns a copy of the `ContextMenu` instance.
`ContextMenu.hideBuiltInItems()`	Most built-in items in the context menu are hidden by this method.
`ContextMenu.customItems`	An undefined array containing `ContextMenuItem` objects. Because `customItems` is an array, the array methods (in particular, `push`) are available to the `customItems` property.

TABLE 7.4

`ContextMenu` **Properties and Events**

OBJECT/HANDLER	DESCRIPTION
`ContextMenu.builtInItems`	A set of built-in properties (`forward_back`, `loop`, `play`, `print`, `quality`, `rewind`, `save`, `zoom`) that can be set to a Boolean value and have a default value of `true`
`ContextMenu.onSelect`	Can be used to initiate a callback before the menu opens

TABLE 7.5

ContextMenuItem **Methods and Events**

METHOD/EVENT	ACTION
ContextMenuItem.copy()	Produces and returns a copy of the context menu item instance
ContextMenuItem.onSelect	Fires when a menu item is selected

TABLE 7.6

ContextMenuItem **Properties**

PROPERTY	CHARACTERISTICS
ContextMenuItem.caption	Specifies the text displayed in the menu item.
ContextMenuItem.enabled	Specifies whether the menu item is enabled or disabled.
ContextMenuItem.separatorBefore	A Boolean value determines whether a separator bar appears above the menu item.
ContextMenuItem.visible	Shows or hides the menu item based on a Boolean value.

The context menu along with custom items for the menu can be added to movie clips as well. To change the default context menu on the Stage, use _level0 or _root when assigning a MovieClip class to the menu.

Working with Text Components

To aid designers and make the process of organizing and building Flash documents simpler, text components were introduced in Flash MX. With Flash MX 2004, you will find additional text field components. The Scrollbar component has been combined into a single TextArea component so that the scrollbar and text field are a single component. Two new text components, TextInput and TextLabel, have been added as well. Later chapters will show these two components used for navigation. In this chapter, they're introduced in their most fundamental formats and application.

The TextArea Component

By combining the Scrollbar component with a text field, the TextArea component makes the job of creating a scrollable text field considerably easier. The scrollbar can be set so that it's only visible when text scrolls beyond the bottom border (auto), or it can be hidden (off) altogether or always present (on).

Like all components, the TextArea component's parameters can be set in either the Property Inspector or the Component Inspector. The latter has more options, but a change in one can cause a change in the other. For example, Figure 7.4 shows that changing the "editable" parameter to false in the Component Inspector causes the same change in the Property Inspector.

Project: Adding a TextArea Component

To see how to use the TextArea component, try this project:

1. Open a new document, setting the Stage size to 800×600. Make three layers, naming them, from top to bottom, Actions, TextAreas, and Labels.

2. Select the TextAreas layer and drag two TextArea components from the Components panel. Size them both to W=350, H=250, naming one `comedy_txt` and the other `tragedy_txt`.

3. Select each, in turn, and in the Parameters tab in the Component Inspector, change the "editable" value to false, as shown in Figure 7.4.

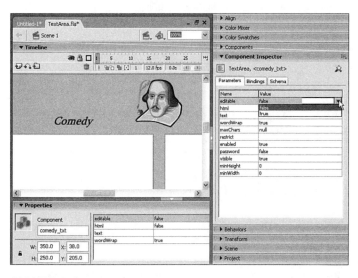

FIGURE 7.4   Setting parameters in the Component Inspector.

4. In the Labels layer, add the labels **Comedy** and **Tragedy** over the TextArea component instances using Figures 7.4 and 7.5 as your guides.

5. Using a text editor such as Microsoft Notepad, enter a scene from your favorite Shakespearean comedy and one from your favorite Shakespearean tragedy. Save the first as `comedy.txt` and the other as `tragedy.txt`. This text should extend beyond the bottom border of the respective TextArea components. Save the FLA file in the same folder as the two text files.

6. Open the Actions panel and add the following script:

```
var com_lv:LoadVars = new LoadVars();
com_lv.onData = function(contents) {
    if (contents.indexOf("\n") != -1) {
```

```
            contents = contents.split("\n").join("");
        }
        comedy_txt.text = contents;
    };
    com_lv.load("comedy.txt");
    var tragedy_lv:LoadVars = new LoadVars();
    //Clean up extra carriage return for Windows
    tragedy_lv.onData = function(contents) {
        if (contents.indexOf("\n") != -1) {
            contents = contents.split("\n").join("");
        }
        tragedy_txt.text = contents;
    };
    tragedy_lv.load("tragedy.txt");
```

7. Once you have it put together, test it. Figure 7.5 shows how both text fields display a scrollbar along the right side of the TextArea components. These can be dragged up and down to reveal the complete contents of the text fields.

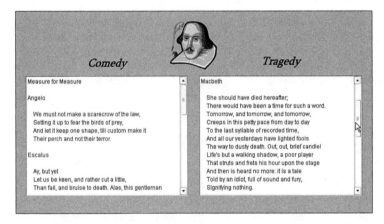

FIGURE 7.5   The text inside the TextArea components can be scrolled using the scrollbars.

The options available in the Property and Component Inspectors make working with the TextArea component fairly simple. However, to get the most out of the component, you need to use the TextArea class and styling with ActionScript 2.0.

The `TextArea` Class

The `TextArea` class's properties have many of the same options you can find in the Component Inspector. However, other options are only available using the `TextArea` class and its properties. Like with other classes, TextArea components can be created dynamically on an object using the following format:

```
object.createObject("TextArea", "someTA_txt", depth)
```

For example, you can use the following script to place a TextArea component on the main Timeline:

```
_level0.createObject("TextArea", "history_txt", 0);
```

Like other methods associated with the TextArea component, the `createObject()` method is actually part of the `UIObject` class, and it's available to all UI components. Likewise, most of the events used by the TextArea component are part of the `UIObject` class. The TextArea component has a single event, `TextArea.change`, which informs listeners of text changes. It also has unique properties, as summarized in Table 7.7.

SHOP TALK

Dealing with the Extra Carriage Return in the Windows OS

One of the many unknowns you'll encounter and must deal with when working with text is how the different operating systems handle text display. When Flash generates text, it includes a carriage return character when it creates a new paragraph. The same is true for text files. At the end of each paragraph is a carriage return.

In the Windows OS, each new paragraph detected invokes a new carriage return. One unintended result is that text will often have two carriage returns, one supplied by the text itself and the other included by the Windows OS. On the screen, instead of a single carriage return leading to adjacent paragraphs, an extra space is added to all paragraphs.

To strip out the added carriage returns, you need to add the following code when loading text using the LoadVars class:

```
loadVarsInstance.onData = function(contents) {
    if (contents.indexOf("\n") != -1) {
        contents = contents.split("\n").join("");
    }
}
```

As the data is loaded, the script looks for the added carriage return (`"\n"`) and strips it out. Macintosh users need not concern themselves with this phenomenon because the Mac OS doesn't add the extra carriage return.

TABLE 7.7

TextArea **Properties**

PROPERTY	DESCRIPTION
TextArea.editable	A Boolean value indicating whether the text field is editable (true) or not editable (false).
TextArea.hPosition	Defines the horizontal position of the text within the scroll pane.
TextArea.hScrollPolicy	The "on", "off", and "auto" values set the status of the horizontal scrollbar.
TextArea.html	A Boolean value for HTML formatting.
TextArea.length	A read-only value storing the number of characters in the text field.
TextArea.maxChars	An integer indicating the maximum number of characters allowed in the text field.
TextArea.maxHPosition	An integer specifying the maximum value of hPosition.
TextArea.maxVPosition	An integer specifying the maximum value of vPosition.
TextArea.password	A Boolean value flagging whether or not the TextArea instance is a password field.
TextArea.restrict	Indicates an individual character or a range of characters allowed in a field. Example: "K-R" (range) or "^K-R" (any letters except uppercase letters *K* through *R*).
TextArea.text	Any text that will be in the text field.
TextArea.vPosition	An integer specifying the vertical position of the scroll in text. (Used to jump to text.)
TextArea.vScrollPolicy	The "on", "off", and "auto" values set the status of the vertical scrollbar.
TextArea.wordWrap	A Boolean value flagging whether or not the text wraps. Defaults to true (the text does wrap).

The change in the properties works like property changes in other classes. For example, as a temporary utility to find where different key points are in a text area, add two more TextArea components to the example of using TextArea in the previous section. Use the dimensions W=100, H=20 for the new TextArea instances, with the instance names comScrol_txt and tragScrol_txt, and add the following script to the bottom of the existing script:

```
_level0.onMouseMove=function() {
    comScrol_txt.text=comedy_txt.vPosition;
    tragScrol_txt.text=tragedy_txt.vPosition;
}
```

Using the values in the two new TextArea instances, you can set up buttons to jump to different parts of the text in the TextArea windows. You can use several other event handlers as well from the UIObject class.

TextArea Styling

Once a text area has been established, you have several options to style the text. Using the format

```
UIObject.setStyle("style", "value");
```

you can add all the styles shown in Table 7.8.

TABLE 7.8

TextArea Styles

STYLE	VALUE
color	The color, using 0xrrggbb hexadecimal format
embedFonts	Font names to embed in the document
fontFamily	The text font family name (for example, Verdana)
fontSize	The value for the font size
fontStyle	"normal" or "italic"
fontWeight	"normal" or "bold"
textAlign	"left", "right", or "center"
textDecoration	"none" or "underline"

The final kind of styling you can apply is coloring the borders of the TextArea component. Using the border properties and the format

```
TXA_in.setStyle("borderProp", "0xrrggbb")
```

you have detailed color styling control. Figure 7.6 shows the different border areas and their property names.

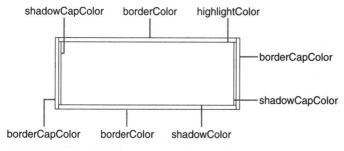

FIGURE 7.6   The border regions all have names for referencing the border color.

To see how this might work, add the following lines to the end of the TextArea example comparing the comedy and tragedy:

```
comedy_txt.setStyle("borderColor", "0xaa0000");
comedy_txt.setStyle("highlightColor", "0xff0000");
comedy_txt.setStyle("shadowColor", "0x550000");
comedy_txt.setStyle("borderCapColor", "0xaa0000");
comedy_txt.setStyle("shadowCapColor", "0x550000");
```

As you can see in Figure 7.5, some of the regions of the border have the same name. Thus, when adding a color scheme, keep in mind that those areas with the same color property name will have the same color.

The TextInput Component

The second important text component is the TextInput component. As the name implies, this component is used for designing documents requiring user input. In looking at the parameters and schema in the Component Inspector, you may be struck by the fact that the "editable" property can be set to false and "read only" can be set to true. Those settings effectively disallow user input. Such settings may seem to defeat the primary purpose of the component, but as you will see in later chapters, in setting up navigation, you may often want to change the functionality of different components, including TextInput components. For example, if you want a user to log in to a site before he or she can enter data, you can set the default "read only" property to true. Then, once the initial material has been entered, the TextInput components become readable. The following shows what such a triggering script may look like:

```
if(entryFlag==true) {
    nameInput_txt.readOnly=false;
    nameInput_txt.editable=true;
}
```

Like the TextArea component, TextInput inherits all methods from UIObject and UIComponent, including the readOnly property. You can also look at other UI classes, such as the UIEventDispatcher to the TextInput component. Whatever events you employ, try to use listener objects such as the following for the UIComponent.focusIn event:

```
var inputListen:Object = new Object();
inputListen.focusIn = function(evtObj) {
    if (evtObj.target == addressInput) {
        addressInput.text = "";
    }
};
addressInput.addEventListener("focusIn", inputListen);
```

Here, evtObj is the object that caused an event. In this case, it's the TextInput component with the instance name addressInput.

Using the Mouse Class

In all Flash Pro movies where the mouse is required, you can use the Mouse class. The class itself is little changed from Flash MX, but you can now employ the mouse wheel in your scripting for your movies. Tables 7.9 and 7.10 show the class elements.

TABLE 7.9

Mouse **Methods**

METHOD	ACTION
Mouse.addListener(obj)	The object (obj) subscribes to onMouseDown, onMouseMove, onMouseWheel, and onMouseUp notification.
Mouse.hide()	Hides the mouse pointer.
Mouse.removeListener(obj)	Removes the subscriber object (obj).
Mouse.show()	Shows the mouse pointer.

TABLE 7.10

Mouse **Events**

LISTENER	EVENT
Mouse.onMouseDown	The Down state of the mouse button triggers notification to listener subscribers.
Mouse.onMouseMove	Any mouse movement triggers notification to listener subscribers.
Mouse.onMouseUp	The Up state of the mouse button triggers notification to listener subscribers.
Mouse.onMouseWheel	The mouse wheel triggers notification to listener subscribers.

Trapping the mouse-related event requires that a listener be established using the following format:

```
someListener=new Object
someListener.onMouseEvent=function() {
    //some actions
}
Mouse.addListener(someListener)
```

You can apply any number of uses by using the Mouse class and its methods and events. For example, you could use a semi-opaque movie clip to act as a text highlighter controlled by the mouse wheel scrolling up or down. The following project is a simple example of using the mouse wheel in this manner:

1. Open a new document and add layers so that you have a total of four—named Actions, Reader Bar, Text Field, and Labels.

2. Place a dynamic text field in the Text Field layer with the dimensions 500×400 and give it the instance name `reader_txt`. Make it a multiline text field with Show Border Around Text selected. Choose 14-point Georgia text and use the hex value color #4C190C for the text color.

3. In the Reader Bar layer, draw a rectangle using no stroke color and the fill color #4C190C. The rectangle's dimensions are W=500, H=20. Align it with the top of the text field. In the Color Mixer panel, change the Alpha value of the rectangle to 15%. Select the rectangle and convert it to a Movie Clip symbol and give it the instance name `line_mc`.

4. In the Labels field, add a 24-point static text labeled **Scroll Reader**, centered over the text field.

5. Click the first frame and add the following script (you can dump the included pseudo-novel noir detective story and substitute any you like):

```
var story:String = new String();
story = "Archer Samuels, private eye, walked into his front office, and she ";
story += " was waiting, dressed to the nines. She wanted something, and it ";
story += " wasn't to find out whether her loving husband was cheating on ";
story += " her. Sam smiled and asked her how he could help. In almost a";
story += " whisper she asked if she could sit down.";
story += "\n \"Forgive me. Of course, sit here,\" Archer, ";
story += "still smiling said.";
story += "\n \"You're very kind,\" she sighed.";
story += "\n \"Can I get you something? Coffee, water, a drink?\"";
story += " Sam inquired.";
story += "\n \"Nothing, thank you,\" again, barely audible.";
story += "\n Archer sat as well and looked at her, still with a friendly";
story += " smile, steadily glued on his puss. Sooner or later she would get ";
story += "around to telling him what she wanted, and he wanted to see how ";
story += " she'd play it out. Women aren\'t like men when ";
story += "it comes to clothes.";
story += " They\'re better at dressing, checking to see ";
story += "if the message they want to convey is getting across. ";
story += "He wondered what message she was sending. ";
```

```
story += "Her clothes were expensive, the jewelry too, but not flashy. "
story += "Her perfume had the same high price ";
story += "aroma as the rest of her, subdued but rich. ";
story += "The only false note in her get-up was that the skirt was "
story += "just a little too short and the neckline ";
story += "a little too low. Not enough to be obvious but enough ";
story += "to notice. The makeup was flawless and gave the impression ";
story += "that she wore none at all. Her skin has a pearl-like ";
story += "glow below the surface. Archer figured the message was that she ";
story += "got what she wanted and was worth every penny on any exchange.";
reader_txt.text = story;
reader_txt.scroll = false;
wheelMover = new Object();
wheelMover.onMouseWheel = function(mover) {
    if (mover == -3) {
        line_mc._y += 20;
    } else {
        line_mc._y -= 20;
    }
};
Mouse.addListener(wheelMover);
```

Figure 7.7 shows the text field with the "reader bar" controlled by the mouse wheel highlighting a segment of text.

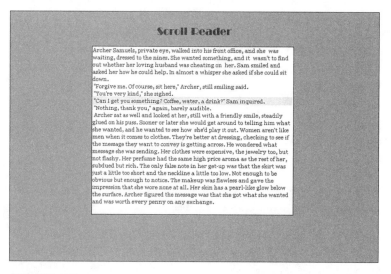

FIGURE 7.7   A reader bar controlled by the mouse wheel highlights each line of text.

In using the `Mouse` class, you are using a different set of tools than you are when a mouse event is part of another class's event set. For example, the line

```
someMc_mc.onMouseMove=function() {
    //some actions
}
```

does not use the `Mouse` class. Rather, it uses the mouse event that's part of the `MovieClip` class. Whether you use the `Mouse` class or an event reading the mouse as an event associated with another class depends on what you need to accomplish. Because you can associate a mouse event with different objects using a listener, the `Mouse` class gives you a good deal of flexibility.

In Brief

- The `Selection` class gives the designer the ability to trap information about selected portions of text.

- With the `PrintJob` class, you can print selected portions of text on a page.

- The `ContextMenu` class provides an additional resource for user input and designer control of a page. No Stage real estate has to be used for pop-up selection of a context menu.

- Text components make it easy to create complex text fields for automatic scrolling, input, and labels in your documents, and you can change their color to fit your design palette.

- The `Mouse` class can be used to listen to different mouse events on the Stage, including changes in the mouse wheel.

Navigation

Flash Navigation Strategies

The major attraction for Web site users is *content*. Good design and smooth navigation to the desired content is a winning combination for any site. So before we delve into the details of using Flash to build different navigation devices, a quick review of Flash navigation strategies will provide a context for understanding the Flash navigation tools.

Keyframes, Scenes, and Buttons

The most fundamental Flash navigation strategy is to provide content stored in different keyframes and scenes. The developer designs the navigation so that when the user clicks a button, the application jumps to a keyframe or scene containing the desired content.

Loading When Needed

A second Flash navigation strategy loads materials from external sources. To avoid long loading times, graphics, movie clips, text and all audio/video files are loaded when requested by the user. All loading times are minimized because the external files are far smaller than a larger SWF file containing all the content. In Chapter 5, "Movie Clip Control," the example that dynamically loads the contact and registration SWF files illustrates such use of external loading. Likewise, Chapter 6, "Viewing and Entering Information with Text Fields," shows how to use the LoadVars class to dynamically load external text.

A new feature in Flash MX 2004 is the ability to load FLV files dynamically. Chapter 10, "Adding Video and Sound," shows how to use the `NetStream` and `NetConnection` classes to do this. With this feature, large video files can be downloaded progressively rather than as part of a large SWF file. These quasi-streaming files can be used to provide information about content, or they can be a direct part of navigation by providing instructions on where to find content. Because FLV video files are not stored in the SWF, even a small, quickly loading SWF file can be used to play the FLV file.

External Links

A third type of navigation strategy using Flash is linking to external Web pages. These pages may or may not contain Flash SWF files, but assuming that they do, an entire Web site can be built with a model not unlike those anchored in HTML. With the full file organization capability provided by programs such as Macromedia Dreamweaver and Adobe GoLive, the navigation and link maintenance can be done in conjunction with Web development applications.

Thinking Buttons and Navigation

In addition to its original humble beginnings as a symbol, the Flash Pro button now has a `Button` class as well as a Button component. Buttons have long alerted users to the fact that they are something special by their ability to change when the mouse moves over their hit area. However, in more sophisticated rich Internet applications (RIAs), buttons often need to provide more information to the user in a navigation context, whether by appearing selected or having a changed status. In the following subsections, the discussion focuses on ways to use buttons in navigation and the Flash Pro capabilities related to button use.

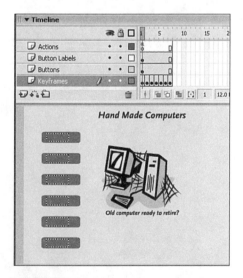

FIGURE 8.1 The navigation menu is seen in all frames.

Simple Button Navigation

The simplest navigation is one where clicking a button jumps the user to a different frame. By placing the menu in a separate layer, you can cause all the keyframes containing unique materials to employ a common set of menu buttons. Figure 8.1 shows a simple setup with six buttons. Each of the buttons, when clicked, stops the movie at a different keyframe.

The Keyframes layer contains seven keyframes. Each button is topped with a dynamic text field for template use. The developer can reuse the template by simply dynamically adding different text content to the text fields. The text fields are assigned sequential instance names, beginning with `nav1_txt` and ending with nav6_txt. The buttons are also named sequentially, from nav1_btn to nav6_btn. If more buttons and text fields are required, both the new labels and additional buttons are easy to add or change within an existing loop. The script in Listing 8.1 shows how different products displayed on the buttons can be placed into an array and then placed in the different text fields.

LISTING 8.1 A Simple Button-Driven Navigation System (NavBtns.fla)

```
stop();
var labelStore:Array = new Array("Accessories", "Printers");
labelStore.push("Monitors", "WebCams", "Software", "Computers");
fullHouse = labelStore.length+1;
for (x=1; x<fullHouse; x++) {
    _level0["nav"+x+"_btn"].enabled = true;
    _level0["nav"+x+"_txt"].autoSize = true;
    _level0["nav"+x+"_txt"].text = labelStore.pop();
}
nav1_btn.onPress = function() {
    gotoAndStop(2);
};
nav2_btn.onPress = function() {
    gotoAndStop(3);
};
nav3_btn.onPress = function() {
    gotoAndStop(4);
};
nav4_btn.onPress = function() {
    gotoAndStop(5);
};
nav5_btn.onPress = function() {
    gotoAndStop(6);
};
nav6_btn.onPress = function() {
    gotoAndStop(7);
};
```

Figure 8.2 shows a typical page selected using this navigation system.

Although this navigation system is simple and quite workable for smaller sites, it is limited. Each of the seven keyframes contains text and graphics and compiles to a file size of about 20KB. This size is well within the acceptable size range, but for a site with more graphic elements, this type of design can quickly become quite heavy.

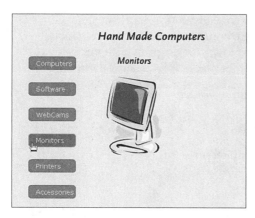

FIGURE 8.2 Each frame displays a different product image.

Project: Adding Flexibility with Event Objects

The Button UI component brings together several different features that allow dynamic change in buttons. Working with the component buttons and the Component Inspector, you can change initial settings dynamically using ActionScript. The navigation strategy is based on changes in the set of navigational buttons and loading external files rather than a series of keyframes, as was done in the previous section. This strategy is flexible so that updating content is simple.

So that you can see how this type of navigational system is set up, this next example demonstrates one set of navigation buttons with two major navigation categories. The user selects from the Dogs and Cats categories, and depending on the selected category, the main set of navigation buttons become enabled and relabeled with the subcategories (breeds, in the example). Once the group category is selected, the selection from the subcategory loads a JPEG image of the breed as a puppy or kitten. Figure 8.3 shows the basic layout of the page along with the relevant layers.

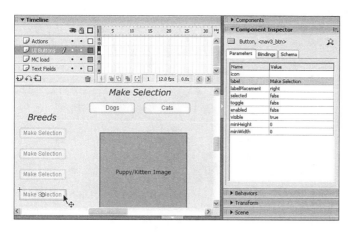

FIGURE 8.3 Setting the UI Button parameters.

Follow these steps to create this dynamic navigational system:

1. Open a new document and create four layers, naming them from top to bottom, Actions, UI Buttons, MC load, and Text Fields.

2. Select the MC load layer, and in the middle of the screen draw a rectangle with the dimensions W=190, H=162. Select the rectangle and press the F8 key to convert it into a movie clip. Give the movie clip the instance name loader_mc. Lock the layer.

3. Select the UI Buttons layer. Drag four UI buttons from the Components panel and place them to the left of the rectangle, as shown in Figure 8.3. From top to bottom, give them the instance names nav0_btn to nav3_btn. In the Component Inspector, add the label value **Make Selection** for each button, and set the "enabled" property to false. When the document is first launched, none of this set of buttons is enabled. The script enables the buttons.

4. Once the first four UI buttons are in place, drag two more UI buttons to the Stage, positioning them at the top of the screen, as shown in Figure 8.3. Label the one on the left **Dogs** and the one on the right **Cats**, using the Component Inspector. Provide the instance names dogs_btn and cats_btn for the left and right buttons, respectively. Leave the other button settings at their default values. Lock the UI Buttons layer.

5. Select the Text Fields layer and add two static text labels, **Breeds** and **Make Selection**, as shown in Figure 8.3.

6. Click the first frame in the Actions layer and add the following script:

```
//Place the label for the dogs and cats into arrays
var dogs:Array = new Array("Collie", "Boxer");
dogs.push("Swissie", "Terrier");
var cats:Array = new Array("Siamese", "Burmese");
cats.push("Exotic", "Korat");
//Create a listener object
var petList:Object = new Object();
petList.click = function(eventObj:Object) {
    var pet:String = eventObj.target.label;
    loadMovie(pet+".jpg", loader_mc);
};
dogs_btn.onPress = function() {
    for (var x = 0; x<dogs.length; x++) {
        _level0["nav"+x+"_btn"].enabled = true;
        _level0["nav"+x+"_btn"].label = dogs[x];
        _level0["nav"+x+"_btn"].addEventListener("click", petList);
    }
};
cats_btn.onPress = function() {
    for (var x = 0; x<cats.length; x++) {
        _level0["nav"+x+"_btn"].enabled = true;
        _level0["nav"+x+"_btn"].label = cats[x];
        _level0["nav"+x+"_btn"].addEventListener("click", petList);
    }
};
```

The script uses an event object. When an event occurs, an event object is passed as a parameter to a listener. Among other things, an event object contains information about the component that broadcasts an event. Thus, by subscribing the UI component buttons to a single listener using an event object instead of creating an unnamed function for each button, you can use a script to find the label name of the button that set off the event. In addition, the script requires less coding, and the navigation system is easier to update. In the script, the section

```
petList.click = function(eventObj:Object) {
    var pet:String = eventObj.target.label;
    loadMovie(pet+".jpg", loader_mc);
};
```

uses an event object to find the label of the button that broadcasts the event. In turn, the label name provides the name of the JPEG file to load into the movie clip, `loader_mc`. By coordinating the names of the files with the label names of the buttons, updating is simply a matter of changing the element names in the arrays. Thus, not only is the navigation system easy to update, it's flexible enough to use in any number of different applications.

When you run the program, the Breeds buttons change dynamically to either dog or cat breeds. When a button is clicked, the appropriate image appears. Figure 8.4 shows what you get when the Dogs option has been selected and the Swissie button is clicked.

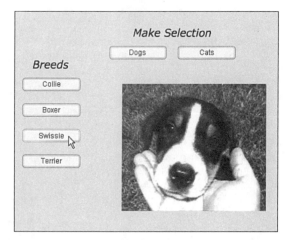

FIGURE 8.4   Button labels and functions change depending on which main category is selected.

The primary advantage of employing this form of navigation system is that not all images are loaded simultaneously in keyframes, and you can use fewer buttons on the Stage to accomplish a far wider range of navigation options. In addition, changing the contents of the navigation buttons is quite simple.

Navigating to External Documents

Navigation in Flash may involve navigating to external sites or to different HTML pages within a single site. Depending on the nature of the site you're building, external navigation can be preferable over using a single Flash page and loading different movie clips and text files. Alternatively, external navigation can be used to open an external page while keeping the current document on the page. Whatever the case, calling external URLs is one of the fundamental options you need to understand.

SHOP TALK

Choosing Between Internal and External Navigation Elements

If you load a large file containing all the images, code, and text in a multiple-frame Flash document in a single load, the user only has to wait through a preloader show once. All navigation after this initial load is "internal"—that is, the user-selected changes are from one keyframe to another, with no new material loaded. The plus side of this kind of navigation system is that once the document is in memory in the user's computer, all navigation is almost instantaneous.

The other navigation strategy is something like simple HTML page navigation using links. Everything is on a separate page, and navigation is a matter of loading one page after another. Heavy pages will take a long time to load, and light pages will be pretty quick on the initial go-round. After the initial viewing, the pages are cached, and the navigation is very quick. With Flash, instead of loading new pages, you can load different movie clips (SWF files), text files, graphics, and video files (FLV files) onto the same page as the user makes selections. However, the process of loading one item at a time also involves having the user wait a moment for each initial viewing.

The best navigation and loading strategy depends on the nature of the files being loaded. If you have a lot of text files the user must navigate among, you should definitely load those separately. If a lot of text is placed in a Flash document, it becomes very sluggish. External text loads very quickly, and as soon as a user clicks a navigation element that will show text, the text comes up almost immediately. If you have a single large graphic that a user may or may not choose to view, it, too, should be external. Unnecessarily loading any optional graphics makes little sense.

Any graphics and text that make up the navigation system or repeated background elements should be loaded when the initial movie loads. For large sites, you may find that a navigation system can be built around a central "mother ship" document used to load and unload movie clips. Using dynamic navigation labels with UI buttons or other UI components, you can maintain a robust site with only the labels in the navigation system changing depending on the user's selections.

For truly professional efforts, sites need to be tested on the different bandwidths likely to be used by the target audience. Testing only on phone modem connections may be fine for some of your audience, but this can lead to a navigational nightmare for users with broadband connections. Testing your navigation only on broadband connections when your audience is a mix of phone modem and broadband users is equally hazardous. Fortunately, Flash provides the flexibility to allow for several different combinations of internal and external navigation options, and you need to test (not just consider) which best fits your audience's needs.

Using getURL for External Navigation

Most experienced Flash users are familiar with the getURL() function for linking to other Web pages. The format for the function is as follows:

```
getURL("url", [window], [variables]);
```

For the most part, the function is used only with the URL or a URL and a window. If the address is within an HTML frameset, the window is the name of the frame. For example, the following line opens the document in a frame named "vacation":

```
getURL("http://www.sandlandmagic.com", vacation);
```

Likewise, the window can be one of these general target names:

- **_self**—The current frame

- **_blank**—A new window

- **_parent**—The parent of the current frame

- **_top**—The current window's top-level frame

For example, one way to keep the current page on the screen while bringing in an external page is to use the _blank window selection.

Where variables are to be passed, the third parameter is GET or POST. The GET method, employed with a small number of variables, simply appends the variables to the end of the URL, whereas the POST method sends the variables as a separate HTTP header. The POST method is favored for longer lists of variables. For example, the following uses the POST method for sending variables:

```
getURL("PHP/contact.php", _self, POST);
```

Flash uses "sandbox security" so that only addresses to the current domain are available without using Flash Remoting. The LoadVars() class is generally favored when passing variables over getURL() because you can send and load variables using LoadVars().

Using the ComboBox Component with External Links

With external links, you may want to minimize occupying the user's screen real estate. After all, clicking an external link may cause the user to leave the current site. One solution is to use a pop-up menu in which a single small object can be opened to reveal a list of link options. The link options are available but don't clutter the document or take up screen space.

The ComboBox UI component is one of Flash's pop-up menus. The ComboBox shares many of the same features as the List UI component (see the next section), so understanding how to use one helps in understanding how to use the other. If you're familiar with using ComboBox from Flash MX, be advised that like most other components in Flash MX 2004, the ComboBox and its associated properties, methods, and event handling have changed.

The basic format for using the ComboBox takes advantage of the change event. Whenever any of the options in a ComboBox is clicked, the option is selected, triggering a change event. Using an event listener object, as soon as the change event occurs, a specified callback function fires. The general format is as follows:

```
var callbackListener:Object = new Object();
callbackListener.change = function() {
    //Callback script goes here
};
ComboBoxInstance_cb.addEventListener("change", callbackListener);
```

Instead of adding a listener, the script uses an event listener (addEventListener) that listens for the specified object's use of an event. Typically, the callback associated with a ComboBox UI component uses either the label or data value, or both. If you're familiar with using the ComboBox UI component in Flash MX, you'll notice some important differences. The label and data values are accessed using the following formats for the selected label and data, respectively:

```
var myData= ComboBoxInstance_cb.selectedItem.label
```

```
var myData= ComboBoxInstance_cb.selectedItem.data
```

The following simple example shows how to use the change event and get data information from a ComboBox component:

FIGURE 8.5 Entering data values for a ComboBox UI component.

1. Open a new document and drag a ComboBox component from the Components panel to the Stage. Provide the instance name links_cb for the ComboBox on the Stage.

2. Open the Component Inspector and click the Parameters tab. Click the Value column in the data row. A Values window opens. Click the plus (+) button and enter a pound sign in quotes ("#"). Keep clicking the plus button and add new values until you have the values shown in Figure 8.5.

3. Repeat step 2 but click the Value column in the labels row of the Values window. Use these values:

- **0**—Select Link
- **1**—Sandlight Productions
- **2**—Design Street
- **3**—Macromedia
- **4**—W3 Consortium

Select Link is displayed in the window of the ComboBox on the Stage. Each of the labels is linked to the data value in the respective row. (For example, the label value Sandlight Productions is linked to the data value www.sandlight.com.)

4. Click the first frame of the sole layer and enter the following script:

```
var linkNow:Object = new Object();
linkNow.change = function() {
    if (links_cb.selectedItem.data != "#") {
        _level0.getURL("http://"+links_cb.selectedItem.data, _blank);
    }
};
links_cb.addEventListener("change", linkNow);
```

Note that the first label, Select Link, simply serves as an instructional label. Its data is the pound (#) sign; when it's selected, the pound sign can be trapped by a conditional statement that won't try to find a Web page by that name.

Using Navigation Tools to Compile Data

Using a broader conceptualization of navigation, the UI components in Flash Pro can be employed in a wider role than simply loading new materials, changing frames, or linking to external pages. The information in one UI component can be passed to another UI component and/or another UI element in Flash. For example, the List component can be used as a selection menu to place information into another List component. The List UI component is very similar to the ComboBox component in that it provides label and data parameters that can be added either in the Component Inspector or dynamically with code.

Project: Passing Information Dynamically

So you can see how to pass label and data information dynamically, this next example uses two List UI components and a dynamic text field. The following steps show you how to set it up:

1. Open a new document and create layers with the following names, working from top to bottom: Actions, List Box, Text Field, and Labels.

2. In the List Box layer, drag two List UI components to the Stage. Provide the instance names menu_lb and order_lb. Select the menu_lb List component, open the Component Inspector, click the Value column in the labels row on the Parameters tab, and add the values Hamburger, Hot Dog, French Fries, Onion Rings, and Soda, as shown in Figure 8.6.

3. With the menu_lb List component selected, click the Value column of the data row on the Parameters tab to open the Values window. Then add the following data values: 0=1.99, 1=1.25, 2=.50, 3=1.00, and 4=.75.

4. Select the Text Field layer and add a dynamic text field with the instance name total_txt.

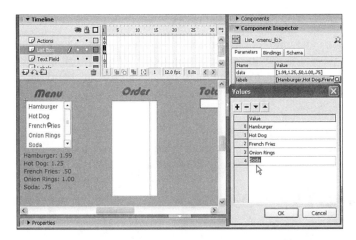

FIGURE 8.6 Adding labels to the `menu_lb` List UI component.

5. Select the Labels layer and add the labels shown in Figures 8.6 and 8.7 to the Stage.

6. Select the first frame of the Actions layer, and in the Actions panel, add the following script:

```
var toOrder:Object = new Object();
var toDelete:Object = new Object();
var amount_num:Number = 0;
var total_num:Number = 0;
var subNow_num:Number = 0;
toOrder.change = function() {
    order_lb.addItem(menu_lb.selectedItem.label, menu_lb.selectedItem.data);
    amount_num = parseFloat(menu_lb.selectedItem.data);
    total_num += amount_num;
    total_txt.text = "$"+total_num;
};
toDelete.change = function() {
    subNow_num = parseFloat(order_lb.selectedItem.data);
    total_num -= subNow_num;
    total_txt.text = "$"+total_num;
    order_lb.removeItemAt(order_lb.selectedIndex);

};
menu_lb.addEventListener("change", toOrder);
order_lb.addEventListener("change", toDelete);
```

In the script, the two List components use two different callbacks:

- **toOrder**—This callback takes the label and data information and passes it to the order_lb List component. In addition, the toOrder callback uses a variable to keep a running total in the text field. Therefore, whenever an item in the menu is clicked, the label and data (price) of the item are cumulatively added to the order list, and the running total is displayed in the text field.

- **toDelete**—This callback simply removes the selected item in the Order List UI component. At the same time, it decrements the running total so that the correct total is maintained at all times. Figure 8.7 shows the completed movie working.

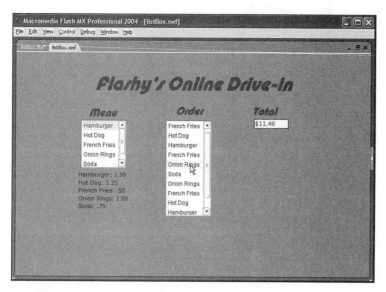

FIGURE 8.7   Two List UI components tracking orders.

The advantage of using UI components beyond standard notions of navigation is that they make it easy for the user to make selections from a broad category of options. At the same time, using components in this manner reduces the amount of development time.

Focus Navigation

When any object on the Stage is selected, it has focus. This section examines the process of arranging how each object comes to the user's focus. Some objects, especially buttons, come into focus because the user selects one by clicking it. Others come into focus when the user presses the Tab key, making the next object in the tab line come into focus. By arranging the ways in which different objects come into focus, the designer can optimize the navigation system and assist the user in navigating through a site.

Setting Tabs

Whenever the Tab key is pressed, the cursor jumps to the next object in the tab index. The tab index for objects on the Stage can be handled in various ways. The most basic settings occur by the order in which they're placed on the Stage, from left to right and top to bottom. The initial objects are given lower settings. Suppose you place eight input text fields on the Stage in two columns of four. The automatic tab index begins with the upper-left object, with tabs jumping first to the right column and then to the next row. However, if you place eight TextInput UI components on the Stage, their tab order follows the order in which they were placed on the Stage. Rather than trying to remember the tab order of different objects placed on the Stage, an easier solution is to establish the order of the objects once they're in their final design positions.

To see the first method for ordering a tab index, follow these steps:

1. Place six TextInput UI components on the Stage. Scramble them so that you don't remember the order in which you placed them, and then organize them into two columns of three each.

2. Select Window, Other Panels, Accessibility to open the Accessibility panel. Select View, Show Tab Order from the main menu.

3. Select the TextInput object you want to use as the first item in the tab index. When you select the object, the Accessibility panel changes to show a Tab Index window at the bottom of the panel. Type the tab index value **1**. As soon as you type a value, that value appears in the upper-left corner of the TextInput instance. Figure 8.8 shows a completed set of TextInput instances with the Show Tab Order option selected.

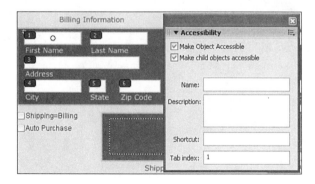

FIGURE 8.8   Viewable tab index.

The visible tab index values only appear on those objects that have their tab index set using the Accessibility window. Those set with the default values of their position or those set using ActionScript 2.0 will not display tab index numbers.

At the same time that the tab index is established using this method, the objects with no instance names are given instance names. UI components are treated as movie clips, and so they're named MovieClip$N$, with N being the value of the tab index. Text fields are named Text$N$, and buttons are Button$N$. If the object has an instance name, no new name is generated.

A final way to set the tab index for objects involves using ActionScript. The format is

```
instanceName.tabIndex = N;
```

where *N* is an integer. This method allows for dynamic change in an instance's tab position.

Custom Focus Navigation

A new feature of Flash MX 2004 is the focus manager and focusManager class. Using the focus manager, you can add more control to the current focus of your document. In addition, the focusManager class allows you to send a button click to a button remotely. When the focus manager is used in conjunction with other UI components, you can summarize your coding in callouts that can be used by more than a single object. For example, some commercial sites have auto-order options that combine several elements, including clicking a Submit Order button. Using the FocusManager, when the Auto Order button is clicked, it in turn "clicks" the Submit Order button.

The class's inheritance path is as follows:

```
UIObject > UIComponent > focusManager
```

Therefore, it's primarily a tool for use with UI components and can't be applied to primitive text fields and buttons. Tables 8.1 and 8.2 summarize the focusManager class methods and properties.

TABLE 8.1

The focusManager **Class Methods**

METHOD	ACTIONS
focusManager.getFocus()	Returns the name of the object that currently has focus
focusManager.sendDefaultPushButtonEvent()	Initiates a click event in the default push button listener
focusManager.setFocus(IN)	Sets focus to instance IN

TABLE 8.2

The focusManager **Class Properties**

PROPERTY	CHARACTERISTICS
focusManager.defaultPushButton	A push button UI instance assigned to this property can be clicked through script that sends the default push button event. This property essentially specifies the default push button for an application.
focusManager.defaultPushButtonEnabled	A Boolean value determines whether the auto push button event is turned on or off.
focusManager.enabled	A Boolean value determines whether Focus Manager tab handling is enabled.
focusManager.nextTabIndex	Sets the next value in a tab index sequence.

When part of a site's navigation involves filling out a form, one helpful step you can take using the Focus Manager is to place the cursor in the first TextInput box. By using the format

```
focusManager.setFocus(instanceName);
```

you cause a blinking I-beam cursor to automatically appear in the specified field. If you make sure that the tab index is set so that the next object is the one that should be filled in or clicked next, the user can easily tab from one task to the next.

Some ebusiness sites make it easier for the user to make a purchase by having an automatic ordering system. Typically, an Auto Order check box or some similar object is used to "click" a Confirm and Order button. Separate callbacks normally would have to be written for such an operation, but using the focusManager class, you can use a single callback to both indicate an automatic order and click the button to complete the order. The script in Listing 8.2 shows the general format for using focusManager in this manner.

LISTING 8.2 Generic Setup for Sending a Click Event to a Button

```
//Assign default push button
focusManager.defaultPushButton = confirm_pb;
//Callback to automatically press button
//Automatically click button
var autoClick:Object = new Object();
autoClick.click = function() {
    if (auto_cb.selected == true) {
        focusManager.sendDefaultPushButtonEvent();
    }
};
auto_cb.addEventListener("click", autoClick);
//PushButton Callback
var completeOrder:Object = new Object();
completeOrder.click = function() {
    //code for completing order
};
confirm_pb.addEventListener("click", completeOrder);
```

After a button has been assigned to be the default, any reference to focusManager.sendDefaultPushButtonEvent() has the effect of clicking the button. Therefore, in the preceding example, if the check box is selected, the callback function that the button is "listening" for is fired.

Project: Controlling the Focus

A simple example will help to show you how all this works in a practical application. Use the following steps to set up this example, which uses TextInput, CheckBox, and PushButton UI components with the `focusManager` class:

1. Open a new document and set it to 650×450 with five layers. From top to bottom, name the layers Actions, Labels, Text Fields, Components, and Background.

2. In the Background layer, draw two rectangles with the dimensions 266×128 and place them next to one another. Beneath the two rectangles, draw one rectangle with the dimensions 233×80 and another 139×65 (see Figures 8.9 and 8.10). Lock the layer.

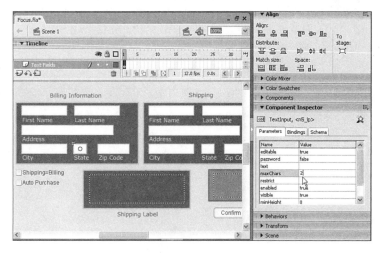

FIGURE 8.9 Setting the maximum characters allowed for a TextInput UI component.

3. Click the Text Fields layer and drag 12 TextInput UI components to the Stage, placing six in the top-left background rectangle and six in the top-right background rectangle, as shown in Figures 8.9 and 8.10. In the Instance Name text box in the Properties panel, name the TextInput UI components `n1_ip` to `n6_ip` in the left rectangle and `ns1_ip` to `ns6_ip` in the right rectangle, proceeding from left to right and top to bottom. Name the bottom-left text field `fullInfo_txt` and the bottom-right text field `cusNote_txt`. Using Figures 8.9 and 8.10 as guides, adjust the widths of the TextInput UI components. Lock the layer.

4. In the Components layer, add two CheckBox UI components, placing them beneath the top-right rectangle. Name the top check box `shipBill_cb` and the bottom one `auto_cb`. Drag a Button UI component to the Stage, placing it beneath the lower-right rectangle, and name it `confirm_pb`. Lock the layer.

5. With the Labels layer selected, add the labels as shown in Figures 8.9 and 8.10.

6. Unlock the Text Fields layer, select the TextInput components labeled State, open the Component Inspector, select the Parameters tab, and type **2** in the Value column next to maxChars. Then select the TextInput component labeled Zip Code and type **5** in the Value column next to maxChars in the Component Inspector. Figure 8.10 shows this process.

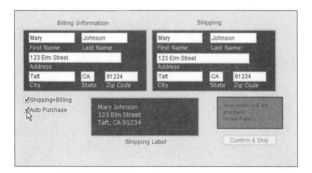

FIGURE 8.10 Once the first information set is completed by the user, the rest can be completed automatically.

7. Click the first frame in the Actions layer and enter the following script:

```
//Enable focus manager and select first input box
focusManager.enabled = true;
focusManager.setFocus(n1_ip);
//Set tab order for check boxes and confirm button
shipBill_cb.tabIndex = 7;
auto_cb.tabIndex = 8;
//Set Tab Order Billing Info
for (x=1; x<7; x++) {
    _level0["n"+x+"_ip"].tabIndex = x;
}
//Set Tab Order Shipping Info
for (x=1; x<7; x++) {
    _level0["ns"+x+"_ip"].tabIndex = x+8;
}
//Set confirm button to default
focusManager.defaultPushButton = confirm_pb;
//Callback for checkbox to see if shipping
//and billings addresses are the same
var checkShipping:Object = new Object();
checkShipping.click = function() {
    if (shipBill_cb.selected == true) {
        for (x=1; x<7; x++) {
```

```
                _level0["ns"+x+"_ip"].text = _level0["n"+x+"_ip"].text;
            }
        }
    };
    shipBill_cb.addEventListener("click", checkShipping);
    //Auto Ship clicks the Confirm and Ship button
    var checkAuto:Object = new Object();
    checkAuto.click = function() {
        if (auto_cb.selected == true) {
            focusManager.sendDefaultPushButtonEvent();
            confirm_pb.enabled = false;
        }
    };
    auto_cb.addEventListener("click", checkAuto);
    //Confirm and Send Order
    var sendOrder:Object = new Object();
    sendOrder.click = function() {
        for (x=1; x<7; x++) {
            if (x == 2 || x == 3) {
                fullInfo_txt.text += _level0["ns"+x+"_ip"].text+newline;
            } else if (x == 1 || x == 5) {
                fullInfo_txt.text += _level0["ns"+x+"_ip"].text+" ";
            } else if (x == 4) {
                fullInfo_txt.text += _level0["ns"+x+"_ip"].text+", ";
            } else {
                fullInfo_txt.text += _level0["ns"+x+"_ip"].text;
            }
        }
        cusNote_txt.text = "Your order will be shipped immediately.";
    };
    confirm_pb.addEventListener("click", sendOrder);
```

Because checking the Auto Purchase check box literally causes the Confirm button to be clicked, the callback that is used to "click" the button also disables it. In this way, the user will not accidentally make double orders by clicking it a second time. This line disables the Confirm button:

```
confirm_pb.enabled = false;
```

One of the interesting aspects of using focusManager.sendDefaultPushButtonEvent() is that it can fire a callback associated with a push button, even if the button is disabled. Therefore, although disabling the button will prevent the user from accidentally clicking it, the disabled button can still be "clicked" by the Focus Manager.

Establishing Mutually Exclusive Options

The main difference between the CheckBox and RadioButton UI components is that radio buttons are designed to be mutually exclusive. That is, if one button in a radio button group is selected, all others are unselected. Used in situations where the designer requires a mutually exclusive or forced choice, the radio button has several applications. For example, in determining individual income, users are far more likely to respond if given a grouping of salary ranges, where only one choice is possible, than if asked to type in their exact annual salaries. Other groups are inherently mutually exclusive, such as gender. If a person is of one gender, she or he is not of the other gender. The following example shows what happens when you place radio buttons in a group where only a single button can be selected:

1. Open a new document with one layer named Actions and the other layer Radio Button.

2. Select the Radio Button layer, drag two RadioButton UI components to the Stage, and provide the instance name male_rb for one and female_rb for the other.

3. In the Parameters tab of the Component Inspector, select each component on the Stage and type **"gender"** for the groupName value. In the Value column of the label row, name one **"Male"** and the other **"Female"**.

4. Finally, select the first frame in the Actions layer and enter the following script:

```
//The radio group "gender" is placed in the
//Component inspector for each instance in
//the group but can be done with code. e.g.,
//male_rb.groupName="gender";
//female_rb.groupName="gender";
//
var radioListen:Object = new Object();
radioListen.click = function() {
    if (male_rb.selected == true) {
        trace("Male");
    } else {
        trace("Female");
    }
};
gender.addEventListener("click", radioListen);
```

When you test the movie, as soon as you select one of the buttons, the other becomes unselected. You can use as many radio buttons in a group as you want, and yet only a single selection is allowed at any one time. If for any reason you need for your radio button instances to change groups or labels, you can perform group and label assignment using code instead of the Component Inspector.

In Brief

- Using keyframes and buttons, you can create simple or sophisticated navigation systems.

- To keep the main movie file size small, you can create navigation by loading external SWF, JPEG, and text files.

- Information can be presented on buttons and other navigation components.

- Event objects allow for sophisticated and "thinking" navigation models.

- Navigation models can include both internal and external links.

- Focus navigation aids the user in moving through a site.

- Mutually exclusive and forced limited option selections can be accomplished using radio buttons.

Producing Online Slide Shows

Using Screen Slides

A new feature available only in Flash MX Professional 2004 is the slide feature. Slides work within a hierarchy, with the highest-level features inherited by the lower-level slides. Using slides makes it easy to create a slide presentation that can be presented sequentially by a speaker or can be self-paced by a user.

In the most fundamental sense, the higher-level slides constitute templates for the lower-level slides. You can place a company logo or some other branding feature on a higher-level slide, and it appears in all lower-level slides, helping to organize a coherent and consistent presentation. Likewise, slides can contain movie clips or other Flash features such as buttons and shapes.

Starting a Screen Presentation

To begin working with a screen document, select Flash Slide Presentation when opening a new document. When you open a screen presentation document, the default page shows a column to the left of the Stage containing icons for two slides with the default instance names *presentation* and *slide1*. (These names can be changed to any instance name you want.)

To create a slide show, all you need to do is to add slides by selecting Insert, Screen from the main menu. To add a screen as a child of another screen, select Insert, Nested Screen. On each slide, you can add graphic and text content, including movie clips. The slide page is just a new blank Flash page; therefore, whatever you can do with a Flash page, you can do with a slide show page.

Working with a Screen Hierarchy

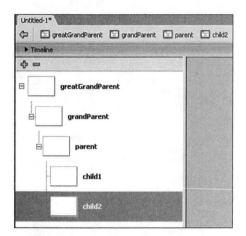

FIGURE 9.1   Each child inherits all the materials from its parental lineage.

In the top-level screen (with the default name *presentation*), you might place a company's logo and other branding or design materials. Likewise, the top-level page can be used to set up a navigation scheme. Because all other pages are nested into the presentation page, whatever is on that page appears on all other pages as well. Another way of putting it is that all children, grandchildren, and their children, *ad infinitum*, inherit the contents of their parental lineage. Figure 9.1 shows screen pages laid out in a parental hierarchy with the screen names reflecting their position in the hierarchy.

The screen at the very bottom of the hierarchy, child2, inherits the characteristics of greatGrandParent, grandParent, and parent. However, it doesn't inherit anything from child1, which is a sibling.

Screen Workflow

The workflow using slide screens is different from that when developing a typical Flash movie, because the layout is structured for a sequence of slides. After you first open a new slide presentation document, the next step is adding slides so that you'll have enough for the sequential screen presentation. Then you add a navigation system.

The navigation system is typically formatted as a Next/Previous slide set of buttons. However, you can set up a menu navigation or any other type you want, depending on the nature of the screens and the options for the user. The first slide after the initial presentation slide can be used as a menu, or a menu can be placed on the presentation slide itself.

The navigation system is set up on the basis of going to a particular slide, or the next or previous slide, not unlike going to a keyframe in the Timeline. Standard buttons can be used to effect navigation. For example, Figure 9.2 shows two graphic button symbols on the Stage used for going to the next and previous slides in a slide presentation designed to show different types of train cars. Because the buttons are placed in the initial slide, all other slides inherit the buttons and their functionality.

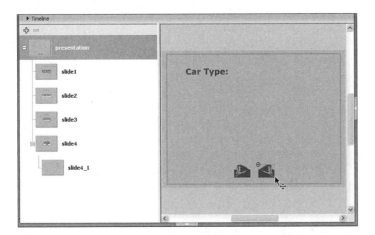

FIGURE 9.2 Navigation buttons placed in the presentation slide are inherited by all other slides.

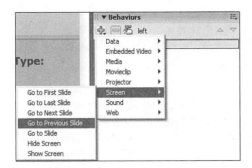

FIGURE 9.3 Adding code to a button on the initial slide.

No matter which child slide employs the buttons in the initial screen, the results are the same—going to the next or previous slide. Setting up the code for going to the next or previous screen, though, is quite different from simple actions to go to the next or previous keyframe. The easiest way to generate the code in this case is to use the Behaviors panel. For example, selecting the right button and adding code to go to the next frame requires only that you select the Add menu in the Behaviors panel and then choose Screen, Go to Previous Slide from the menu. Figure 9.3 shows this process.

Once the code has been added to the highest-level slide, it's employed by the button on all slides on all levels. As shown in the following code generated for the left button, the target is the screen instance of the `mx.screens.Slide` object:

```
on (release) {

    // GoTo Previous Screen behavior
    var screen = null;
    var target = this;
    while((screen == null) && (target != undefined) && (target != null))
    {
     if(target instanceof mx.screens.Screen)
     {
```

```
   screen = target;
  }
  else
  {
   target = target._parent;
  }
 }
 if(screen instanceof mx.screens.Slide)
 {
  screen.rootSlide.currentSlide.gotoPreviousSlide();
 }
 // End GoTo Previous Screen behavior
}
```

SHOP TALK

Are Slide Shows Just Like PowerPoint Presentations?

Flash Pro slide shows are to Microsoft PowerPoint as an Abrams tank is to a BB gun. First of all, PowerPoint has been the target of well-aimed assaults by both information design critics and educators for being a tool for transmitting shallow knowledge. (In fact, one PowerPoint presentation was dragged before a Congressional committee and cited as the reason why engineers were unable to communicate that the problems with the Columbia Space Shuttle were so severe that remedies should have been put into place to avert the re-entry disaster.) Perhaps Microsoft can borrow one of the NRA's slogan makers—PowerPoint doesn't cause crummy information; presenters do! Hence, comparing Flash slide shows with PowerPoint slide shows too closely sets them up to the same criticisms.

Aside from the fact that PowerPoint has been misused dreadfully and that it can be quite useful when employed judiciously, the comparison between Flash slide shows and PowerPoint slide shows envisions two different audiences. Flash is fundamentally a Web application, whereas PowerPoint is an application to be used "live." Using PowerPoint, a presenter with a laser pointer and a voice stands before a live audience and guides the hapless assemblage through a series of bulleted points and canned graphics they've seen in other presentations with totally different topics. With Flash slide shows, a speaker typically is not available, so the information needs to be rich enough so that the viewer need not wonder about a set of bulleted points consisting of what may appear to be disconnected thoughts. In fact, bulleted points should only appear in certain contexts and not forced on every page as PowerPoint templates encourage—a list of topics covered in the presentation should exhaust the bullets' usefulness. The reader can linger on a single "slide" in Flash presented over the Web or speed through a Flash slide presentation. Unlike live PowerPoint presentations, where the audience is forced to muzzle their cell

Going to the previous screen is a method within the screen class, shown in this line:

```
screen.rootSlide.currentSlide.gotoPreviousSlide();
```

Therefore, although the code is generated in the Behaviors panel, it can be done in the Actions panel with standard ActionScript 2.0.

Adding Content to Slides

The purpose of a slide presentation is to show content. Using the different tools available, anything that can be added to a Flash page can be added to a slide. For example, Figure 9.4 shows a slide (slide4) with a graphic (the tanker car), text (Tanker), and a button (the encircled *i* in the upper-right corner). The graphic was imported from a FreeHand drawing in its original vector graphic format.

phones and appear to be engaged, a Web audience not only can yak on the phone, they can respond to instant messages, eat a meatball sub, and change their kid's diapers while your slide show is making its debut. So the approach to a slide in a Flash slide show should be something more than a graphic and a list of information-poor bulleted points.

For anyone who has viewed the templates for the slide shows that accompany Flash MX Professional 2004, the comparison between Flash slide shows and PowerPoint presentations is clear. These templates serve to illustrate why Flash slide presentations should not attempt to ape PowerPoint presentations. (The use of 3D graphics in the Tech Slide presentation in depicting a pie chart only underlines the inability of the designer to select the right graphic to display information in the slide show—the pie chart looks like an oil storage tank at the moment it's struck by a smart bomb.) Although the templates certainly illustrate good-looking pages, they're as shallow in information as PowerPoint presentations. What's more, the PowerPoint presenter has the advantage of actually explaining a misunderstood point, whereas the Flash slide show must be dynamic and engaging without a charismatic speaker.

So for those of you wondering whether Flash slide presentations are something like PowerPoint, the answer is no. Flash has too many powerful tools to inform the viewer in both static and dynamic media to employ either the deadly dull bulleted list or the constrained graphics characteristic of PowerPoint presentations. Flash slide presentations have all the resources of Flash at hand. Also, keeping in mind that the Flash slide presentation viewer is sitting in an environment of other distractions, the slide show created in Flash needs to use the graphics, text, UI controls, FLV files, movie clips, ActionScript, and other tools at hand to get the information to the viewer while keeping his or her attention.

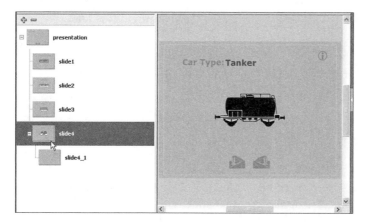

FIGURE 9.4   Added content and dimmed materials from parent slide.

Note that the features from the presentation slide can be seen in the background. All materials from parent slides that can be seen are "dimmed" (that is, they're visible but not on the slide itself). They cannot be moved or changed on the child slide.

If a slide is selected and you choose Insert, Nested Screen from the main menu, the inserted screen becomes a child of the selected slide. In Figure 9.5, all the features of both the parent slide (slide4) and the grandparent slide (presentation) are dimmed on the child slide (slide4_1).

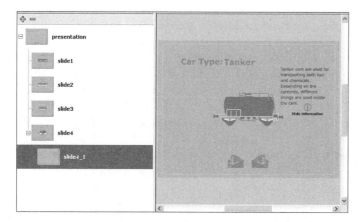

FIGURE 9.5   Added content and dimmed materials from the parent slides.

You can make the text block on slide4_1 visible or invisible by making the slide visible or invisible. The button on slide4_1 makes the slide invisible with the following script:

```
on (release) {
  // Hide Screen behavior
  if((this != undefined) && (this != null))
  {
```

```
    this.setVisible(false);
    }
    // End Hide Screen behavior
}
```

Generated in the Behaviors panel, the code is self-referent to the entire slide, not just the button. In other code, you'll see that the screen object contains the code, working like code assigned to a movie clip. (It works something like selecting a movie clip and then entering a script in the Actions panel for that clip.)

Creating Slide Transitions and Screen Events

A final feature that designers and developers can add to a slide show is a *transition*. You can add different types of transitions to your slides using the Behaviors panel, or you can create them using ActionScript 2.0. The entire slide is the target of the generated ActionScript, based on different events.

To create a transition, follow these steps:

1. In the Screen Outline pane, select the slide you want to use for the transition.

2. In the Behaviors panel, select the plus (+) sign, Screen, Transition. The Transitions dialog box appears, displaying transition options.

3. Select the transition you want in the transition window on the left of the dialog box. As you click each transition, a preview shows what the transition looks like with the default settings.

4. Set the standard parameters, including Direction, Duration, and Easing, as well as any special parameters unique to that transition. For example, Rotate can be set to Clockwise or Counterclockwise and the number of degrees. Figure 9.6 shows the settings for a Fade-in transition with a 1-second duration.

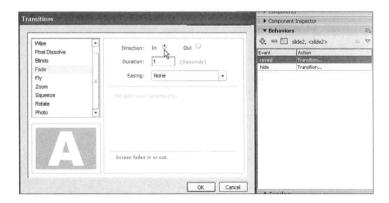

FIGURE 9.6 Setting a transition.

In the Event column of the Behaviors panel, the fade-in is set to occur when the slide is first revealed; therefore, the reveal event is selected. To create a fade-out effect (that is, when the slide show moves to another slide, it hides the current slide), you can create a second transition using the hide event that simply uses the same transition, except rather than the In radio button for Direction, you select the Out button instead. Once the transition settings have been completed, the following script appears in the Actions panel:

```
on (reveal) {
    // Transition behavior
    if (!eventObj.target._isSlide || (eventObj.target._isSlide &&
    ➥eventObj.target.currentSlide)) {
        mx.transitions.TransitionManager.start (eventObj.target,
            {type:mx.transitions.Fade,
            direction:0, duration:1, easing:mx.transitions.easing.None.easeNone,
            param1:empty, param2:empty});
        eventObj.target.__transitionManager._triggerEvent = eventObj.type;
    }
    // End Transition behavior
}
on (hide) {
    // Transition behavior
    if (!eventObj.target._isSlide || (eventObj.target._isSlide &&
    ➥eventObj.target.currentSlide)) {
        mx.transitions.TransitionManager.start (eventObj.target,
            {type:mx.transitions.Fade,
            direction:1, duration:1, easing:mx.transitions.easing.None.easeNone,
            param1:empty, param2:empty});
        eventObj.target.__transitionManager._triggerEvent = eventObj.type;
    }
    // End Transition behavior
}
```

To work with screens and events independent of the Behaviors panel and code them directly in the Actions panel, you may find it helpful to understand the different hierarchies involved. The events that are part of the Slide class are actually part of different hierarchies. First, the "pure" Screen class (API) is part of the following hierarchy:

```
UIObject > UIComponent > View > Loader > Screen
```

The events in the Behaviors panel or in the Flash Screen classes show far more than the events in the Screen API. Only the following are actually part of the Screen class:

- allTransitionsInDone
- allTransitionsOutDone
- mouseDown
- mouseDownSomewhere
- mouseMove
- mouseOut
- mouseOver
- mouseUp
- mouseUpSomewhere

To see how to invoke an event with script on a slide, add a new slide to a slide presentation and then draw a large *X* using the Paintbrush tool on the slide. Then select the slide and enter the following script:

```
on(mouseUp) {
    trace("The mouse on slide " + eventObj.target._name + " is up.");
}
```

When you test the movie, the hand icon indicating a hot spot appears only if the cursor is over the *X*. This indicates that the slide itself is not the entire slide area as far as the mouseUp event is concerned. However, if you employ the mouseUpSomewhere event, you can click anywhere on the slide to invoke the event.

The other events employed with the slide object and part of the Screen class include the following, shown with their hierarchies:

```
UIObject: MovieClip > UIObject
UIComponent: UIObject > UIComponent
Loader: UIObject > UIComponent > View > Loader
Slide: UIObject > UIComponent > View > Loader > Screen > Slide
```

The following events make up the rest of the events used with the Screen API, shown with their root classes:

- complete (Loader)
- draw (UIobject)
- focusIn (UIComponent)
- focusOut (UIComponent)
- hide (UIObject)
- hidechild (Slide)
- keyDown (UIComponent)
- keyUP (UIComponent)
- load (UIObject)
- move (UIObject)
- progress (Loader)
- resize (UIObject)
- reveal (UIObject)
- revealChild (Slide)
- unload (UIObject)

The majority of screen events are associated with other root classes.

Using Screen Forms

Forms are used for creating application states and used as graphic element containers. An *application state* refers to some condition that the application displays under given circumstances. For example, one application state may display a streaming video, and another application state may show a price list. Each individual application can be used to create any application state you want.

As graphic containers, forms can hold anything from standard graphics, such as JPEG photos, to graphic user interfaces. The forms themselves help organize the graphics, no matter what they are. Laid out in the Screen Outline pane, all the different parts of an application are visible to the designer.

Forms and slides are both part of the Screen class. Here is the form hierarchy:

```
UIObject > UIComponent > View >Loader > Screen > Form
```

The Slide and Form classes share identical higher-level hierarchies, both inheriting directly from the Screen class.

Organizing Materials in an Application with Forms

One way to think of forms and their use is as something like a vertical Timeline. Instead of the different application states or graphic elements contained in a keyframe, each one resides in a different form. Because you can only view a single keyframe at a time (because the playhead can be in only one place at a time), organizing a project with forms helps you to visualize an application during its development. The Screen Outline pane is the visual equivalent of the Timeline, except that you can see all the keyframes in a single eye span.

Each form element in a project can be visible or invisible at any one time. As a result, you can set up a project so that you can see some of the forms, all of them, or none at any one time. Navigation becomes a matter of hiding and showing different forms depending on what the user is doing.

Using Forms as Placeholders

One of the more dysfunctional temptations using forms is to create a wholly visual environment full of graphics, UI components, and other "heavy" elements (ones that take several kilobytes of space). The resulting SWF file may do everything you want, but the delay in loading the file is so long that users will be unhappy.

One solution to this problem is to use forms as placeholders. As a placeholder, the form serves to act as a loading platform for an external SWF or other file that can be loaded into Flash. As a result, the heaviest element will be the single heaviest item loaded and not the sum of all the elements loaded.

To create a simple but very functional form application using placeholders, just open a new form document and add five screens. You will now have a master form named *application* and five forms named with a sequence of names beginning with *form1*. The master form will serve as a navigation system that makes the different forms visible. Figure 9.7 shows a layout with five empty placeholder forms.

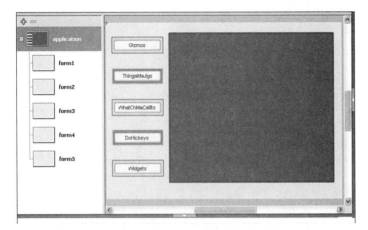

FIGURE 9.7 Empty forms as placeholders.

To load any external content into the form requires a simple line:

```
formInstance.contentPath="url";
```

This will do the trick because the Form class extends the Screen class, which in turn extends the Loader class. By using the reveal event as a trigger, whenever a form is selected, the external materials will load. For example, the following script, which is in the form itself, loads a SWF file called gizmo.swf:

```
on (reveal) {
    this.contentPath = "gizmo.swf";
}
```

The navigation system, made up of several UI Button components, needs only to show the right form when the user makes a selection. The handy Behaviors panel can be used to show a screen. For example, select Behavior Panel, plus (+) sign, Screen, Show Screen, and then select the screen you want in the Select Screen dialog box. Selecting form1 results in the following script:

```
on (click) {
// Show Screen behavior
        if((this._parent.form1 != undefined) && (this._parent.form1 != null))
```

```
        {
          var screen = null;
          var target = this;
          while((screen == null) && (target != undefined) && (target != null))
          {
            if(target instanceof mx.screens.Screen)
            {
              screen = target;
            }
            else
            {
              target = target._parent;
            }
          }
          this._parent.form1.setVisible(true);
if((screen != null) && (this._parent.form1 != screen.rootSlide.currentSlide))
          {
            screen.rootSlide.currentSlide.setVisible(false);
          }
        }
        // End Show Screen behavior
}
```

If each button is provided in the preceding script, when a button is clicked, the appropriate
screen is revealed. However, all the other forms must close as soon as any other screen is
revealed so that they're not mixed. Therefore, using the code generated in the Behaviors
panel, you need to add the following code for all other possibly open forms:

```
// Hide Screen behavior
      if((this._parent.form2 != undefined) && (this._parent.form2 != null))
      {
        this._parent.form2.setVisible(false);
      }
      // End Hide Screen behavior
```

The hiding screen behavior script will have to be added for all other forms other than the
one currently being opened. All the code for revealing the desired form and hiding the others
needs to be within a single click event for each button.

Although the Behaviors panel makes it easy to generate complex code, sometimes less is more. For example, rather than using the code generated by the Behaviors panel, the following script was created in the Actions panel and associated with each button. The following script is for the button that opens form1:

```
on (click {
    this._parent.form1.visible=true;
    this._parent.form2.visible=false;
    this._parent.form3.visible=false;
    this._parent.form4.visible=false;
    this._parent.form5.visible=false;
}
```

The visible property is part of the Form class (inherited from UIObject), and by setting it to true or false, you can cause any selected form to appear or hide. Once the form is made visible, the reveal event fires, loading the external file. For example, Figure 9.8 shows an FLV file playing in a media component inside an externally loaded SWF file.

FIGURE 9.8   An external SWF file loaded into a form playing an FLV file.

The linkage to the file being played as a progressive download has the sequence Form > SWF file with media player > FLV file. The complete SWF file with the five placeholder forms is only 35KB, and most of the file size is due to the Button component, not the five forms. The ThingaMaJig button in this example loads a 67KB SWF file containing a single MediaPlayback component (see Chapter 10, "Adding Video and Sound," for more information on this component), and it progressively downloads a 476KB FLV file that was compressed from a 41MB AVI file. Had the AVI file been imported directly into one of the forms for DSL/cable modem speed at 256KB, the entire movie including all the other placeholder forms would have compressed to about 396KB. A 396KB movie is far too large for use on the Internet, but one less than 10% that size (35KB) will work nicely.

Although forms may seem unwieldy at first glance, they can actually provide a very "thin" method of creating rich Internet applications (RIAs). The trick is to use forms as placeholders to load external materials. Any external videos should be streamed or delivered as progressive downloads to minimize the amount of time a user has to wait to see the materials being delivered. Likewise, other heavy content can be loaded from external sources as needed.

In Brief

- Slides allow developers to quickly construct presentations using simple "Next Slide" or sophisticated navigation systems.

- The screen hierarchy nests different elements in a presentation so that a single screen can acquire materials from both parent and child slides.

- The workflow for slides is unique in that the individual slides are the content containers rather than keyframes.

- Slides are designed for sequential presentations.

- Special-effect slide transitions are easily created using the Behaviors panel.

- Forms are used for creating application states and for graphic element containers.

- Using forms makes it easier to visually construct RIAs.

- Forms can be used as placeholders to keep an application's size small.

Adding Video and Sound

10

Adding Sound to Flash Movies

In the standard configuration without QuickTime 4 or later installed, you can import and play WAV (Windows only), AIFF (Macintosh only), or MP3 files for use with Flash Pro. A new Flash MX 2004 feature allows you to import AVI files; an option is available to separate the sound as a component in the Library panel. You can then use it for adding sound to your movie, discarding the video portion of the file. If you have QuickTime 4 or later installed, you can import the following:

- AIFF (Windows or Macintosh)

- QuickTime movies with sound only

- Sound Designer II (Macintosh)

- Sun AU

- System 7 Sounds (Macintosh)

- WAV (Windows or Macintosh)

The QuickTime player can be freely downloaded from www.apple.com; its main benefit is allowing the popular WAV files to be developed on Macintosh computers and AIFF files on Windows.

The three major types of sounds for use in Flash movies include music, sound effects, and narration. You can set most sound effects and narration files to very-low-quality mono settings without losing effective quality. The lower-quality and mono settings generate much smaller file sizes and reduce loading time. Music, however, is a different matter. Often, the left and right stereo tracks add important dimensions to music, and many of the subtle effects of music require higher KHz rates, resulting in larger file sizes. A stereo setting requires double the space of mono settings; if the sound you're using doesn't absolutely require stereo, don't use the stereo setting. Most of the important pondering decisions involve settings for music files. Narration and sound effects should be set to mono at the lower ranges.

Importing and Setting Sounds

You can best optimize your files if you take care of their file size settings before importing them into Flash. Flash has a limited number of sound settings, and although some of the settings are key ones, you're better off optimizing sound in your sound editor.

Importing sound is quite easy. Select File, Import to Library from the main menu. (If you select Import to Stage, the sound will be imported to the library. You can use the Ctrl+R shortcut to import to the Stage, and it will work just like selecting a file for library import.) When you're importing multiple sound files, importing them to the library first helps to organize them. Once the files are in the library, you can then select the layer and/or keyframe where you want the sound to begin. Select the sound file you want, and the file is imported.

If you want to use sound from an AVI file, the process is very similar, but you need an additional step to separate the sound file from the video. Use the following steps:

1. Select File, Import to Library and select an AVI file to import. The Video Import Wizard opens.

2. Select the Import the Entire Video option and then click the Next button. If you want to edit the video file first, select the Edit the Video option, and you can choose only the portion needed for the sound.

3. In the Editing Encoding window, select any speed you want in the Compression Profile drop-down menu. The compression profile size at this stage is not important because you will be deleting the video portion of the file, changing the audio portion to MP3, and then setting the bit rate and sound quality in Flash.

4. In the Advanced Settings pop-up menu, select Create New Profile. The Encoding (Advanced Settings) window opens. In the lower-left corner under Track Options, select Separate from the Audio Track drop-down menu, as shown in Figure 10.1.

5. Once you've made all these settings, click Finish. In the Library panel, you should see two files: the video file and the audio file from the same original AVI file. A speaker icon identifies the sound file, and a video camera icon identifies the video file. Figure 10.2 shows separate audio and video files from an AVI file with the name `narration.avi`.

After the import of sound from an AVI file is complete, delete the video portion from the Library panel if all you need is the sound portion. In other applications, you may need to throw out the separated sound portion and rerecord the sound or not use it at all.

FIGURE 10.1   Separating the audio and video tracks.

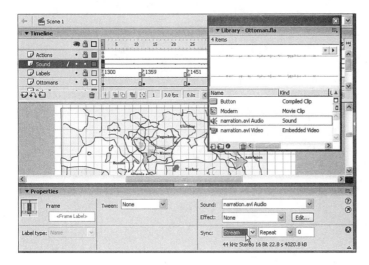

FIGURE 10.2   Sound from an AVI file in a Flash movie.

Setting Sound Properties

Once you have placed a sound file into the Library panel, especially if the file is not an MP3 file, you should reduce the file to the smallest possible size for effective use. Select the sound in the Library panel and click the information icon at the bottom of the Library panel to open the Sound Properties dialog box. You will see the information about the original file size. For example, the extracted sound from the AVI file showed the following information:

```
44 kHz Stereo 16 bit 22.8 s 4020.8 kB
```

MP3 has the best file-compression format, so selecting MP3 from the Compression drop-down menu generally offers the best file size reduction while maintaining quality. Checking the Preprocessing check box converts a stereo file to mono (only available for bit rates of 20Kbps or greater). The bit rate can be set from 8Kbps to 160Kbps. You can see that it has a major effect on the file size. For example, at 8Kbps, a 4MB file converted to MP3 is about 23KB. However, at 160Kbps, the same file is about 456KB, or 20 times as large.

Once the settings have been made, the new file size is shown at the bottom of the Sound Properties dialog box. From the original size information of the extracted AVI file, the size now shows as follows:

```
8 kbps Mono 22.8 kB, 0.6% of original
```

Figure 10.3 shows how the Sound Properties dialog box appears after the adjustments have been made.

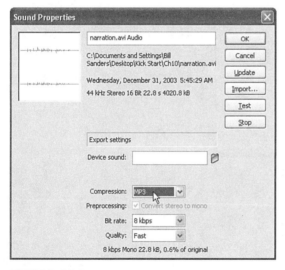

FIGURE 10.3   Sound properties settings.

Further settings for sound can be made in the Publish Settings dialog box. Select File, Publish Settings and click the Flash tab. Clicking the Set button for either the Audio Stream or Audio Event settings will provide setting choices similar to those found in the Sound Properties dialog box. You can then elect to override the sound settings. One primary use of overriding the settings made in the Sound Properties dialog box is for quickly testing different settings without having to reset them in the Sound Properties dialog box.

Once you have added a sound to a movie, you can use the Edit Envelope window to change the beginning and ending position of the sound by moving the Time In and Time Out controllers. Also, you can set the left and right channels to one of the following effects:

- Left Channel (only)
- Right Channel (only)
- Fade Left to Right
- Fade Right to Left
- Fade In
- Fade Out
- Custom

You can set one of these effects by selecting it from the Effect drop-down menu in the Property Inspector or the Edit Envelope window. Using the Edit Envelope window, you set custom effects by dragging anchor points left and right and up and down. The top sound pane sets the left channel, and the bottom pane sets the right channel. Dragging the anchor points increases or decreases the volume for each channel. You can create a total of eight anchor points for each channel by clicking on the volume line. Figure 10.4 shows the Edit Envelope window with custom effect settings. The Time In controller has been moved to the right so that the sound will start playing after the first portion has been skipped. The shaded area of the sound wave shows the part of the sound that will not be played.

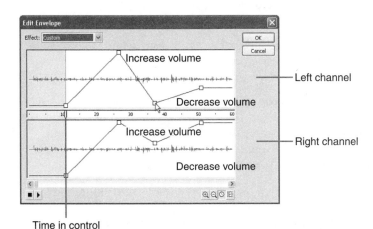

FIGURE 10.4 The Edit Envelope window.

As noted, the Edit Envelope window cannot be used until the sound has been loaded into the movie. The next section shows the different methods available for adding sounds to movies.

Adding Sounds to Movies

Once you have imported sound into a document's library, placing it into the movie is simple. Click the keyframe where you want the sound to begin playing. Then, in the Property Inspector, select the sound you want in the Sound drop-down menu (Figure 10.2 shows the sound "narration.avi Audio" in both the Library panel and in the Property Inspector). Next, you can choose either Event or Stream in the Sync drop-down menu. An event sound downloads completely before it begins playing and needs only a single frame. A stream sound, on the other hand, uses a progressive download method of playing and will start playing after only a few frames are downloaded, resulting in the sound beginning much sooner. In addition, a stream sound is tied to the Timeline. Whereas an event sound requires only a single frame, a stream sound requires frames for the entire sound. The playhead moves at the speed of the sound, and if the computer cannot draw the animation fast enough to keep up with the sound, Flash will skip frames to make it do so. Table 10.1 shows the differences between the two types of sound.

TABLE 10.1

Stream and Event Sounds

SOUND	DOWNLOAD	TIMELINE COORDINATED	FRAMES REQUIRED
Event	Complete	No	One
Stream	Progressive	Yes	The number necessary to encompass the entire sound

An event sound will play after the movie has stopped, whereas a stream sound stops as soon as the playhead stops. Therefore, long after a movie has reached its last frame or a stop() action, an event sound can keep on playing, even repeatedly.

Besides selecting Event or Stream in the Sync drop-down menu, you can select the Start and Stop options. The Start and Stop options are typically used in pairs. One keyframe is used to start the sound, and another is used to stop the sound. Selecting the Start option without using a Stop option functions like selecting an event sound. You can also add a Stop option in the layer where you have placed your sound with an event or stream sound.

The Repeat/Loop option's primary use is for looping event sounds. Loops simply repeat a sound a specified number of times, and they shouldn't be used with stream sounds. Using loop sounds is the main method employed to load high-quality music to a Flash movie at minimum load time costs. Basically, the idea is to use a single music loop that keeps repeating itself but sounds like a single continuous song. For example, a high-quality sound set at 44KHz that loops 12 times is loaded only once but plays music the length of time a single sound file 12 times its size would play. Thus, instead of having to reduce the quality of the music, the developer simply uses a single, shorter, high-quality music file that repeats itself. The smaller length of the musical piece is where file size is kept small, rather than sacrificing quality. However, this method is only successful when used with loops.

Free Sounds

You can download hundreds of different music loops free from `www.flashkit.com`.

Using the Behaviors Panel to Load Sounds

Using the Behaviors panel, you can load and play sounds from external sources or the library. You can stop sounds globally and stop specific sounds as well. Table 10.2 shows the behaviors available for sound.

TABLE 10.2

Sound Behaviors

BEHAVIOR	ACTION
Load Sound from Library	Uses a linkage name to load and/or play sound imported to the library
Load Streaming MP3 File	Uses progressive download to load and/or play an external MP3 file
Play Sound	Plays sound identified by an instance name
Stop All Sounds	Stops all sounds on all layers
Stop Sound	Stops only sound identified by a linkage name and instance name

Using the Behaviors panel to add sound and to start and stop it is quite simple. Use the following steps to set up and play a sound file for access by the code generated through the Behaviors panel:

1. Import a sound file to the library.

2. Select the sound file in the Library panel and, from the Library menu or context menu, select Linkage.

3. In the Linkage Properties dialog box, check Export for ActionScript and provide an identifier (no spaces) for the sound.

4. Place a Button component on the Stage and label it **Play Sound**. With the button selected, click the plus (+) button in the Behaviors panel and then select Sound, Load Sound from Library.

5. In the Load Sound from Library dialog box, type the linkage name and then type some other name for the code to use as a sound instance reference. (Any name will do.) Check the check box labeled Play This Sound When Loaded. Before clicking the OK button, you might want to jot down the linkage and instance names because you will need them both in step 7.

6. On a different layer, drag another Button component to the Stage and label it **Stop Sound**. With the button selected, click the plus (+) button in the Behaviors panel and then select Sound, Stop Sound from Library.

7. In the Stop Sound dialog box, enter the same linkage name and sound instance name you used in the Load Sound from Library dialog box in step 5.

Now test the movie. When you click the Play Sound button, you should hear the sound, and as soon as you click the Stop Sound button, the sound should stop.

One of the more useful actions to quickly generate with the Behaviors panel is streaming external MP3 files. By using external streaming, you can lessen the size of the SWF file, thereby reducing file size and load time. Because external files that will be streamed in don't add to the file size of the document, you can use any size MP3 file you want, and it won't delay the loading of your document. (The process used to "stream" MP3 files is actually progressive downloading, but the term *stream* is used because when you select the behavior from the Behaviors panel, you select the option Load Streaming MP3 File.) However, once an MP3 begins to play, the audio must take a little time to load a portion into the buffer.

Using the Sound Class

The code generated by the Behaviors panel shows how Flash Pro uses the many different elements of the Sound class. Tables 10.3–10.5 summarize the methods, properties, and events, respectively, of the Sound class.

TABLE 10.3

Sound Class Methods

METHOD	ACTIONS
soundInst.attachSound("id")	Attaches the sound identified by the linkage name *id* to the instance.
soundInst.getBytesLoaded()	Returns the number of bytes in the sound instance that's currently loaded.
soundInst.getBytesTotal()	Returns the total number of bytes in the sound instance.
soundInst.getPan()	Returns the current pan value established by setPan().
soundInst.getTransform()	Returns the value from the last setTransform() call.
soundInst.getVolume()	Returns the current volume setting.
soundInst.loadSound("url", Boolean)	Loads the MP3 file identified by *url* with the option of streaming (Boolean true) or event (Boolean false).
soundInst.setPan(n)	The pan value (*n*) is set in terms of negative values up to –100 for the left speaker and positive values up to 100 for the right speaker. Mid balance is 0.
soundInst.setTransform(Obj)	Establishes the amount of the two channels that will be played in left and right speakers. (*Obj* is an object containing the channel properties for left/right speakers.)
soundInst.setVolume(n)	The volume (*n*) can be set from 0 to 100, where 0 indicates the sound is off.
soundInst.start(s,l)	The sound begins playing with these optional parameters: start position in seconds (*s*) and number of times to loop (*l*).
soundInst.stop()	Only stops the sound instance's sound.

TABLE 10.4

Sound Class Properties

PROPERTY	CHARACTERISTICS
soundInst.duration	Returns the number of milliseconds in a sound instance.
soundInst.id3.*tagName*	A read-only property to access different ID3 1.0/2.0 tags (*tagName*) in an MP3's metadata.
soundInst.position	Returns the number of milliseconds for which a sound has been playing.

TABLE 10.5

Sound Class Events

EVENT	DESCRIPTION
soundInst.onID3	Fires after the load sequence and ID3 data become available.
soundInst.onLoad	When a sound is loaded, the event fires.
soundInst.onSoundComplete	Fires once the sound has stopped playing.

The Sound class provides two methods to access sound: attachSound() and loadSound(). When you use attachSound(), you need to first import a sound into the Library panel and give it a linkage name. Using loadSound(), you can load the sound file directly from the server, either as an event sound or a stream sound. When you select a stream sound, the sound begins playing shortly after the loading begins.

All instances of the Sound class must first be instantiated using the Sound constructor, such as in the following line:

```
var soundBarrier:Sound = new Sound();
```

Once the Sound class is instantiated, its different methods, properties, and events can be attached to the instance. Using the Sound class, you have far more control over sound than with any other technique available in Flash Pro.

Project: Experimenting with Sound

To show you how several Sound class features can be employed, the following application uses UI component buttons to start and stop a sound and sliders to control the volume and pan. A single MP3 file named jazz1.mp3 is employed, but any MP3 file can be used in its place. The following steps show how to create the application:

1. In a new Flash document, create six layers named, from top to bottom, Actions, Labels, Buttons, Levers, Grooves, and Background. Provide a gray background color (#A6A6A6).

2. Using Figure 10.5 as a guide, in the Grooves layer draw a vertical line with settings H=100, X=100, Y=140, and a horizontal line with settings W=200, X=200, Y=200 using color code #A699E6. Then in the Background layer, add solid black rectangles. In the

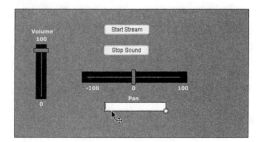

FIGURE 10.5   Sound controllers.

Buttons layer, drag two UI component buttons to the stage, providing the labels Start Stream to the top button and Stop Sound to the bottom button. Add the instance name `stream_btn` to the top button and `stop_btn` to the bottom button.

3. In the Labels layers, add static text labels as shown in Figure 10.5. Also, in the Labels layer centered beneath the Pan label, add a dynamic text field and provide the instance name soundStatus_txt.

4. Select the Levers layer and draw a rectangle with the dimensions W=31, H=8. Select the rectangle and press F8 to convert it into a movie clip with the name `lever`. Give it the instance name `vol_mc`. From the Library panel, drag a second instance of the movie clip. Rotate the second lever 90 degrees, and give it the instance name `pan_mc`. Place the `vol_mc` instance at the top of the vertical groove line and place `pan_mc` in the middle of the horizontal groove line, as shown in Figure 10.5.

5. Click the first frame of the Actions layer. Open the Actions panel and add the following script:

```
//Instantiate sound instance
var soundHere:Sound = new Sound();
//Load a streaming sound
stream_btn.onPress = function() {
    soundHere.loadSound("jazz1.mp3", true);
};
soundHere.onLoad = function() {
    soundStatus_txt.text = "Sound streaming";
};
//Stop the streaming sound
stop_btn.onPress = function() {
    soundHere.stop();
    soundStatus_txt.text = "Sound stopped";
};
//Volume Control
vol_mc.onPress = function() {
    this.startDrag(false, 115, 140, 115, 240);
};
vol_mc.onRelease = function() {
    stopDrag();
};
```

```
var hearVol:Object = new Object();
hearVol.onMouseMove = function() {
    soundHere.setVolume(240-vol_mc._y);
};
Mouse.addListener(hearVol);
//Pan Control
pan_mc.onPress = function() {
    this.startDrag(false, 195, 184.5, 395, 184.5);
};
pan_mc.onRelease = function() {
    stopDrag();
};
var hearPan:Object = new Object();
hearPan.onMouseMove = function() {
    soundHere.setPan(295-pan_mc._x);
};
Mouse.addListener(hearPan);
//Signal end of sound
soundHere.onSoundComplete = function() {
    soundStatus_txt.text = "Sound finished";
};
```

The volume slider control is set to generate values from 0 to 100, and the pan slider control is set to generate values from –100 to 100. The two buttons invoke methods to begin the progressive download (streaming) and to stop the sound instance. The onLoad() event handler indicates that the progressive download has "loaded" as soon as enough of the file has entered the buffer to begin playing. Therefore, only a small part of a stream sound needs to be loaded to fire the onLoad() event handler, whereas an event sound must be fully loaded to invoke the same event.

In tests with the sample file (a 940KB MP3 music file), the buffering time ranged from 3 to 7 seconds on high-speed connections (cable and DSL). The longer test periods were on DSL lines between the Eastern U.S. and Europe, whereas the shorter time was to and from an East Coast U.S. city. With slower Internet speeds, the buffering time could increase significantly, and a "buffering" message lets the user know that something is happening while he or she is waiting for the file to begin playing.

A new feature added to the Sound class is the ID3 property and event handler. ID3 information is optionally added to an MP3 file, but if the information is available, you can incorporate it into your document. The read-only information in the ID3 property can be used in conjunction with the onID3 event handler in the following format:

```
soundInstance.onID3 = function() {
    ID3info_txt.text = soundInstance.id3.tag;
}
```

With 47 different ID3 properties (tags) available, from album name to the name and the
length of the song, you can find a good deal of information you may want to incorporate
into your Flash document. Figure 10.6 shows a partial list of the ID3 properties you can select
from the Sound class pop-up menu.

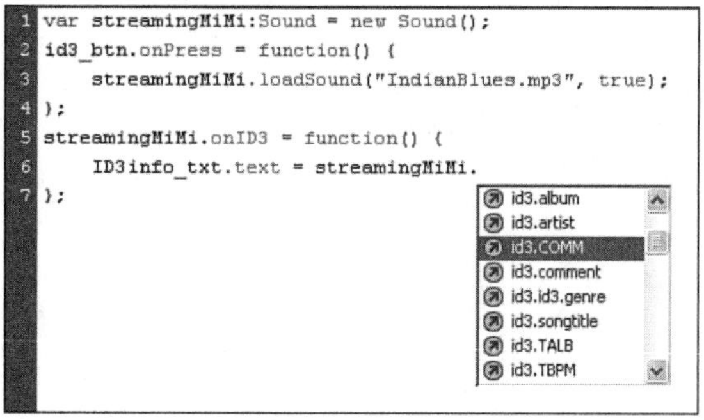

```
1  var streamingMiMi:Sound = new Sound();
2  id3_btn.onPress = function() {
3      streamingMiMi.loadSound("IndianBlues.mp3", true);
4  };
5  streamingMiMi.onID3 = function() {
6      ID3info_txt.text = streamingMiMi.
7  };
```
```
id3.album
id3.artist
id3.COMM
id3.comment
id3.id3.genre
id3.songtitle
id3.TALB
id3.TBPM
```

FIGURE 10.6 A pop-up menu shows the different ID3 properties.

Many MP3 files have minimal or no ID3 information at all. When no ID3 information is
detected using the onID3 event handler, you will either get an "undefined" response, indicating that some ID3 information is in the MP3 file but not the property you requested, or an
"empty" ID3 response, indicating that no ID3 information at all is available in the file.

Using Media Components

A major new feature in Flash MX Professional 2004 is the ability to progressively download
FLV files. In Flash Pro, the following three media components aid in this process:

- MediaController
- MediaDisplay
- MediaPlayback

The MediaController component must be used in conjunction with the MediaDisplay
component because its only purpose is to provide controls for the media display. The
MediaPlayback component is a complete media display and controller in a single component.

Converting Media to FLV Files

The media components are set up to progressively download FLV files. The first step in using
these components is to convert a video file in a format supported by Flash (such as AVI or
MOV) to the FLV format. Fortunately, Flash Pro can export any supported video file to the

FLV format. You can create FLV files directly using Flash Communication Server or a third-party application such as Sorenson Squeeze. Table 10.6 shows all the file types you can import into Flash Pro and export as FLV movies.

TABLE 10.6

Supported Video

EXTENSION	FILE TYPE
AVI	Audio Video Interleaved
MPEG/MPG	Motion Picture Experts Group
MOV	QuickTime movie
WMV/ASF	Windows Media file

The AVI, MPEG, and MOV files require QuickTime 4+ installed for either Windows or Macintosh computers. On Windows computers, DirectX 7+ allows for AVI, MPEG, and WMV movies. Windows users can easily create a video using the Windows Movie Maker found in the Accessories folder, and Macintosh users can do the same using iMovie, which is shipped with Macs.

To convert video media to FLV format, use the following steps:

1. Open a Flash document and select File, Import to Library.

2. When the Video Import Wizard opens, select Import the Entire Video and click Next.

3. In the Encoding window, select the compression profile you want to use, and in the Advanced settings, be sure that Audio Track is set to Integrated.

4. Click Next and then Finish. You should now see the video file in the Library panel.

5. Select the video in the Library and right-click (Control-click on the Mac) to open the context menu. Choose Properties in the context menu.

6. In the Embedded Video Properties dialog box, click the Export button. The default save format is FLV. Provide a filename and click Save. (The .flv extension is added automatically.)

Once the FLV is saved on your hard drive or server, you can access it like any other external file.

Adding FLV Files and Working with a Preferred Media Size

Once you have a file in FLV format, all you need to do to get started is to drag a MediaDisplay component to the Stage, open the Parameters tab of the Component Inspector, and in the URL box, add the path to the FLV file. For example, if you save your Flash file in

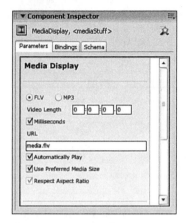

FIGURE 10.7   Media Display settings for an FLV file.

the same folder as an FLV file named `media.flv`, all you would enter into the URL window is `media.flv`. Figure 10.7 shows the settings in the Component Inspector.

The default aspect ratio of movies is 4:3, length to height. The most common USB Webcam aspect ratio is 160 by 120, and digital camcorders and IEEE 1394 (FireWire) Webcams are 320 by 240. The default window size of the Media Display window is 300 by 200, which is most likely not the size you want. (It is out of the 4:3 aspect ratio.) However, by selecting the Use Preferred Media Size option in the Parameters tab in the Component Inspector, you can automatically resize the component to the preferred size for the recorded file. For example, Figure 10.8 shows two different FLV files, one formatted at 160 by 120 and the other at 320 by 240.

160 x 120

320 x 240

FIGURE 10.8   Different size videos in the same application.

Each of the two videos was run on the same application. The solid rectangle area behind the image on the left shows the default 300-by-200 size of the MediaDisplay component.

Watch Out for Distortion

In designing a site that incorporates a streaming FLV file, you should resize the MediaDisplay component to reflect the format size in which you will be displaying the video. If you resize a smaller format to a larger output window, the video's quality is severely degraded; however, if you reduce the size of a larger video format to a smaller window, the output is fine. Keeping the 4:3 aspect ratio is important so that the video doesn't appear warped.

Both the MediaDisplay and MediaPlayback components connect to FLV files in the same way. However, whereas the playback controls are built in to the MediaPlayback component, the MediaDisplay component needs to be associated with the MediaController component to achieve any control over the playback of FLV files. This association is accomplished using

ActionScript. Both the MediaController and MediaDisplay components need an instance name. Then, using the ActionScript format

```
controllInstance.associateDisplay(MediaDisplayInstance);
```

you can associate the two components with one another. Using the controller, you can pause, rewind, and start the video in the display. In addition, the controller provides volume control.

Working with Media Classes

Using ActionScript 2.0's new media classes, you can effect far more precision than with any of the other tools available in Flash Pro. However, at the same time, many of the classes require Flash Communication Server for them to be of much use. Included in the media classes are the following:

- Camera
- Microphone
- NetConnection
- NetStream
- Sound
- Video

In looking at the classes within the media classes' ActionScript folder, you can see that only a portion can be applied without other programs. The first part of this chapter covered the Sound class, so that class will not be repeated here. The Camera and Microphone classes primarily are made up of a large number of read-only properties, and the methods and properties that

SHOP TALK

Which Media Component?

Some designers may wonder, why have the MediaController in the mix of media components? If you need a controller, just use the MediaPlayback, and if you don't, use the MediaDisplay. Seems like a no-brainer!

However, after some work with these components, you'll see that the separate display and controller turns out to be a very good idea. First, when you set the size of the display, you get exactly what you need for the design, and you maintain the 4:3 aspect ratio of the video. Once it has been sized, you can then add the controller separately. When you size the MediaPlayback component, though, the size includes both the display screen and the attached controller, so it's difficult to get an exact fit.

Second, unlike the MediaPlayback component, the MediaController is not connected to the display screen, so you can put it where you want. You can even change its orientation from horizontal to vertical if needed. So what may at first appear to be an unnecessary media component turns out to be an important design component.

allow writing are of little value without outward streaming or recording. Without Flash Communication Server, the only streaming that occurs is the progressive downloads of FLV files. Therefore, the remainder of this chapter shows how to employ the `NetConnection`, `NetStream`, and `Video` classes.

Playing FLV Files with ActionScript 2.0

Prior to ActionScript 2.0, the only way you were able to play an FLV file was using Flash Communication Server. With Flash Pro using script, you can create very small files that can progressively download and display an FLV file. For example, a simple movie that steams an FLV file can be created in less than 1KB, whereas the minimum using components is about 67KB.

To get started, all you need on the Stage is a single embedded video object. The following steps show how to use the `NetConnection` and `NetStream` classes in conjunction with the `Video` class to display an FLV video:

1. Open a new Flash document and then open the Library panel. Add a total of three layers named, from top to bottom, Actions, Video, and Background.

2. In the Library panel, open the panel's pop-up menu and select New Video. An embedded video icon appears in the library.

3. Open the Color Mixer and in the large color pane, add the color #5C0B08 (dark maroon). Then open the Color Mixer's pop-up menu and select Add Swatch. Do the same thing with the colors #D4B707 (dark mustard) and #EADFC2 (light tan). Use the light tan as the background color for the movie.

4. Select the Background layer. In the middle of the Stage draw a rectangle with a dark mustard 3.75 stroke and a dark maroon fill. Use the Align tools to center the rectangle in the middle of the Stage. Lock the Background layer.

5. Select the Video layer and then drag an instance of the embedded video object to the center of the stage. In the Property Inspector, lock the object dimensions and change the W value to 300. (The H value should automatically change to 225.) Then, using the Align panel tools, center the Embedded Video object in the middle of the stage and give it the instance name `flashVid_video`.

6. Select the Actions layer and in the Actions panel, add the following script, substituting `media5.flv` for an FLV file in the same folder where you saved your FLA file:

```
//Make NetConnection
var makeConn_nc:NetConnection = new NetConnection();
makeConn_nc.connect(null);
//New NetStream
var netWork_ns:NetStream = new NetStream(makeConn_nc);
//Connect to Video instance
flashVid_video.attachVideo(netWork_ns);
netWork_ns.play("media5.flv");
```

Once you save the FLA file, test it. Its size is only 291 bytes (that's bytes, not kilobytes!). Because bandwidth is measured in bits instead of bytes, multiply the size by 8 to get the number of bits being shipped over the Internet—only about 2.3Kb—not even enough to get a 56K phone modem wheezing. The main bandwidth usage will come from progressively downloading the FLV file, but because this is done progressively, only a little at a time has to be sent and processed.

NetStream Controls

Once you have an embedded video instance displaying a progressively downloaded FLV file, you can use the properties, methods, and events associated with the NetStream class to provide your users with additional information or just to grab their attention.

So that you understand the difference between true video streaming and progressive downloads, we'll use the NetStream.seek() method, which is both instructive and useful. The seek() method moves the play forward or backward the number of seconds specified in the argument. The general format is as follows:

```
streamInstance_ns.seek(seconds);
```

Therefore, if you have a 60-second FLV video, the following setting would jump to the halfway point of the video:

```
streamInstance_ns.seek(30);
```

The only problem with using seek() and progressive download is that it cannot seek beyond the portion that has been downloaded. Therefore, a 60-second video that has played 30 seconds can only seek to 30 seconds or less. It could not, for example, seek to 45 seconds. (Flash Communication Server uses true streaming, so the user can seek to any position, no matter how long the FLV file has streamed.) To "rewind" the video, set the seek() value to 0.

The FLV files are played using cached memory, so when you play a smaller-size FLV file, the entire video may be stored in cached memory. If you play the file a second time, it can seek ahead to the limit of the cache. For example, if 45 seconds of a 60-second video are in cached memory, you can seek any part of the 45 seconds, no matter how few seconds of the video have played.

For a quick demonstration of how seek() affects a video, revise the application from the previous section using the following steps:

1. Change the size of the embedded video object to 160 by 120. This change will give you more room on the Stage for the Button and TextInput components.

2. Drag a Button component onto the Stage, providing it with the label **Seek** and the instance name seek_btn.

3. Directly beneath the Seek button, add a TextInput component with the instance name seek_txt.

4. Click the first frame of the Actions layer and add the following code to the existing script in the Actions panel:

```
var seekHear:Object = new Object();
seekHear.click = function() {
    var seeker:Number = parseFloat(seek_txt.text);
    netWork_ns.seek(seeker);
};
seek_btn.addEventListener("click", seekHear);
```

When you test the program, if you put in a value higher than the number of seconds the video has played, the video won't jump ahead. Once the video has played all the way through, type **0** in the text field and click the Seek button. Then, type in a value in seconds that's greater than the video has played. On this second time, it will jump ahead because the FLV file has been cached.

In addition to the seek() method, NetStream has several other methods and properties you can use. In order to examine as many of these methods and properties as possible, this next example shows several properties, some methods, and the NetStream event handler, onStatus(). To keep things as simple as possible, use the previous example's application and remove everything from the Stage except for the embedded video instance and the background images. It will serve as a foundation for this next example.

To make it interesting, you'll employ a horizontal slider to change the seek position and a moving "playhead" to move along with the NetStream.time property. Depending on the length in seconds of the video, an offset variable adjusts the movement of both the "playhead" and the lever for changing the seek position. The following steps explain setting up the document:

1. Start with the document from the previous section and remove everything from the movie except the Embedded Video instance and background. Add a Controls layer right above the Background layer.

2. In the Background layer, add two "groove" lines for the lever and the time playhead. Each line should be exactly 200 points in horizontal length. Position the top line at X=175, Y=69, and the bottom line at X=175, Y=294. Use Figure 10.9 as a guide. Lock the Background layer.

3. All instance names in this step are in parentheses and refer to those shown in Figure 10.9. In the Controls layer, add a Button component and label it **Buffer** (buffer_btn). Beneath the Buffer button, add an InputText component (buffer_txt). To the right of the InputText component, add a dynamic text field (time_txt), and above it use static text to type the label, **Time**. Position the Embedded Video instance (flashVid_video) at the left center and add a TextField component to the right (status_txt). Add a Button component to the bottom center and label it **Pause** (pause_btn).

buffer_txt   buffer_btn   timeline_mc

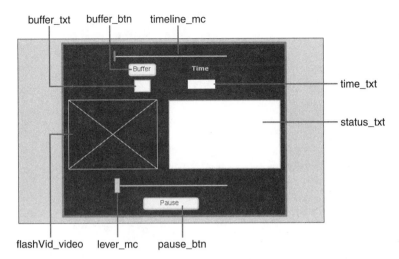

time_txt

status_txt

flashVid_video   lever_mc   pause_btn

FIGURE 10.9   Objects and their instance names.

4. Still in the Controls layer, draw a vertical line (V=15) using a 4-point stroke. Convert it to a movie clip (timeline_mc) and position it on the left side of the top groove line (X=175, Y=61). Draw a rectangle (W=9, H=25), convert it to a movie clip (lever_mc), and position it at X=174, Y=281.

5. Click the first frame in the Actions layer and add the following script:

```
//Make NetConnection
var makeConn_nc:NetConnection = new NetConnection();
makeConn_nc.connect(null);
//New NetStream
var netWork_ns:NetStream = new NetStream(makeConn_nc);
//Connect to Video instance
flashVid_video.attachVideo(netWork_ns);
//Set Buffer and Start Play
var bufferHear:Object = new Object();
bufferHear.click = function() {
    var buffer:Number = parseFloat(buffer_txt.text);
    netWork_ns.setBufferTime(buffer);
    netWork_ns.play("media6.flv");
};
buffer_btn.addEventListener("click", bufferHear);
//Pause
var pauseHear:Object = new Object();
pauseHear.click = function() {
    netWork_ns.pause();
};
```

```
pause_btn.addEventListener("click", pauseHear);
//Time
var timeHear:Object = new Object();
timeHear.click = function() {
    time_txt.text = netWork_ns.time;
};
time_btn.addEventListener("click", timeHear);
//Drag
lever_mc.onPress = function() {
    this.startDrag(false, 175, 281, 375, 281);
};
//Calculate offset
//Length of groove and time line (200)
//divided by number of seconds in movie.
var timeOfMovie:Number = 124;
var offset:Number = 200/timeOfMovie;
lever_mc.onRelease = function() {
    stopDrag();
    netWork_ns.seek((lever_mc._x-175)*offset);
};
//Status
netWork_ns.onStatus = function(netInfo) {
    status_txt.text += "Status: "+netInfo.code+newline;
    status_txt.text += "Buff Length: "+netWork_ns.bufferLength+newline;
    status_txt.text += "Bytes Loaded: "+netWork_ns.bytesLoaded+newline;
};
//Track Time
function timeCallback() {
    time_txt.text = netWork_ns.time;
    timeLine_mc._x = 174+(netWork_ns.time*offset);
}
setInterval(timeCallback, 50);
```

This movie is a learning project in that you can test your FLV file with different values in the buffer and change the seek position by moving the bottom slider. The time is constantly displayed (every 50 milliseconds), and the different status codes, buffer length, and bytes loaded are displayed in the text field, which can be scrolled to review all the data generated. The NetStream.onStatus event handler can be used to capture the information that triggered the event. Because we used an argument in an unnamed function, the argument has both code and level properties. The code property contains the result of the handler, and the level property contains either status or error. In this example, only the code property is used because it's more informative. Figure 10.10 shows the kind of information displayed when the movie plays.

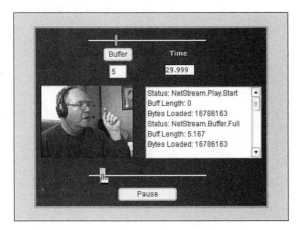

FIGURE 10.10 Information displayed as movie plays.

The NetStream.pause() method is an interesting one because it's a true toggle. The first time it's invoked, it stops the playback, and when it's invoked while the playback is stopped, it starts the playback again. You don't have to add any special code. Just set up the code to call this method with no parameters, and it will serve to start and stop the playback.

In Brief

- Sounds can be imported from a wide variety of sources into Flash.

- Sounds can be embedded in a Flash movie or dynamically loaded while the movie plays.

- Sound editing from within Flash can control volume levels in two channels.

- Sounds can be separated from digital files by Flash and used in a Flash movie without the video.

- Built-in code for working with sound can be generated easily with the Behaviors panel.

- The media components in Flash Pro make it easy to progressively download FLV files and play them in a Flash movie.

- The media classes have several methods, properties, and events that can control video.

- Several aspects of a streamed FLV file can be used as information for feedback and for triggering other Flash actions.

Formatting and Calculating

Using the `String` Class to Format Text

Strings are nothing more than characters treated as text. They are not words, phrases, sentences, or paragraphs. Think of strings as different arrangements of characters—spaces, numbers, punctuation marks, even graphic characters in specialized fonts such as Webdings—and you'll find that working with the `String` class makes a lot more sense.

The `String` class in ActionScript 2.0 contains a single property and only a dozen methods, but it's an extremely important class. Several previous chapters have shown examples incorporating `String` class methods. This section covers the key uses of the `String` class we haven't yet examined.

The `String` class has a single property, which is a nonzero integer specifying the number of characters in the `String` object:

`String.length`

Table 11.1 provides a quick overview of the `String` class methods.

TABLE 11.1

The String Class Methods

METHOD	ACTIONS
String.charAt(i)	Returns the character at location i. Zero-based location.
String.charCodeAt(i)	Returns the code for the character at location i. Zero-based location.
String.concat(s1,s2,sn)	Combines all the strings in the parameters into a new string. (s1, s2, and sn represent any number of strings.)
String.fromCharCode(c1,c2,cn)	Creates a single string made up of ASCII or Unicode character values. (c1, c2, and cn represent any number of numeric code values.)
String.indexOf(s, [si])	Returns a zero-based location in the string of the first instance of string s with an optional starting index (si).
String.lastIndexOf(s, [si])	Returns a zero-based location in the string of the last instance of string s with an optional starting index (si).
String.slice(b,e)	Returns a new string from the current string by taking a slice out of the original string beginning at the b zero-based position and ending at the e zero-based position in the string.
String.split(s, [limit])	Creates an array with the delimiter s serving as a breakpoint. Any string can serve as a delimiter, and the array will be as large as the number of delimiters identified in the string or an optional limit number.
String.substr(b, length)	Returns a substring beginning at b for a length of length.
String.substring(b, e)	Returns a substring beginning at b and ending at e.
String.toLowerCase()	Converts all characters in the string to lowercase without affecting the values of the original string.
String.toUpperCase()	Converts all characters in the string to uppercase without affecting the values of the original string.

String Formatting

A typical use of string methods is to compare a user's response to a key string for verification. For example, in an online quiz, the user may have the correct answer but typed the word using an unrecognized combination of lowercase and uppercase. If a question asks for the state capital of Connecticut, for example, the following are typical responses:

- Hartford
- HARTFORD
- hartford

Rather than entering this in a conditional statement, as shown here, you can convert any input into a single case and use a single term for comparison:

```
if(answer=="Hartford" || answer=="HARTFORD" || answer=="hartford") {...
```

The following simple project shows you how to employ string information in this manner:

1. Open a new document and create the following layers, from top to bottom: Actions, Button, Text Fields, and Background. Draw a rectangle with the dimensions W=235, H=265 in the Background layer to serve as a backdrop. Lock the layer.

2. In the Text Fields layer, add one input text field with the instance name input_txt and one dynamic text field with the instance name output_txt. Above the input text field, in static text, type this question, using Figure 11.1 as a guide:

   What is the capital of Connecticut?

   Lock the layer.

3. In the Button layer, drag one UI Button component to the Stage. Give the button the instance name response_btn (see Figure 11.1). Lock the layer.

4. In the Actions layer, click the first frame and add the following script:

```
//Function to fire on pressing button
response_btn.onPress = function() {
    //Response strings
    var correctAnswer:String = "Yes, Hartford is the correct answer.";
    var incorrectAnswer:String = new String();
    incorrectAnswer = "No, "+input_txt.text+" is not ";
    incorrectAnswer += "Connecticut's capital. Hartford is.";
    //Create a string for response and change to lowercase
    var answer:String = input_txt.text;
    var answer = answer.toLowerCase();
    //Evaluate answer and send out appropriate response
    if (answer == "hartford") {
        _level0.output_txt.text = correctAnswer;
    } else {
        _level0.output_txt.text = incorrectAnswer;
    }
};
```

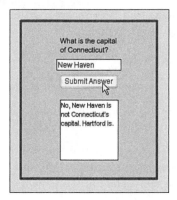

FIGURE 11.1   All user feedback displays the original string input by the user.

This simple script creates a number of string objects and combines these strings with the text from the input text field. The key method employed is `String.toLowerCase()`, which takes any combination of characters entered and changes them all to lowercase. In this way, no matter what case combination the user enters as an answer to the question, if the string is the correct one, the response displayed in the dynamic text field indicates a correct answer. At the same time, an incorrect response uses the literal response, irrespective of cases, to inform the user that the answer is incorrect. Figure 11.1 shows what the user sees with one possible incorrect response.

Substrings

The real power of the `String` class's methods and property lies in examining a string for substrings. A substring is nothing more than a set of characters within a string; however, such sets typically make up words, phrases, names, addresses, or other meaningful chunks of a string.

One of the key uses of substrings is to locate and possibly change a segment of a string. The string methods available in ActionScript 2.0 allow just about any segment of a string to be found, changed, or used in some manner. To explore how you can employ substrings and other string possibilities with the `String` class, the following project shows how to quickly find one name and replace it with another:

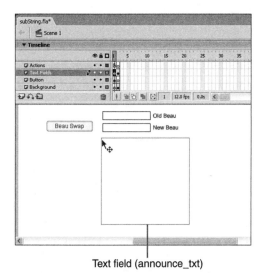

Text field (announce_txt)

FIGURE 11.2   Set up three text fields and a UI Button component on the Stage.

1. Open a new document and create the following four layers, naming them from top to bottom: Actions, Text Fields, Button, and Background. Add a second frame so that all layers have two frames.

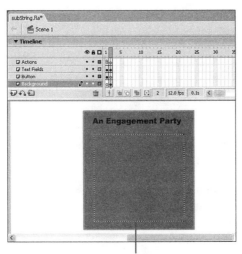

Text field (announce_txt)

FIGURE 11.3 In the second frame, only the large text field remains, but it now has a background graphic.

2. In the first frame, click the Text Fields layer and add two input text fields and one multiline dynamic text field. Label the top text field **Old Beau**, giving it the instance name oldBeau_txt, and the bottom one **New Beau**, with the instance name newBeau_txt. Lock the layer. Figure 11.2 shows the initial layout.

3. Click the first frame of the Button layer and drag a UI Button component to the Stage. Set the label to **Beau Swap** and give it the instance name beauSwap_btn.

4. Add keyframes to the second frame for all layers except the Actions layer. In the second keyframe of the Text Fields layer, remove the two input text fields and add the static header **An Engagement Party**, as shown in Figure 11.3. In the Button layer, in the second frame, remove the UI Button component. In the Background field, add a rectangle with the dimensions W=235, H=246, with a 3-point stroke, a fill color of #998066, and a stroke color of #8CFF99.

5. Click the first frame of the Actions layer and add the following script in the Actions panel:

```
stop();
announce_txt.wordWrap = true;
var invite:String = new String();
invite = "Mr. and Mrs. Frank Jones announce the ";
invite += "engagement of their daughter, Penelope, ";
invite += "to Mr. Carl Smith."+newline+newline;
invite += "You are cordially invited to a reception ";
invite += "for the couple at the University Club on ";
invite += "Wednesday, January 15 at 5:30 pm.";
beauSwap_btn.onPress = function() {
    var searchName:String = oldBeau_txt.text;
    var replaceName:String = newBeau_txt.text;
    for (var x = 1; x<invite.length; x++) {
        var search:String = invite.substring(x, x+searchName.length);
        if (search == searchName) {
```

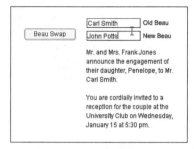

FIGURE 11.4   In the first page, the name of Penelope's old beau is replaced with the name of her new beau.

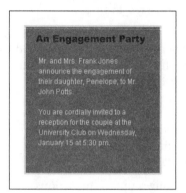

FIGURE 11.5   All the text remains the same except for the name.

```
        invite = invite.split(searchName).join
        ➥(replaceName);
        gotoAndStop(2);
        announce_txt.wordWrap = true;
        announce_txt.textColor = 0x8CFF99;
        announce_txt.text = invite;
      }
    }
};
announce_txt.text = invite;
```

When you run the application, type the name in the existing text (**Carl Smith**) in the top input text field; in the second input text field, type another name, as shown in Figure 11.4.

When you click the Beau Swap button, not only is the name changed, but an engagement invitation is generated. (This application is a must for parents with fickle daughters.) Figure 11.5 shows how the new text looks after the beaus have been swapped.

SHOP TALK

Where Are the Regular Expressions?

For those of you who have dabbled with Perl or even the more recent versions of JavaScript, you may be wondering, "Where are the regular expressions?" When it comes to finding and replacing strings, nothing beats regular expressions, primarily because they were designed precisely for accomplishing those tasks.

One of the goals of ActionScript 2.0 is conformity with the ECMA-262 standards set by the European Computer Manufacturers Association for Internet languages, such as JavaScript. For example, a very nice string method in JavaScript is `replace()`. To replace one string with another, all that's necessary is the following generic line:

```
String.replace(RegExp,NewString)
```

Compare that to the loop and conditional statement that has to be used to make a replacement in the script in the previous example to sniff out the desired substring. If ActionScript 2.0 had regular expressions, the following line would have done the job of the loop and conditional statement:

```
invite = invite.replace(/Carl Smith/g, "John Potts");
```

Because the script looks for one substring and replaces it with another, any substring can be swapped for another. For example, try substituting Penelope with Mercedes. Now the parents not only can swap beaus, they can swap daughters.

Performing Math Calculations

Many Flash designers and developers have an aversion to math, so this section concentrates on a few key examples that show specific uses of the Math class with the purpose of illustrating practical applications for common usage.

Need Help with Math?

For an excellent book on using math with Flash, see *Flash Math Creativity* (Friends of Ed, 2002) by David Hirmes, et al. Even through it's written for Flash 5, this book transcends the different Flash versions with its algorithms.

For a quick overview, Tables 11.2 and 11.3 simply show what the methods compute and the names of the constants, respectively. If you don't know what a tangent is, further description here won't help. Therefore, the tables summarize only.

Far more complex searches and replacements can be carried out using regular expressions. Regular expressions were developed primarily for searching through strings of data going into and out of databases, and as a result they have been heavily associated with middleware programs, especially Perl. However, many occasions arise in which client-side searches can speed the process of data entry and extraction, or client-side text blocks can be employed in regular expressions. Data validation prior to leaving the client speeds the process of going through the middleware and seeking data records from a database. Likewise, simple client-side validation is greatly enhanced using regular expressions.

One of the holdups in implementing regular expressions in ActionScript is that it will add about 20KB to the size of the Flash Player. For users with broadband connections, the extra 20KB would not be noticed, but for users with a 56Kbps phone modem, it might be. Rather than risking fewer people downloading and using the Flash Player, holding off allows those with slower bandwidth connections to upgrade to broadband connections. (Hurry up, guys!)

TABLE 11.2
Math Methods

METHOD	COMPUTATION
`MathInstance.abs()`	Calculates the absolute value
`MathInstance.acos()`	Calculates the arccosine
`MathInstance.asin()`	Calculates the arcsine
`MathInstance.atan()`	Calculates the arctangent
`MathInstance.atan2()`	Calculates the angle from the x axis to the point
`MathInstance.ceil()`	Returns the number rounded up to the nearest whole number
`MathInstance.cos()`	Calculates the cosine
`MathInstance.exp()`	Calculates the exponential value
`MathInstance.floor()`	Calculates the number rounded down to the nearest whole number
`MathInstance.log()`	Calculates the natural logarithm
`MathInstance.max()`	Returns the larger of the two whole numbers
`MathInstance.min()`	Returns the smaller of the two whole numbers
`MathInstance.pow(x,y)`	Calculates x raised to the power of y
`MathInstance.random()`	Generates a random number between 0.0 and 1.0
`MathInstance.round()`	Rounds to the nearest whole number
`MathInstance.sin()`	Calculates the sine
`MathInstance.sqrt()`	Calculates the square root
`MathInstance.tan()`	Calculates the tangent

TABLE 11.3
Math Constants

CONSTANT	VALUE
`Math.E`	The base of natural logarithms (Euler's constant)
`Math.LN2`	The natural logarithm of 2
`Math.LOG2E`	The base 2 logarithm of e
`Math.LN2`	The natural logarithm of 10
`Math.LOG10E`	The base 10 logarithm of e
`Math.PI`	The circle's circumference divided by its diameter (a constant ratio of 3.14159 to 1)
`Math.SQRT1_2`	The reciprocal of the square root of 1/2
`Math.SQRT2`	The square root of 2

In working with the different `Math` methods, you will find one in particular to be very useful: `Math.random()`. Generating a pseudo-random value between 0 and 1 may not sound like much of a range, but you can use multiples and offsets to create any range you want. For example, suppose you want to move a movie clip across the stage in random increments between 2 and 6 pixels. The following code will generate those values in integers:

```
var moveX=Math.round(Math.random()*(6-2)) +2
```

In looking at the `Math.random` portion of the code, you'll see that the high end of the range is coded as the result of subtracting the high end from the low end and then adding the low end. To my mind, that's about as clear as mud. Trying to remember that isn't intuitive. Therefore, using a little OOP, we can create a new class to generate a better random number method. The little script shown in Listing 11.1 does just that.

LISTING 11.1   Extending the `Math` Class for a Better Random Number Method (`NewMath.as`)

```
class NewMath extends Math {
    function betterRandom(b:Number, e:Number) {
        return (Math.random()*(e-b))+b;
    }
}
```

Now, with this new class, all you have to do is to write something like the following to specify a range of random numbers:

```
var myRandom:New Math= new NewMath();
var ranNum:Number = myRandom.betterRandom(2,6);
```

Instead of having to recode the random number generator to get a range, all you need to do is to put the beginning of the range in the first parameter and the maximum range value in the second parameter. To generate integers, all that's required is that you use `Math.round`, `Math.ceil`, or `Math.floor` for integer conversion. To show how such a class might be used in a Flash application, this next project uses the class in a horse race:

1. Open a new Flash document and create five layers, naming them from top to bottom, Actions, Horses, Start Button, Winner, and Background. Set the Stage size to 700×300 pixels and use #00CC66 for the background color. Add a second frame to all layers.

2. In the Background layer, using Figure 11.6 as a guide, draw a tan rectangle the entire width of the stage (W=700 and H=190). The rectangle depicts the racetrack. Center the rectangle vertically on the stage. On either side of the rectangle, draw two parallel 3.75-point black lines to depict rails. Finally, draw a vertical line at about horizontal position 565 (x=565). Label the line **Finish** with static text. Lock the layer.

3. In the Horses layer, add two movie clips depicting racehorses and riders. Place their starting point at the left side of the racetrack, as shown in Figure 11.6. Provide the instance name `topHorse_mc` for the horse movie clip on top and `bottomHorse_mc` for the one on the bottom. Lock the layer.

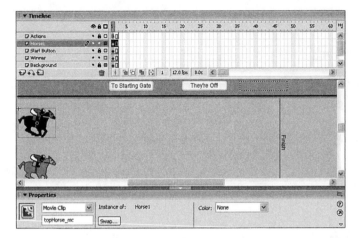

FIGURE 11.6   The Stage depicts a racetrack with two horses in the running.

4. In the Start Button layer, using Figure 11.6 as a guide, place two UI Component buttons on the Stage. Set the label on the left one to **To Starting Gate** and give it the instance name gate_btn, and label the right button **They're Off!**, with the instance name run_btn. Lock the layer.

5. In the Winner layer, add a dynamic text field above the finish line, giving it the instance name winner_txt. Set the text color to white. Lock the layer.

6. Click the first frame of the Actions layer and type the following script:

```
//Stop until Start button pressed
var starter:Boolean;
if (starter == false || starter == undefined) {
    stop();
}
run_btn.onPress = function() {
    starter = true;
    play();
};
//Back to starting gate
gate_btn.onPress = function() {
    topHorse_mc._x = 0.5;
    bottomHorse_mc._x = 0.5;
    winner_txt.text = "";
};
//Get improved random
var horseMove:NewMath = new NewMath();
var horse1:Number = Math.round(horseMove.betterRandom(1, 5));
```

```
var horse2:Number = Math.round(horseMove.betterRandom(1, 5));
topHorse_mc._x += horse1;
bottomHorse_mc._x += horse2;
if (topHorse_mc._x>=486.5) {
   winner_txt.text = "Topper won!";
   starter = false;
   stop();
} else if (bottomHorse_mc._x>=486.5) {
   winner_txt.text = "Low Boy won!";
   starter = false;
   stop();
}
```

Be sure to publish the movie in the same folder where the NewMath.as script was saved. The script references the NewMath class, and unless you set up a special path to the class, you'll have to save it in the same folder as the SWF file. When you play the movie, the horses inch forward as the values are randomly generated. The ranges can be varied any way you want—you simply enter the minimum value in the first parameter and the maximum value in the second parameter. Figure 11.7 shows what you should see at the end of the race. (Note the name of the winning horse displayed above the finish line.) To start over, just click the button labeled To Starting Gate.

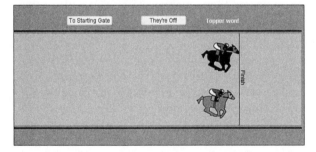

FIGURE 11.7   The randomly generated forward movement makes the application into a real horse race.

In looking at the code in the horserace project, you'll notice that different Math methods are used to create a new class and an altered random method. A more elaborate application of the Math class can be applied to creating geometric shapes. Using both Math methods and constants, you can create classes that contain "packaged" shapes with variable parameters. For example, the script in Listing 11.2 creates a Circle class that uses a movie clip on the Stage to draw a circle with parameters available for the instance name of the movie clip, the circle's radius, and its location on the Stage (x and y positions.)

LISTING 11.2   A Class for Drawing Circles with User-Controlled Position and Size (`Circle.as`)

```
class Circle {
    function drawIt(mc:String, radius:Number, xLoc:Number, yLoc:Number) {
        var cPoint:Number;
        var xPoint:Number;
        var yPoint:Number;
        for (cPoint=0; cPoint<360; cPoint++) {
            xPoint = radius*Math.cos(cPoint*Math.PI/180)+xLoc;
            yPoint = radius*Math.sin(cPoint*Math.PI/180)+yLoc;
            var mcDot:String=mc+cPoint;
            _root[mc].duplicateMovieClip(mcDot, cPoint);
            _root[mcDot]._x = xPoint;
            _root[mcDot]._y = yPoint;
        }
        _root[mc]._x = xPoint;
        _root[mc]._y = yPoint;
    }
}
```

With all the code that goes into the class, very little needs to be done elsewhere. On the Stage, add a movie clip made up of a 2×2 paint or pencil drawing. Give it the instance name dot_mc. Add the following script in the first frame and then save the FLA and SWF file in the same folder as the `Circle.as` file:

```
var ring:Circle = New Circle();
ring.drawIt("dot_mc", 45, 200, 150);
```

By changing the value of the parameters, you can alter the size and position of the circle. You can use any movie clip you want to fashion a circle, but shapes other than dots may result in surprising spheres.

Working with the Number Class

The `Number` class is something like a formatting class compared to the `Math` class. Its two methods simply return a Number instance's value as a string or primitive value. The following script illustrates that a string can be assigned a number value using the `Number.toString()` method:

```
var someWord:String = new String("5599");
var someNumber:Number = new Number(44);
someWord = someNumber.toString();
trace(omeNumber.valueOf()+" "+ someWord.length);
```

Degrees and Radians

In Flash, points around a circle are calculated in *radians* instead of degrees. Although you may know that 360 degree points from a center point with a common radius make up a circle, you probably don't know (or care) that 360 degrees is equal to 2*PI radians.

Without going into a geometry lesson, you will find it helpful to know that one degree equals PI/180 radians. Using the cosine of 360 degrees, you can determine the x position, and using the sine value, you can determine the y position. Therefore, in the Circle class definition, the lines

```
xPoint = radius*Math.cos(cPoint*Math.PI/180)+xLoc;
yPoint = radius*Math.sin(cPoint*Math.PI/180)+yLoc;
```

calculate the degree points using radians. The offsets (xLoc and yLoc) determine where on the Stage the circle will be located. Because the class is designed to use a movie clip anywhere on the Stage, the final step is to incorporate the original movie clip as part of the circle. To do this, the "dot" is tucked into the circle with the following lines:

```
_root[mc]._x = xPoint;
_root[mc]._y = yPoint;
```

Otherwise, the original movie clip looks like a loose dot on the Stage.

Most of the values associated with the Number class are constants. Tables 11.4 and 11.5 provide a summary of the methods and constants, respectively, of the Number class.

TABLE 11.4
Number **Methods**

METHOD	ACTION
NumberInstance.toString()	The Number instance's value is passed as a string.
NumberInstance.valueOf()	The Number instance's value is passed as number primitive.

TABLE 11.5
Number **Constants**

CONSTANT	VALUE
Number.MAX_VALUE	The largest number that can be represented.
Number.MIN_VALUE	The smallest number that can be represented.
Number.NaN	An assignable value that is Not a Number (NaN).
Number.NEGATIVE_INFINITY	Negative infinity.
Number.POSITIVE_INFINITY	Positive infinity.

Like the Math class, the Number class has a constructor, and an instance is created with or without a value. Here are examples:

```
var heavy:Number = new Number();
```

```
var heavy:Number = new Number(789);
```

Also like in the Math class, when a constant is assigned to a Number instance or numeric variable, the constant is expressed as Number.CONSTANT and not NumberInstant.CONSTANT. For example, the following will result in an error message:

```
var lambda:Number=new Number();
var chi:Number = lambda.MIN_VALUE;
trace(chi);
```

Instead, you would write this:

```
var chi:Number = Number.MIN_VALUE;
```

So remember that you can use the Number constants without constructing Number instances.

Static and Dynamic Uses of the Date Components

Flash has had a wide range of time and date options since Flash 5. Using both date and time are useful for any number of applications, and you can always put a display of the time and date on a site so that people will use it to look up the current date and time. The Date class constructor is conventional, and new instances are created like other class objects:

```
dateInstance:Date = new Date();
```

The methods in the Date class fit into four categories, based on what they do. The methods do the following:

- Get the local date/time
- Set the local date/time
- Get the UTC date/time
- Set the UTC date/time

Virtually all modern computers have built-in date and time devices that can be accessed to get the current date and time. The objects created with the Date class get the date and time from these built-in calendars and clocks. So, for the most part, scripting with the Date class is a matter of creating a Date instance and assigning different get methods to be used to assign the date and time details to be displayed. However, because the information supplied is numeric, the names of months and days of the week need to be substituted for numbers. If you don't want a 24-hour display of time in military style but instead prefer an a.m./p.m. display, further work needs to be done.

In order for you to see how to apply the main date and time elements, creating a small application will be useful. (Most of the material in the FLA file is code.) Here are the steps to follow:

1. Open a new Flash document and set the Stage size to 250×20.

2. On top of the long narrow Stage, place a dynamic text field that takes up the entire Stage, giving it the instance name `dateTime_txt`.

3. Open the Actions panel, click the first frame, and type the `clearClock.fla` script:

```
function showDate() {
    var clearClock:Date = new Date();
    //Create a clear month
    var Month:Array = new Array();
    Month.push("January", "February");
    Month.push("March", "April", "May", "June", "July");
    Month.push("August", "September", "October");
    Month.push("November", "December");
    var Day:Array = new Array();
    Day.push("Sunday", "Monday", "Tuesday", "Wednesday");
    Day.push("Thursday", "Friday", "Saturday");
    var nowMonth:String = Month[clearClock.getMonth()];
    var nowDate:Number = clearClock.getDate();
    var nowDay:Number = Day[clearClock.getDay()];
    var nowYear:Number = clearClock.getFullYear();
    var nowCalendar:Object = nowDay+" "+nowMonth+" ";
    nowCalendar += nowDate+", "+nowYear;
    //Create clear time
    var nowHour = clearClock.getHours();
    var normEve:String;
    if (nowHour>12) {
        nowHour = nowHour-12;
        mornEve = "pm";
    } else {
        mornEve = "am";
    }
    var nowMinute:Object = clearClock.getMinutes();
    if (nowMinute<10) {
        nowMinute = "0"+nowMinute;
```

```
    }
    var nowSecond:Object = clearClock.getSeconds();
    if (nowSecond<10) {
        nowSecond = "0"+nowSecond;
    }
    var nowTime:Object = " Time:"+nowHour+":"+nowMinute;
    nowTime += ":"+nowSecond+" "+mornEve;
    dateTime_txt.text = nowCalendar+" "+nowTime;
}
setInterval(showDate, 1000);
```

When you run the program, the time is displayed in a clear format, as shown in Figure 11.8.

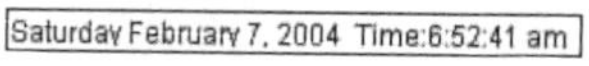

Saturday February 7, 2004 Time:6:52:41 am

FIGURE 11.8   The time display uses names for the month and the day of the week and an a.m./p.m. time format.

Whenever you have an application where you want to load a complete date and time display, you can load the SWF file using the MovieClipLoader class. (Think of it as a SWF component!) Also, you might want to make some adjustments to the code and create a clear clock class.

Coordinated Universal Time (UTC)

If you look at the methods for the Date class in the Actions panel's Toolbox pane, you will see a mirror image of all the get and set methods prefaced by UTC, which stands for *Coordinated Universal Time*. UTC time is the time at the zero meridian. Originally established at the Greenwich Observatory outside of London, the time is often referred to as *GMT (Greenwich Meridian/Mean Time)*. Pilots use the term *Zulu time* (Zulu for zero meridian) and employ it in their flight plans. For example, when flying from Paris to New York, the pilots need not change their watches or time reference if they use Zulu time. Paris and New York have a 6-hour conventional time difference, but when using UTC, the time is the same in both places.

If your application requires UTC, an important method is getTimezoneOffset. This method compares the current time in your computer's clock and returns the number of hours difference. For example, if you live in California, the offset shows 480, representing an 8-hour difference. Those on the East Coast of the United States see 300, or a 5-hour difference. Paris, France, though, shows -60, because it's one hour ahead of Greenwich time. Likewise, all time zones East of Greenwich and west of the International Date Line show negative offsets. For example, the following script displays two different times:

```
var nowTime:Date = new Date();
var local:Number = nowTime.getHours;
var UTC:Number = nowTime.getUTCHours;
trace("local:"+(local*60)+ " ¦ UTC:"+UTC);
```

The difference between the local and UTC times reflects the value found using `Date.getTimezoneOffset`. (For residents of India, the UTC offset is 5 hours and 30 minutes—displayed as -330 minutes! Likewise, Afghanistan and Iran, among others, have half-hour offsets.)

Date Components

Flash MX Professional 2004 (only) has two `Date` components: DateField and DateChooser. Both of these components are simple to use. In fact, they both can be simply dragged to the Stage and employed without any alterations other than styling changes.

The DateField component serves as an on-Stage calendar. The default setting for DateField is the current month, day, and date displayed as part of a monthly calendar. The DateChooser looks like a pop-up menu, except instead of displaying a menu, it displays a calendar like the DateField calendar. Once a date is selected in the DateChooser, it's displayed in a small window. Figure 11.9 shows both components displayed on the Stage.

FIGURE 11.9 Both the DateField and DateChooser components display calendar dates.

Like all components, the Date components have default styles. However, the default styles often don't fit in with a design. In Figure 11.9, the text color of the DateField was changed to red. The change is accomplished by providing the instance name `calendar` to the DateField instance and adding the following code:

```
calendar.color=0xFF0000;
```

However, as you may have noticed in other examples throughout this book, a component may need a lot of style changes to be consistent with other design elements in a document. The next section explains how to change the style of various components and how to find root component elements that need to be addressed to change styles.

Formatting Component Styles

For those familiar with styling components in Flash MX, you'll find some differences in styling Flash MX 2004 components. Depending on the nature of your project, styles can be general or specific to individual components. However, an overall style for a page has certain characteristics in common, and the styles can be set globally. The following sections examine different ways and scopes for styling components.

Global Component Styling

Once the designer has a color palette, all the different parts that make up a Flash application can be created with the colors in the palette. However, up to this point, styling has been ignored when it comes to components. To make up for this apparent slight to designers, global styling of components makes it easy to make them fit in with the rest of the design. What's more, the global styles apply to all components, not just a single type.

Table 11.6 provides a summary of the attributes that can be changed dynamically and the types of values they can be assigned. All color codes are represented as generic hexadecimal values formatted as 0xRRGGBB. Figure 11.10 shows the parts of RecBorder that make up certain components, such as the UI Button and List components.

TABLE 11.6
Global Properties and Value Types

PROPERTY	VALUE TYPE
BackgroundColor	0xRRGGBB.
borderColor	See Figure 11.10.
borderCapColor	See Figure 11.10.
borderStyle	"none", "inset", "outset", or "solid".
buttonColor	0xRRGGBB.
color	Text color (0xRRGGBB).
disabledColor	Disabled text color (0xRRGGBB).
fontFamily	"fontFamily".
fontSize	Integer.
fontStyle	"normal" or "italic".
fontWeight	"normal" or "bold".
highlightColor	See Figure 11.10.
highlightCapColor	See Figure 11.10.
marginLeft	Number.
marginRight	Number.
scrollTrackColor	0xRRGGBB.
shadowColor	See Figure 11.10.
shadowCapColor	See Figure 11.10.
symbolBackgroundColor	The backgrounds of check boxes and radio buttons (0xRRGGBB).
SymbolBackgroundDisabledColor	The disabled backgrounds of check boxes and radio buttons (0xRRGGBB).
SymbolBackgroundPressedColor	Check boxes and radio buttons when selected (0xRRGGBB).
symbolColor	The color of the check in a check box or the button in a radio button. It is also the color of the check box's or radio button's background (0xRRGGBB).
SymbolDisabledColor	The color of the check in a check box or the button in a radio button. It is also the color of a disabled check box's and radio button's background (0xRRGGBB).
TextAlign	"left", "right", or "center".

TABLE 11.6

Continued

PROPERTY	VALUE TYPE
textDecoration	"none" or "underline".
textIndent	The number affecting the first line indent of the paragraph.
themeColor	"haloGreen", "haloOrange", "haloBlue" or custom.

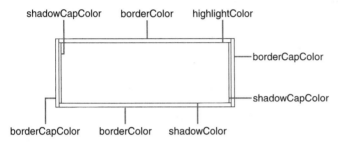

FIGURE 11.10   Location of the RecBorder style properties.

In setting a global style, you don't need to reference an instance name because global styles apply to all instances. Use the following format:

```
_globalStyle.setStyle("feature", value);
```

Some values are in quotation marks and others are not, but all style features must be between quotation marks. Color values expressed as hexadecimal values (0xRRGGBB) don't require quotation marks.

One of the first things you'll discover when using global settings is that they don't work with all components. Although some global settings (such as text color) affect all components, others (such as background color) seem to affect some but not others when used in a global application. To see some examples, place the following components with the associated instance names on the Stage:

- TextArea (myText_txt)
- CheckBox (myCheckBox)
- List (myList_lb)
- ComboBox (myCombo_cb)
- Button (myButton_btn)

Put these items anywhere you want on the Stage. After you set them up with the appropriate instance names, add the script in Listing 11.3.

LISTING 11.3   Dynamic Global Style Settings for Components (basicGlobal.fla)

```
//Establish Global styles
_global.style.setStyle("highlightColor", 0x222f44);
_global.style.setStyle("backgroundColor", 0x222f44);
_global.style.setStyle("textAlign", "left");
```

LISTING 11.3   Continued

```
_global.style.setStyle("scrollTrackColor", 0x222f44);
_global.style.setStyle("borderColor", 0x999999);
_global.style.setStyle("highlightCapColor", 0x222f44);
_global.style.setStyle("shadowColor", 0x000000);
_global.style.setStyle("shadowCapColor", 0x000000);
_global.style.setStyle("color", 0xFF9900);
_global.style.setStyle("symbolColor", 0xFF0000);
_global.style.setStyle("fontFamily", "Arial");
_global.style.setStyle("fontSize", 11);
_global.style.setStyle("themeColor", "haloOrange");
//Add Content to List and ComboBox
var contents:Array = new Array("Flash MX Pro 2004", "Get it now!");
contents.push("Book Downloads", "MP3 Sound");
contents.push("Video", "Horse Race");
for (x=0; x<contents.length; x++) {
   myCombo_cb.addItem(contents[x]);
   myList_lb.addItem(contents[x]);
}
myCombo_cb.rowCount = contents.length;
//Add content to TextArea
var info:String = "In this space you can see how the ";
info += "style affects the text in a TextArea component.";
info += " In order for the scroll bar to appear, the text ";
info += "must extend beyond the bottom of the TextArea  ";
infor += "component's visible area.";
myText_txt.text = info;
```

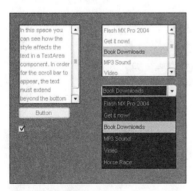

FIGURE 11.11   The global style settings affect only some of the features of the components.

When you test the movie, all the components have the right color text and the haloOrange is extant with all components. However, although the background color is established in the ComboBox component, it hasn't affected the others. The check mark in the CheckBox component is not the correct symbolColor (red). Moreover, none of the scroll tracks are colored. Figure 11.11 give you an idea of what's affected and what isn't.

Instance Styling

At the base of UI components are the UIObject and UIComponent objects, and all UI components inherit their properties, methods, and events. However, because the UIObject, a child of the MovieClip class, implements styles, that object will be the next focus. You can add styling features with the UI component instance.

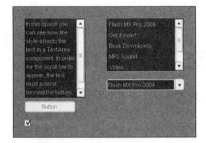

FIGURE 11.12 Instance settings can establish features that may not be set with global settings.

In the previous section, when you used global style declarations, not all style settings took hold. However, if you set the style with the instance of the component, the style will sometimes be implemented. For example, add the following code to the end of the global setting in Listing 11.3.

```
myText_txt.setStyle("backgroundColor", 0x222f44);
myList_lb.setStyle("backgroundColor", 0x222f44);
```

When you test the application, both the TextArea and List components have the background color as well. Figure 11.12 shows these changes.

Adding Styles

Some of the components, such as the UI Button component, have different responses to styling, depending on the style context. The default style context exists when the theme HaloTheme.fla is in use (HaloTheme.fla is the default theme, and only some of the styles available to V2 components can be used). Flash MX Professional 2004 has a second theme you can employ in SampleTheme.fla. This second theme adds to what HaloTheme.fla contains; therefore, this second style context can be discussed as an added style context.

To set up the added style context, you must add library folders from the SampleTheme.fla library to the library of your current project. To do so, follow these steps:

1. On your PC or Mac, find the Flash MX 2004 First Run folder. In that folder is the ComponentFLA folder in which you'll find SampleTheme.fla. (On my Dell, the path is Program Files, Macromedia, Flash MX 2004, en, First Run, ComponentFLA. On my Mac, the path is Applications, Macromedia Flash MX 2004, First Run, ComponentFLA. The path may be slightly different on your system.)

2. Open SampleTheme.fla and then open its Library panel.

3. Open a new Flash document and open its Library panel.

4. In the SampleTheme.fla Library panel, open Flash UI Component 2, Themes. In the Themes folder is the MMDefault folder. With both Library panels open, drag the MMDefault folder into your new document's Library panel. When you drag the MMDefault folder into the new document's library, you'll also see the BoundingBox, UIObject, and UIObjectExtensions movie clips as well as the MMDefault folder. The three additional movie clips are added automatically when you drag the MMDefault folder into the Library panel. Close SampleTheme.fla but don't save it.

After going through this process, your components behave in a different manner than previously. To see an example, follow these steps:

1. Open a new Flash document and place a UI Button component in the middle of the stage. Give the button the instance name myButton_btn.

2. Add the following script to the first frame:

```
myButton_btn.setStyle("buttonColor", 0x222f44);
myButton_btn.setStyle("color", 0xff9900);
myButton_btn.label = "Click Here";
```

3. Save the FLA as defaultStyle.fla and test the movie. The button with an orange Click Here label appears in the middle of the screen. The background is the default, and the button has rounded corners.

4. Using Save As, save the file as addedStyle.fla.

5. Following the earlier steps for adding the MMDefault folder to the Library panel, place the MMDefault folder into the addedStyle.fla library. Everything else should be exactly the same.

6. Test the movie a second time. Now the button should have a dark brown background color and squared corners rather than rounded ones. Figure 11.13 shows the buttons in the different tests.

FIGURE 11.13   The styles of the default and added style contexts lead to very different results.

Besides a different look, the file sizes differ. The defaultStyle.swf file should be about 26KB, and the addedStyle.swf file about 40KB. Therefore, while the added style context generates more style features in components, it also adds to the file size.

Setting Styles for Components

A final aspect of component styling to examine is something like a global style. However, instead of creating a set of global style settings, this method is very much like CSS. In fact, it uses the CSSSTyleDeclaration() method. Rather than making several style settings for individual instances, you can save time and generate better consistency by using a single style containing several attribute settings. The general format is as follows:

```
var someStyle = new mx.styles. CSSStyleDeclaration();
someStyle.styleName="someName";
_global.styles.someName=someStyle;
//settings for someStyle
myInstance.setStyle("someName", "someStyle");
```

To see how this works, place a UI ComboBox and List on the Stage and provide the instance names myCombo and myList. Then, enter the script in Listing 11.4.

LISTING 11.4   Using CSS Type of Style Definition for Components (componentStyle.fla)

```
var myStyle:Object = new mx.styles.CSSStyleDeclaration();
myStyle.styleName = "billzStyle";
_global.styles.billzStyle = myStyle;
//Style settings
myStyle.fontFamily = "Verdana";
myStyle.fontSize = 11;
myStyle.backgroundColor = 0x222F44;
myStyle.color = 0xFF9900;
myStyle.setStyle("themeColor", "haloOrange");
//Applying style to instances
myList.setStyle("styleName", "billzStyle");
myCombo.setStyle("styleName", "billzStyle");
//Filler items for components
var listStuff:Array = new Array(1, 2, 3, 4, 5, 6, 7);
for (x=0; x<listStuff.length; x++) {
    myList.addItem(listStuff[x]);
    myCombo.addItem(listStuff[x]);
}
```

When you test the application, the two components are styled identically. Note that in the format, a _global object is assigned the style object. Therefore, although aspects of CSS are included in styling the component, the _global object still plays a role.

In Brief

- The various methods of the String class can be used in scripts to change text for consistent comparisons.

- Substrings can be found in and used in larger strings.

- The Math methods can be used in Flash animation for controlling objects on the Stage.

- Geometrical shapes can be drawn using the available Math methods and constants.

- The Date class provides both standard and UTC date methods for calculating, using, and displaying the date and time.

- The DateField and DateChooser components simplify embedding a calendar in a document.

- Components can be styled using both global and instance settings.

- Components have extended style features available in a folder that can be added to any document's Library panel.

Dealing with External Data and Objects

Loading and Using Variables from Text Files

Chapter 5, "Movie Clip Control," showed you how to load external movie clips, and in Chapter 6, "Viewing and Entering Information with Text Fields," you saw how to load external text files. Besides loading text files as whole files to be displayed, you can also use text files to store data in the form of variables. Flash has a special format for embedding variables and their values in a text field:

```
variableA=Any text data.&variableB=More text data.
```

All data between the assignment operator (=) and the separation operator (&) are assigned to the variable to the left of the assignment operator. When distilled from the text file, the results are as follows:

```
variableA  =  Any text data.
variableB  =  More text data.
```

One of the features of this type of data storage is that all data is treated as text, and therefore no quotation marks are required to distinguish text. Another feature is that absolutely no spaces are allowed between either the assignment operator (=) or the separation operator (&) and the text.

To get a variable and its data from a text file and place it somewhere useful in Flash, use the LoadVars() class. When the text is loaded into an instance of LoadVars(), you can then pass the data as separate variables to any type of output you want. Typically, the output is displayed in a dynamic text field, but it can be used for any purpose for which any variable may be used. The following shows the generic format for loading variables and their contents from an external text file into a text field:

```
var someLoader_lv:LoadVars = new LoadVars();
    someLoader_lv.onLoad = function() {
        someFieldA_txt.text = this.variableA;
        someFieldB_txt.text = this.variableB;
};
someLoader_lv.load("textFile.txt")
```

The LoadVars() object contains all the variables of the text file, and each variable becomes a property of the LoadVars() object. In the generic listing

```
this.variableA
```

could be written as follows:

```
someLoader_lv.variableA
```

This shows more clearly that the variable in the text file has become a property of the LoadVars() object.

To show the use of the LoadVars() class in a practical example, the following project stores customer names, addresses, and their Web site URLs in text files that are extracted and presented in a Flash document:

1. Make two text files. Remember that no spaces can be placed on either side of either type of operator. Also, just type everything on one big long line that wraps around. Don't add any carriage returns (new paragraphs).

2. Save the following text in two separate files (name the first file SamKelley.txt and the second SuzyQueue.txt):

   ```
   fname=Sam&lname=Kelley&address=123 Elm Street&city=Taft&state=CA&
   ➥zip=93268&web=http://www.sandlight.com
   ```

   ```
   fname=Suzy&lname=Queue&address=321 Apple Lane&city=Roseville&state=WA&
   ➥zip=98377&web=http://www.suezeeque.net
   ```

   You can create the text files with a text editor such as Notepad, or you can use Save As Text in a word processor.

3. Open a new Flash document and create the following layers, from top to bottom: Actions, Text Fields, Button, and Background. Set the background color to #D9E6CC.

4. In the Background layer, using the Rectangle tool with no fill color and a .50-point stroke line colored #008080, draw a rectangle 420×267 and center it to the Stage. Select the rectangle, make a copy of it, and then select Edit, Paste in Place. In the Transform panel, select the Constrain option and type in **95%** for the reduction size. You should now have a frame made up of two rectangles. Using the Ink Bottle tool, change the color of the interior rectangle to #FF0040. In the center of the frame, draw a rectangle with no stroke line using #FF0040 for the fill color. Set the size to 212×96. Center the rectangle. Finally, in 24-point Black Arial font using the color #008080, type in **Customer Information** using static text. Use Figure 12.1 as a guide for the drawings and text placements. Lock the layer.

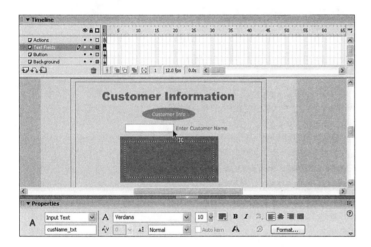

FIGURE 12.1   The objects on the Stage are arranged to accept information passed from external text files.

5. In the Text Fields layer, place an input text field above the red rectangle in the middle of the Stage. Give it the instance name cusName_txt. Use #008080 for the input text box's font color, and set the font size to 10 and the font to Verdana. (Make sure that the Show Border Around Text option is selected.) Next, place a dynamic text field right in the middle of the big red rectangle. Use 10-point white Verdana text and set the field size to 190×75. Give it the instance name customer_txt1 and select Multiline for the line type. Finally, using static text, next to the input field, add the label **Enter Customer Name** using 10-point #008080 Verdana font. Lock the layer.

6. Select the Button layer and, using the Oval tool, create an elongated oval. Use #E68926 for the fill color and use no stroke. Select the oval and press F8 to open the Convert to Symbol dialog box. Double-click the button object to edit it. In the symbol-editing

mode, add a second layer, and in the top layer using a white 10-point Verdana font, type **Customer Info** centered over the oval. Add frames for the Over and Down frames. Then insert a keyframe first in the Down frame and then in the Over frame. In the Over frame, change the color of the font from white to #D9E6CC. Exit the symbol-editing mode and lock the layer.

7. Click the first frame of the Actions layer and enter the following script:

```
getCus_btn.onPress = function() {
    var cus_lv:LoadVars = new LoadVars();
    //Use the onLoad event to separate out variables
    cus_lv.onLoad = function() {
        var cname:String = this.fname+" "+this.lname;
        var address:String = this.address;
        var loc:String = this.city+", "+this.state+" "+this.zip;
        var website:String = this.web;
        var cr = newline;
        customer_txt.text = cname+cr+address+cr+loc+cr+website;
    };
    //Find and remove the space between first and last names
    var customer:String = cusName_txt.text;
    for (x=1; x<customer.length; x++) {
        if (customer.charAt(x) == " ") {
            var cus:String = customer.substr(0, x);
            var tomer:String = customer.substring(x+1, customer.length);
            customer = cus+tomer+".txt";
        }
    }
    cus_lv.load(customer);
};
```

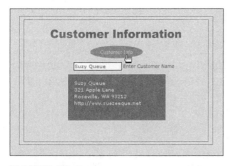

FIGURE 12.2   Data from the external text file appears in the output window.

When you test the application, you enter the first and last name of one of the persons in the text file "database." The two sample text files are saved as SamKelley.txt and SuzyQueue.txt; however, you can enter their names as "Sam Kelley" and "Suzy Queue" in the input field. The script separates out the space between the first and last names and appends the .txt extension using String class methods. You can add as many text files as you want, but all files must be named using the first and last names with no space between the names and the .txt extension. Figure 12.2 shows what happens when Suzy Queue's name is entered.

This "poor person's database" has limited functionality, but it serves to take data from external files, separate the information from the variables, and make it available in a Flash application. Flash doesn't write text files, but a data-entry module could be patched together with some duct tape and Notepad. Basically, you would create a Flash application where you enter the data and then have an output window with selectable text formatted using Flash's text file variable format. Then you could cut and paste the outcome from the text field into Notepad or some other text editor and save it as a text file. (No patent pending on this idea, so feel free to use it in any way you see fit.)

Using the LoadVars Class for External Data

Besides serving as a portal through which text file data can be sent and received, the LoadVars class can be used for communicating between a Flash front end and middleware. The middleware sends the requests from the front end to databases. Tables 12.1 through 12.3 provide an overview of the LoadVars class and its methods, properties, and events, respectively.

TABLE 12.1

LoadVars **Class Methods**

METHOD	ACTIONS
LVinstance.addRequestHeader(hn,hv)	In POST operations, this method changes or adds the http header with the provided header name (hn) and header value (hv).
LVinstance.getBytesLoaded()	When the load() or sendAndLoad() method is invoked, this method returns the number of bytes currently loaded.
LVinstance.getBytesTotal()	When the load() or sendAndLoad() method is invoked, this method returns the total number of bytes to be loaded.
LVinstance.load(URL)	Variables downloaded from URL.
LVinstance.send(URL[,t,m])	Variables from the LoadVars() instance are sent with an optional target frame (t) and a GET or POST method (m) to URL.
LVinstance.sendAndLoad(URL,lvO[,m])	Variables from the LoadVars() instance are sent to URL, with loaded returning variables sent to the LoadVars() instance (lvO) with an optional GET or POST method.
LVinstance.toString()	Automatically encodes in the MIME content code all the properties of the LoadVars() instance containing variable data.

TABLE 12.2

LoadVars **Class Properties**

PROPERTY	CHARACTERISTICS
LVinstance.contentType	The MIME type of the data in the LoadVars() instance.
LVinstance.loaded	A Boolean true value assigned when the load operation is completed. This property defaults to undefined, but it changes to false when the load operation begins prior to being completed.

TABLE 12.3

LoadVars **Class Events**

EVENT HANDLER	EVENT
LVinstance.onData	Once data is fully downloaded, the event fires. This event is also invoked if an error occurs during a data-download operation.
LVinstance.onLoad	When the load or sendAndLoad operation is complete, this event fires.

The most important use of the LoadVars() class is communication with server-side scripts that can connect with a database. The LoadVars() objects serve to pass data from user input on the front end to the middleware and then to a database. At the same time, LoadVars() instances are used to extract data from a database and return it to a Flash front end—typically through a dynamic text field.

For you to see how to use the LoadVars() class's methods, properties, and event handlers with a server-side script, the server-side script needs to be written specifically to accommodate the way in which Flash handles data. Recalling the work in the previous section with text files, you'll remember that variables are embedded in the text in the following format:

```
variableName=Some kind of data
```

In the same way, data is passed from middleware such as Perl, ASP, PHP, or any other server-side script language to Flash. For example, in PHP, variables have a dollar-sign ($) prefix. Here's the difference:

- **Flash**—fname="Jack";

- **PHP**—$fname="Jack";

When LoadVars() sends a variable named fname to PHP, it automatically changes it to $fname. To send a message from PHP to Flash, all variables must be placed into the same format used with the text files you saw in the previous section. Therefore, if you have a variable in PHP called $greeting that you want to send to a LoadVars() instance in Flash, you need to format it as follows:

```
$toFlash="flashVar=$greeting";
echo $toFlash;
```

In PHP, echo is an output statement that sends the data back to the front end, whether it's HTML or Flash. When $toFlash arrives in the LoadVars() instance, the variable flashVar is a property of the LoadVars() instance. The contents of flashVar are the contents of $greeting. Therefore, the data is accessed as follows:

```
myLoaVars.flashVar
```

To see a simple example of how this works, use the PHP script in Listing 12.1. (If you're unfamiliar with PHP or aren't set up on either your own system or a server to run PHP, you can follow the logic or transfer it to middleware you're more comfortable with.)

LISTING 12.1 A PHP Script to Be Called from Flash (`helloFlash.php`)

```php
<?php
$greeting = "Hello, " . $fname . " from the server!";
$output="fromPHP=$greeting";
echo $output;
?>
```

In Listing 12.1, the `$greeting` variable is made up of literal text and the variable `$fname`. The dots (.) in PHP are operators used to concatenate strings—like the plus (+) operator in ActionScript 2.0. The variable `$fname` is passed from Flash and used here to illustrate how variables can be sent from the front end to the back end using `LoadVars()`. The key Flash formatting in the script is the line

```
$output="fromPHP=$greeting";
```

The variable, `fromPHP`, is like the text file variables discussed earlier. That special variable will become a property of the `LoadVars()` instance.

On the Flash end of the equation, all we need are a couple text fields and a button. Create one input text field with the instance name `input_txt`, a dynamic text field with the instance name `fromServer_txt`, and a UI Button component with the instance name `sender_btn`. (See Figure 12.3 to get an idea of the general arrangement of the text fields and the button.) Now, just click the first frame and enter the code in Listing 12.2 in the Actions panel.

LISTING 12.2 Flash Front End Sending and Receiving Data from the Back End (`sendAndLoad.fla`)

```
sender_btn.onPress = function() {
    var getIT_lv:LoadVars = new LoadVars();
    getIT_lv.fname = _level0.input_txt.text;
    getIT_lv.onLoad = function() {
        _level0.fromServer_txt.text = this.fromPHP;
    };
    //URL should be the one your actually use.
    getIT_lv.sendAndLoad("http://www.someURL.com/helloFlash.php", getIT_lv);
};
```

If you're setting up your PHP script on your system or a remote server, you have to change the URL in the next-to-last line. If you place the SWF file and PHP file in the same folder on your system or a server, you can simply address it as `"helloFlash.php"` in the script.

FIGURE 12.3   The message from the server-side script uses data from the front end as well as data it provides.

One of the very helpful methods in the `LoadVars()` class is `sendAndLoad()`. With it you can send any variables from Flash and, at the same time, load data from the back end. The first parameter of the method is simply the URL of the server-side script. The second parameter is the name of the `LoadVars()` instance into which to place the data being sent from the server side. In the example, a single instance is used for both sending and receiving data, but you can use separate `LoadVars()` objects if you want. Just remember, all variables become properties of the `LoadVars()` object, and the variables are the ones defined in the special MIME format used by Flash, originally shown in use with the text files in the previous section. Figure 12.3 shows what happens when Delia Jean puts her dual name into the input box and clicks the button.

SHOP TALK

Sandbox Security

You may have heard of Flash's sandbox security. Further, you may have wondered what it is and why it has been planted in Flash. First off, it's called *sandbox security* because it's a security system based on materials being in the same domain—or sandbox, as it were. Second, the system is put into place to aid in securing data from hackers and data theft. If a SWF file residing in domain A is called from domain B, the called file will not load because of sandbox security.

To allow a SWF file to be loaded from a "foreign" domain, you have to set the `System` class setting, as follows:

```
System.security.allowDomain("ForeignDomainName");
```

Therefore, if I have a SWF file on `www.sandlight.com` and I want to load a SWF file on `www.room99.co.uk`, I would enter this:

```
System.security.allowDomain("www.room99.co.uk");
```

If you're not getting all of this, don't worry. It helps if you've played around with server-side languages using HTML. If this is of no interest to you at this time, at least you know where to start when you're ready to work with server-side materials and Flash. However, for those of you who have been looking to use Flash as a general front end, you now have the keys to the kingdom of the back end.

Working with the Data Components

Flash MX Professional 2004 has a set of data components not available in the standard version of Flash MX 2004. With these data components, you can easily load data from external sources into a Flash application. The following sections show representative examples of the key data components and how they're used to bring in external data to the Flash pages.

WebServiceConnector

One of the more interesting types of data is provided by Web services. These services provide everything from stock quotes to the current weather. By connecting to these services with the WebServiceConnector component, you can easily create applications that provide dynamic information for your sites.

Also, you can place an XML file on the domain you're using to target the domain you want to allow. For example, the following XML file, saved as `crossdomain.xml`, would allow www.sandlight.com access from any server it was placed on:

```
<?xml version="1.0"?>
<!-- http://www.foo.com/crossdomain.xml -->
<cross-domain-policy>
  <allow-access-from domain="www.sandlight.com" />
</cross-domain-policy>
```

That's fine and good for SWF files, but what about server-side files? Unfortunately, it won't work when a SWF file on one domain attempts to access a server-side file on another domain. To do so would defeat the sandbox security system. To work with SWF files in one domain and server-side files on another domain, you have to use Flash Remoting MX, a separate Macromedia product.

One workaround if you don't have Flash Remoting MX is to keep a SWF file in the domain where you have your server-side files. The path would be SWF_domainA, SWF_domainB, ServerSide_domainB. The `LoadVars()` class would need to be in the SWF file in the same domain as the server-side file, but with some attention to levels or movie clip paths, you can make the jump.

The first step is finding a Web service. Using a search engine such as Google or Yahoo!, you can find several different Web services available on the Web. For example, the following Web service returns the current temperature for a given ZIP Code:

`http://www.xmethods.net/sd/2001/TemperatureService.wsdl`

Using the WebServiceConnector, you can place a little weather station in your Flash document using that Web service. The following project steps you through the process. It's a little different from what you've seen in previous projects, so take it a step at a time:

1. Open a new Flash document and create the following layers from top to bottom: WebServiceConnector, Input/Output, Trigger, and Background. Then select Window, Development Panels, Web Services to open the Web Services panel. Don't place the Web Services panel in the panel dock but rather leave it free-floating on the Stage.

FIGURE 12.4   Adding the Web service in the Define Web Services dialog box.

FIGURE 12.5   Adding a method call to the function automatically adds the WebServiceConnector to the Stage.

2. Click the globe icon in the upper-left corner of the Web Services panel to open the Define Web Services window. Click the Add (+) button and type the following in the text box:

    `http://www.xmethods.net/sd/2001/`
    `➥TemperatureService.wsdl`

    Figure 12.4 shows how the dialog box looks when successfully completed. Click OK to display the Web Services icon with the label TemperatureService.

3. Select the WebServiceConnector layer. Then, in the Web Services panel, click the expand icon (+) next to the Web Services icon to show a plug icon labeled `getTemp()`. Right-click the `getTemp()` icon (Control-click on the Macintosh). A context menu opens, as shown in Figure 12.5. Select the Add Method Call command from this menu.

4. As soon as you select Add Method Call, a WebServiceConnector icon appears on the Stage. You can put it anywhere you want because it's not visible when the application is launched. Select the WebServiceConnector icon and provide it with the instance name `weatherSer` in the Property panel. Lock the layer.

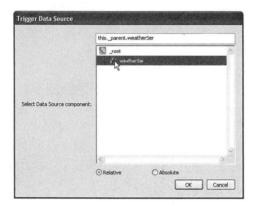

FIGURE 12.6 Selecting the WebServiceConnector instance to trigger with the button.

5. In the Input/Output layer, add a UI TextInput component and set its dimensions to W=60, H=22. Provide it with the instance name zip. Then add a TextArea instance below the TextInput component. Set its dimensions to W=30 and H=20, and give it the instance name temp. Lock the layer.

6. In the Trigger layer, add a PushButton component, giving it the label **Get Weather** and the instance name showWeather_btn. Then, with the PushButton component selected, open the Behaviors panel and select Add Behavior (the + icon), Data, Trigger Data Source. In the Trigger Data Source window, choose the weatherSer instance, as shown in Figure 12.6.

After you have completed this procedure, open your Actions panel. With the button still selected, you'll see that the following code has been generated:

```
on (click) {
    // Trigger Data Source Behavior
    // Macromedia 2003
    this._parent.weatherSer.trigger();
}
```

Unlike the bulk of code you have seen in this book, this code is connected directly to the button rather than in code stored in a frame. Lock the layer.

7. In the Background layer, above the TextInput component, add the static text label **Zip Code**, and above the TextArea component, add the label **Temperature**. Place backdrops behind both Text components and the Button component and then label the Stage **Weather Station**. Figure 12.7 shows where all the parts go on the Stage. Lock the layer.

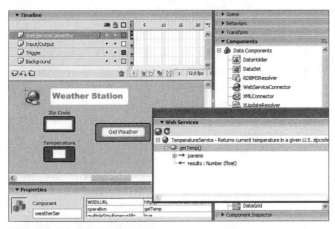

FIGURE 12.7   All the objects for the application are on the Stage, including the WebServiceConnection icon that disappears when the application launches.

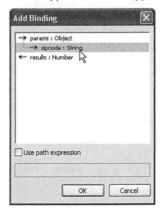

FIGURE 12.8   Choosing the binding for the WebServiceConnector.

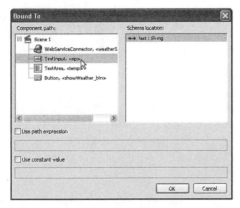

FIGURE 12.9   Binding the `zipcode:String` to the TextInput component with the instance name `zip`.

8. Unlock the WebServiceConnector layer and select the WebServiceConnector component. Open the Component Inspector panel and select the Bindings tab. Click the Add Binding button (the + icon). This will open the Add Binding window. Select `zipcode:String`, as shown in Figure 12.8, and click OK.

9. When you click OK, `params.zipcode` appears in the Bindings window. Select it. Then, in the Bindings tab, click the Value column of the Bound To row. This will open the Bound To window. Select `TextInput, <zip>`, as shown in Figure 12.9, and click OK.

10. Repeat steps 8 and 9, except choose `results:Number` in the Add Binding window and select `TextArea, <temp>` in the Bound To window. Once this is done, you have successfully bound the TextInput component to the ZIP Code used by the Web service, and you have bound the TextArea component to the result (a temperature) from the Web service.

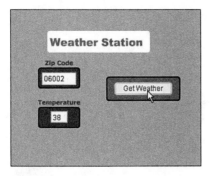

FIGURE 12.10 You can enter any ZIP Code from any location on the Web and find the temperature.

When you test the application, enter a ZIP Code and click the Get Weather button. You will experience a slight delay. Then, in the TextArea component, you will see the current temperature displayed. Figure 12.10 shows an example of what you can expect to see.

DataHolder

The DataHolder component is something like a middleware component. It acts to connect a data source with a data display component. For example, the DataHolder can be used to connect data between the DataGrid component and a data source in an array. In general, the DataHolder component is required only when you cannot directly bind data to a component that outputs data.

Curb Your Web Service

One possible use of the temperature service and other Web services is to add them to your site to encourage viewer traffic. However, before you start slapping Web services willy-nilly on your sites, note that even a simple Web service setup can add significantly to your bandwidth costs. For example, the simple little example with the ZIP Code and weather reading has a SWF file size of 85KB. About half of the file size is added by the WebServiceConnection component, and the rest by the UI components. That's not much of an issue for broadband users, but some guy in Nome, Alaska with a 56K phone modem may get frostbite before he loads that extra 85KB for a Web service that tells him it's 100 below zero.

In order for you to see how the DataHolder component works, the following project shows how to bind array data to a DataGrid component via a DataHolder component:

1. Open a new Flash document, creating the following layers from top to bottom: Data/Actions, DataHolder, and DataGrid. Set the background color to #00F300.

2. Select the DataHolder layer and drag a DataHolder component from the Components panel and place it on the left side of the Stage. Provide the DataHolder the instance name holdData.

3. Select the DataGrid layer and drag a DataGrid component from the Components panel and place it in the horizontal and vertical center of the Stage. Give the component the instance name showData in the Property Inspector. Set the size of the DataGrid to W=200, H=150.

4. Select the Data/Actions layer and click the first frame. Open the Actions panel and enter the following script:

```
showData.setStyle("themeColor", "haloOrange");
showData.setStyle("color", 0xE60000);
showData.setStyle("backgroundColor", 0xFFE600);
holdData.soccerTeam = [{Age:6, Name:"Jimmy"}, {Age:8, Name:"Suzy"}];
holdData.soccerTeam.push({Age:5, Name:"Bill"}, {Age:9, Name:"Maria"});
holdData.soccerTeam.push({Age:7, Name:"Jack"}, {Age:7, Name:"Jill"});
```

Lock the layer.

5. Select the DataHolder layer and select the DataHolder instance on the Stage. Open the Components Inspector, click the Schema tab, and then click the Add Component Property (+) button. As soon as you click the button, you'll see new field:String in the top pane. Next, click the field name row in the bottom pane, and in the Value column enter the value **soccerTeam**. Then, in the Value column of the Data Type row, select Array from the pop-up menu that appears when you click the Value column.

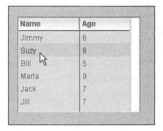

6. With the DataHolder component still selected, click the Bindings tab and then click the Add Binding (+) button. In the Add Binding dialog box, select new soccerTeam:Array and click OK. In the lower pane of the Bindings tab, click the Value column of the Bound To row. When the Bound To window opens, select DataGrid, <showData> and click OK.

7. Save the movie as dataHolder.fla and test it. You'll see the display shown in Figure 12.11.

FIGURE 12.11   The DataHolder component passes data from an array to a DataGrid component that displays it on the Stage.

The DataHolder works similarly to the DataSet component, and depending on the project, you can use one or the other. Each uses the same general set of steps, so moving from one to the other is relatively simple.

XMLConnector

Because XML data is standardized, storing data in XML format makes it easy to update materials on a Web site. Rather than having to reformat the movie, all you need to do is to update the XML. Some services provide information not unlike Web services with the data stored in XML files.

Using the XMLConnector requires a precise set of steps to be successfully employed, so this next project uses a simple XML file to show and explain how to bring in data from an XML file using the XMLConnector component.

Before starting on the project, you need to have a minimum understanding of XML files. For those new to XML, you'll find these files very easy to create and work with. They are tag-based like HTML files; however, you get to name all the tags! Data is organized in a nested hierarchy, and just like HTML, when you open a container, you have to close all the enclosed containers before closing the parent container. A container is the material between an opening and closing tag, such as

```
<myData> Information goes here </myData>
```

where `<myData>` is the container name. The rules that cover opening and closing tags in nested applications apply to XML in the same way as HTML. If you place a container within another container, the inner container must open and close before the outer container closes. All references are to the name of the tag within any other container the tag may be nested. XML files have attributes and other features, including data type definitions called *schema*. However, for use with Flash, you don't need a schema because Flash works out the schema for you.

This project is extremely simple so that you can best see how to use the XMLConnector component, but you can handle far more complex XML files and a variety of different UI components. Here are the steps to follow:

1. Create the following XML file using a text editor such as Notepad or using Save As Text in your word processor:

    ```
    <project>
     <step1>The first step in creating a good Flash application is to gather
    ➥all of the necessary tools. You will need a bag of chips, some Jolt Cola,
    ➥and a headset so that you can listen to music.</step1>
     <step2>The second step is playing a few video games. This will warm you up
    ➥for the task at hand and remind you that the guy who created the games
    ➥you're playing made a bundle.</step2>
    </project>
    ```

    Save the file as `flashProjXML.xml` in the same folder where you'll be saving your FLA file. Even though the XML file is simple, it's well formed. However, you can use XML files of any complexity.

2. Open a new document in Flash and create four layers with the following names, from top to bottom: Actions XMLconn, Output, and Background. Save the file as `connectXML.fla`. (Remember to save it in the same folder as the just-created XML file in step 1.)

3. Open the Components panel, and in the XMLconn layer, drag an instance of the XMLConnector to the Stage. Like other data components, it cannot be seen at runtime, so place it off to the side where it won't get in the way. In the Property Inspector, with

the XMLConnector selected, give it the instance name projXML. Also in the Property Inspector, you'll see a list of parameters to set. The top one is URL. Set it to flashProjXML.xml and then set the Direction parameter to receive.

4. With the XMLConnector component selected, open the Component Inspector and click the Schema tab. Click the arrow button on the Schema tab—it shows Import a Schema from a Sample XML File when the mouse passes over it. When you click the button, the XML file's schema appears in the top pane of the Schema tab, as shown in Figure 12.12.

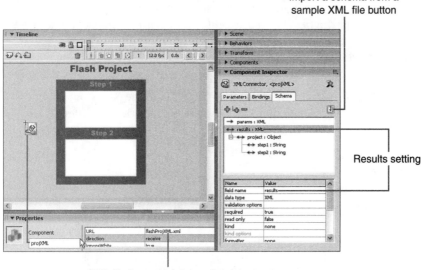

FIGURE 12.12   Flash generates the XML file's schema automatically.

5. In the Output layer, drag two TextArea components and place them on the Stage, one above the other, as shown in Figure 12.12. Set the size to W=200, H=100 for both, and center them on the Stage. Provide the instance name projOut for the top one and projOut2 for the bottom one. For both, set the HTML line in the Properties Inspector to True. (The XML text acts something like HTML text when read by Flash, so double-check to be sure that the HTML line in the Parameters tab in the Property Inspector is "on.")

6. Select the XMLConnector component (projXML). In the Component Inspector, under the Schema tab, select the schema line that reads results:XML, as shown in Figure 12.12. When you select the line in the top pane of the Scheme tab, you will see that the field name in the bottom pane also shows you have selected results.

7. With the XMLConnector component still selected, click the Bindings tab in the Component Inspector and then click the Add Binding (+) button. When the Add Binding box opens, select step1:String and click OK. In the bottom pane of the Bindings tab, set the Direction to out and then click the Value column of the Bound To row to open the Bound To dialog box. Select TextArea,<projOut>, as shown in Figure 12.13, and then click OK.

8. Repeat step 7 to add a second binding, but this time select step2:String in the Add Binding box and TextArea,<projOut2> in the Bound To box.

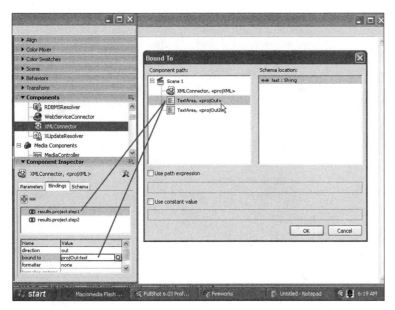

FIGURE 12.13 Binding the XMLConnector to the TextArea components.

9. Click the first frame on the Actions layer. In the Behaviors panel, click the Add Behavior button and select Data, Trigger Data Source. That generates the following script in the Actions panel:

```
this.projXML.trigger();
```

When the application is launched, the XMLConnector pulls the data out of the XML file and places it in the appropriate TextArea component triggered by the script in the first frame.

10. Lock all the layers except the Background layer. Draw a rectangle with the dimensions W=250, H=280 behind the two TextArea components using the color #D40022 with no stroke line. Then, using an 18-point Arial Black font colored #F0D513, type **Step 1** above the top TextArea component and **Step 2** above the bottom one. Finally, with a 24-point Arial Black font colored #61261E, type **Flash Project** above the red rectangle. Lock the layer and test the application. Figure 12.14 shows what you'll see.

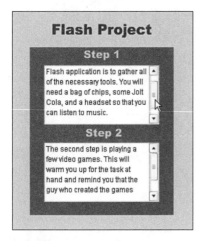

FIGURE 12.14   Binding the XMLConnector to the TextArea components.

The other data components not discussed in this chapter are for use with different Web services. The XUpdateResolver and RDBMSResolver are used to update changes made to data from some type of Web service or other source, where changing data is passed to a SWF file. They're typically used in conjunction with the WebServiceConnector and DataSet components for handling continually changing data sets.

However, for kick starting your work with external data sources in Flash MX Professional 2004, you should now have a good collection to get you off and running. In addition to using the data components, you can deal more directly with their classes by using the properties, methods, and events associated with these classes to fine-tune your own creation!

In Brief

- You can store and recover variables and their values from text files as a "poor person's database."

- With the LoadVars() class, Flash can communicate with middleware and, through the middleware, to SQL databases.

- Using sandbox security, Flash allows only same-domain files to be loaded without special permission or Flash Remoting.

- Using the WebServiceConnector component, Flash can easily connect a document to a live Web service for external data that's dynamically updated.

- The DataHolder component helps to take different types of data and pass it to output sources in Flash.

- XML files are easily accessed and displayed as data using the XMLConnector component.

Index

Symbols

A

B

C

calculations

Math class, 271-277

Number class, 276-78

calendars, Date class components, 281

Camera class, 257

capabilities object, 82

caption property, ContextMenuItem class, 197

carriage returns, text display, 200

cartoon animations, coordination, 117

banner ads, 120-128

copying and pasting frames, 119-120

parts planning, 117-118

position selection, 118-119

Cascading Style Sheets. *See* CSS

case sensitivity

codes, 70

conditional statements, 85

case statement, 86

ceil() method, Math class, 272

cels, 19-20

Celsius, Fahrenheit conversion application, 66-67

Cent Formatter listing, 89

center points, motion tweens, 106-108

CentFormat class, 90

change event

ComboBox UI component, 217

TextArea class, 200

change handlers, replaced with listeners, 81

Character Position option, Property Inspector, 158

charAt(i) method, String class, 266

charCodeAt(i) method, String class, 266

Check Syntax button, Actions panel, 68

Clarkson, Mark, *Flash 5 Cartooning*, 117

classes

built-in, 78

constants, 80

events, 80-81

listeners, 81

methods, 80

objects, 82

properties, 78-79

Button, 210-214

ContextMenuItem class, 196-197

creating, 58-60

encapsulation, 60

inheritance, 60-61

polymorphism, 62

Date, 278-280

components, 281

UTC (Coordinated Universal Time), 280-281

focusManager, 222-226

Form, 238-239

Loader, 239

LoadVars(), 166, 209

external data, 293-297

text file variables, 289-293

disabledColor property, 282

display CSS attribute, 180

Distort option, 44

do while loop, 83

Document Properties dialog box, Stage size, 18

document tabs, 17

Don't Close Gaps option, 44

dragging, mask layers, 115

draw (UIObject) event, Screen class, 237

drawing methods MovieClip class, 151-153

_droptarget property, MovieClip class, 147

duplicateMovieClip(nn,d,[io]) method, MovieClip class, 143

duration property, Sound class, 251

dynamic text fields, 34, 157, 163-166

    HTML text flow around graphic image, 166-167

    JPEGs, 167-168

    SWF file, 167-168

    TextFormat class, 169

E

E constant, Math class, 272

echoing layers, 112-113

ECMA (European Computer Manufacturers Association), 55

Edit Character Options, Property Inspector, 158

Edit Envelope window, 247

Edit Format Options, Property Inspector, 158

Edit menu commands, 37-38

    Keyboard Shortcuts, 41

    Paste in Place, 107

Edit toolbar, 45

editable property, TextArea class, 201

else statement, 85

else if statement, 86

embedFonts property, TextField class, 172

embedFonts style, TextArea, 202

enabled property

    ContextMenuItem class, 197

    focusManager class, 222

    MovieClip class, 147

encapsulation, OOP, 60

endFill() drawing method, MovieClip class, 152

Envelope option, 44

equality operator (==), 76

Erase Fills option, 44

Erase Inside option, 44

Erase Lines option, 44

Erase Normal option, 44

Erase Selected Fills option, 44

Eraser tool, 44

European Computer Manufacturers Association (ECMA), 55

event handlers, MovieClip class, 150-151

Event sounds, 248

events

    built-in classes, 80-81

    ContextMenu class, 196

    ContextMenuItem class, 197

    LoadVars class, 294

focusEnabled property, MovieClip class, 147

focusIn (UIComponent) event, Screen class, 237

focusManager class, 222-226

focusOut (UIComponent) event, Screen class, 237

_focusrect property, MovieClip class, 147

font

    outlines, static text fields, 160

    property, TextFormat class, 186

    symbols, 32

font-family CSS attribute, 180

font-size CSS attribute, 179

font-style CSS attribute, 179

font-weight CSS attribute, 179

fontFamily property, 282

fontFamily style, TextArea, 202

fontSize property, 282

fontSize style, TextArea, 202

fontStyle property, 282

fontStyle style, TextArea, 202

fontWeight property, 282

fontWeight style, TextArea, 202

for loops, 83

for..in loops, 83

forced limited option selections, radio button navigation, 227

Form class, 238-239

formatting

    component styles

        added style context, 285-286

        CSS style declaration, 286-287

        global, 282-284

        instances, 284-285

    text, String class, 265-271

forms, screen slides, 238

    organizing project, 238

    placeholders, 238-242

frames, scenes, 19-20, 26-27, 99

_framesloaded property, MovieClip class, 147

Free Transform tool, 44, 49, 103-104, 108

fromCharCode(c1,c2,cn) method, String class, 266

functions, global, 87-88

    unnamed, 90

    user-defined, 88-90

G

general operators, 74

GET method, 216

getBounds(cs) method, MovieClip class, 143

getBytesLoaded() method

    LoadVars class, 293

    MovieClip class, 143

    Sound class, 250

getBytesTotal() method

    LoadVars class, 293

    MovieClip class, 143

    Sound class, 250

getCount() method, TextSnapshot class, 161

getDepth() method

    MovieClip class, 143

    TextField class, 170

H

menus

    Commands, 38-39

    Control, 39

    Edit, 37-38

    File, 37

    Help, 40-41

    View, 38

    Window, 40

methods

    buildReg, 175

    built-in classes, 80

    ContextMenu class, 196

    ContextMenuItem class, 197

    focusManager class, 222

    LoadVars class, 293

    Math class, 272

    Mouse class, 204

    MovieClip class, 143-147

    MovieClip.createTextField(), 175

    MovieClipLoader class, 136

    Number class, 277

    objects, 57

    PrintJob class, 192

    Register.buildReg, 176

    Sound class, 250

    String class, 266-268

    TextField class, 170-171

    TextField.StyleSheet class, 179

    TextSnapshot class, 161

Microphone class, 257

Microsoft PowerPoint versus Flash Pro slide shows, 232-233

MIN_VALUE constant, Number class, 277

min() method, Math class, 272

Minimum Area parameter, Trace Bitmap dialog box, 98

Miscellaneous Operators folder, 77-78

Modify menu commands

    Bitmap, 30, 97

    Break Apart, 159

    Shape, 102

modulo operator (%), 75

morphs, animation, 99-103

motion tweens

    animation, 103

        center point repositioning, 106-108

        gradual point size changes, 103-104

        guide layers, 109-110

        imported vector graphics, 104-106

        layers, 110-111

    changes, 104

Mouse class, 204-207

mouseDown event, Screen class, 237

mouseDownSomewhere event, Screen class, 237

mouseMove event, Screen class, 237

mouseOut event, Screen class, 237

mouseOver event, Screen class, 237

mouseUp event, Screen class, 237

mouseUpSomewhere event, Screen class, 237

mouseWheelEnabled property, TextField class, 172

MOV files, 29

move (UIObject) event, Screen class, 237

moveTo(x,y) drawing method, MovieClip class, 152

N

T

U

UI components

focus manager, 222

passing information dynamically, 218-220

UIComponent class, TextInput components, 203

UIObject class, 200-203

Undefined data type, 71

underline property, TextFormat class, 187

Undo option, 38

unload (UIObject) event, Screen class, 237

unloadClip(target_mc/levelN) method, MovieClipLoader class, 136

unloadMovie() function, 134

unloadMovie() method, MovieClip class, 144

unloadMovieNum() function, 135

unnamed functions, 90

_url property

MovieClip class, 148

TextField class, 173

TextFormat class, 187

useHandCursor property, MovieClip class, 148

user classes, linking to movie clips, 153-154

user-defined functions, 88-90

users

banner ads, 121

input text fields, 34

text fields

basics, 157-168

Stylesheet class, 179-186

TextField class, 169-178

TextFormat class, 186-188

UTC (Coordinated Universal Time), 280-281

UtilsClasses class, 53

V

valueOf() method, Number class, 277

Variable option, Property Inspector, 158

variable property, TextField class, 173

variables

Actions panel, 70-71

converting data types, 72-74

data types, 71-73

text files, 289-293

vector graphics, 30

conversion from static text field, 159-160

motion tweens, 104-106

versus bitmapped graphics, 96-99

Video class, 257

Video Import Wizard, 244

videos, 35, 245

View menu commands, 38

Preview Mode, 160

Rulers, 102

View Options button, Actions panel, 69

_visible property

ContextMenuItem class, 197

Form class, 241

MovieClip class, 148

TextField class, 173

visible tab index, 221

void operator, 78

vPosition property, TextArea class, 201

vScrollPolicy property, TextArea class, 201

W-X-Y-Z

KICK START

< QUICK >
< CONCISE >
< PRACTICAL >

Radio UserLand Kick Start
Rogers Cadenhead
0672325632
$34.99 US/$52.99 CAN

Mono Kick Start
Hans-Jürgen Schönig & Ewald Geschwinde
0672325799
$34.99 US/$52.99 CAN

Microsoft .NET Kick Start
Hitesh Seth
0672325748
$34.99 US/$52.99 CAN

ASP.NET Kick Start
Stephen Walther
0672324768
$34.99 US/$52.99 CAN

ASP.NET Data Web Controls Kick Start
Scott Mitchell
0672325012
$34.99 US/$52.99 CAN

Microsoft Visual Basic .NET 2003 Kick Start
Duncan Mackenzie, et al
0672325497
$34.99 US/$52.99 CAN

Microsoft Visual C# .NET 2003 Kick Start
Steven Holzner
0672325470
$34.99 US/$52.99 CAN

XQuery Kick Start
James McGovern, et al
0672324792
$34.99 US/$52.99 CAN

Your Guide to Computer Technology

GL

www.informit.com

Sams has partnered with **InformIT.com** to bring technical information to your desktop. Drawing on Sams authors and reviewers to provide additional information on topics you're interested in, **InformIT.com** has free, in-depth information you won't find anywhere else.

ARTICLES

Keep your edge with thousands of free articles, in-depth features, interviews, and information technology reference recommendations—all written by experts you know and trust.

POWERED BY

Safari

ONLINE BOOKS

Answers in an instant from **InformIT Online Books'** 600+ fully searchable online books. Sign up now and get your first 14 days **free**.

CATALOG

Review online sample chapters and author biographies to choose exactly the right book from a selection of more than 5,000 titles.

SAMS   www.samspublishing.com